THE CHEQUER'D SHADE

The Chequer'd Shade

REFLECTIONS ON
OBSCURITY IN POETRY

JOHN PRESS

Let standard-Authors, thus, like trophies born,
Appear more glorious as more hack'd and torn,
And you, my Critics! in the chequer'd shade,
Admit new light thro' holes yourselves have made.
ALEXANDER POPE, *The Dunciad*, Book IV, 123–6.

LONDON
OXFORD UNIVERSITY PRESS
NEW YORK TORONTO
1958

*Oxford University Press, Amen House, London E.C.*4
GLASGOW NEW YORK TORONTO MELBOURNE WELLINGTON
BOMBAY CALCUTTA MADRAS KARACHI KUALA LUMPUR
CAPE TOWN IBADAN NAIROBI ACCRA

PRINTED IN GREAT BRITAIN

CONTENTS

ACKNOWLEDGEMENTS

Permission to use quotations from copyright works is gratefully acknowledged to the following authors, publishers, and other copyright-holders.

W. H. AUDEN: *Poems; The Dog Beneath the Skin; Letters from Iceland; Another Time; New Year Letter; Collected Shorter Poems 1930–44; The Age of Anxiety; Nones; The Shield of Achilles:* Messrs. Faber and Faber, Ltd., and Random House, Inc., New York.

LAWRENCE DURRELL: *A Private Country; Cities, Plains and People; The Tree of Idleness:* Messrs. Faber and Faber, Ltd.

T. S. ELIOT: *Collected Poems 1909–1935; Four Quartets:* Messrs. Faber and Faber, Ltd., and Harcourt, Brace and Co., Inc., New York.

WILLIAM EMPSON: *Collected Poems:* Messrs. Chatto and Windus, Ltd., and Harcourt, Brace and Co., Inc., New York.

DAVID GASCOYNE: *Poems 1937–42:* Messrs. Pearn, Pollinger and Higham, Ltd.

EZRA POUND: *Selected Poems,* Copyright 1926: Messrs. Faber and Faber, Ltd., Messrs Shakespear and Parkyn, Solicitors, and New Directions, Norfolk, Connecticut.

DYLAN THOMAS: *Collected Poems,* Copyright 1952, 1953: Messrs. J. M. Dent, Ltd., and New Directions.

RICHARD WILBUR: *Poems 1943–56:* Messrs. Faber and Faber, Ltd., and Harcourt, Brace and Co., Inc., New York.

W. B. YEATS: *Collected Poems:* Mrs. W. B. Yeats, Messrs. Macmillan and Co., Ltd., A. P. Watt and Son, and the Macmillan Co., New York.

Introduction

Persius who you use to say, you do not know whether he be a
good poet or no, because you cannot understand him, and who therefore (I say) I know to be not a good poet.
ABRAHAM COWLEY, 'The Dangers of Procrastination'

But the source of bad criticism, as universally of bad philosophy, is
the abuse of terms.
RICHARD HURD, *Letters on Chivalry and Romance*

ON 11 March 1955 Lord Samuel spoke at a Foyle's literary
luncheon during which John Betjeman received an award of
£250 for his book of poems *A Few Late Chrysanthemums*.
According to a report in the *Daily Telegraph* of 12 March,
Lord Samuel denounced

this fashion of deliberate and perverse obscurity. On going through
the anthologies of several years I was appalled to find the degree to
which this vice of obscurity was afflicting British poetry. I could
give several examples but I will read only one . . .

> A grief ago
> She who was who I hold, the fate and flower
> Or, water-lammed, from the scythe-sided thorn
> Hell wind and sea
> A stem cementing, wrestled up the tower,
> Rose maid and male
> Or, masted venus, through the paddler's bowl
> Sailed up the sun.

Accepting the cheque for £250, John Betjeman said: 'I
don't know who wrote the thing Lord Samuel read out.'
Another poet, Stephen Spender, who knew that the thing
had been written by Dylan Thomas, and who left the room
when Lord Samuel began to quote the stanza, later said that
somebody should have thrown an egg at Lord Samuel. He
also remarked, again according to the *Daily Telegraph*, that

'although the Dylan Thomas poem was obscure, it was also very beautiful. There were many occasions when phrases from it came into one's head. In any case, it was not fair to lift a piece out of the context for criticism.'

This farcical episode admirably illustrates in miniature the present relationship between poetry and the reading public. An elder statesman of cultivated tastes, asked to talk about modern verse, isolates one stanza from a poem and describes it as typical of the mystification and self-conscious posturing in which so many contemporary poets indulge. Of the poets present, one does not recognize the source of the quotation and one, after walking out in baffled rage, can advance no argument likely to convince the average Philistine that Lord Samuel is in the wrong. For to say that a poem is beautiful though obscure will confirm many sensible people in their suspicion that poetry is an airy-fairy cult; and numerous lines recur to one's memory precisely because they are unforgettably banal or ludicrous. Finally, a middlebrow newspaper which would not normally dream of giving much space to modern verse devotes a column and a half of its centre page to this brawl, obviously believing that poetry has news value only as a comic turn.

In fairness to Lord Samuel one must admit that the majority of even the fully literate reading public would echo his jeremiad about the state of contemporary poetry. Most people, if asked, would say that they do not read modern verse because it is obscure, implying that they habitually read and instantly understand the works of Shakespeare, Donne, Milton, Blake, and Shelley. Indeed the very notion of obscurity in poetry is one of those convenient Platonic abstractions—comfortable and sanitary dug-outs as Aldous Huxley calls them—into which men retreat to guard their prejudices from the blast of uncomfortable facts. Leslie Stephen said of Nature that it is 'a word contrived to introduce as many equivocations as possible into all the theories, political, legal, artistic or literary into which it enters'. This is true of obscurity also.

There is a popular belief that what conservatives like to call real poetry was perfectly straightforward until some unspecified date, when poets suddenly changed into reckless bunglers or deliberately set out to bamboozle plain, honest readers with mumbo-jumbo. Nobody knows exactly when this catastrophe took place, although the shrewdest observers maintain that the decline began when they themselves were about twenty-five years old.

Even intelligent critics have lent colour to this delusion. In the course of some valuable remarks about obscurity T. S. Eliot says:

> Or difficulty may be due just to novelty: we know the ridicule accorded in turn to Wordsworth, Shelley and Keats, Tennyson and Browning—but must remark that Browning was the first to be *called* difficult; hostile critics of the earlier poets found them difficult, but called them silly.[1]

The epigram, despite its superficial persuasiveness, is misleading. For example, the early critics of Shelley's *Alastor* announced that its readers would have to consult a glossary and, as I shall try to show in a later chapter, Wordsworth, Keats, and Tennyson were categorically accused of being difficult and obscure. On this point Randall Jarrell seems to me nearer the truth than Eliot: 'When critics first read Wordsworth's poetry they felt that it was silly, but many of them *said*, with Byron, that "he who understands it would be able—To add a story to the Tower of Babel".'[2]

In his inaugural lecture as Professor of Medieval and Renaissance Literature, C. S. Lewis advances a more elaborate and subtle contention, which is part of his wider argument that since the Napoleonic Wars we have been living in a radically new kind of civilization:

> To say that all new poetry was once as difficult as ours is false; to say that any was is an equivocation. Some earlier poetry was difficult, but not in the same way. Alexandrian poetry was difficult because it presupposed a learned reader; as you became learned you found the answers to the puzzles. Skaldic poetry was unintelligible if you did not know the *Kenningar*, but intelligible if you did. And —this is the real point—all Alexandrian men of letters and all skalds would have agreed about the answers. I believe the same to be true of the dark conceits in Donne; there was one correct interpretation of each and Donne could have told it to you. . . . I do not

---

[1] *The Use of Poetry*, p. 150.   [2] *Poetry and the Age*, p. 19.

see in any of these the slightest parallel to the state of affairs disclosed by a recent symposium on Mr. Eliot's *Cooking Egg*.[1] Here we find seven adults (two of them Cambridge men) whose lives have been specially devoted to the study of poetry discussing a very short poem which has been before the world for thirty-odd years; and there is not the slightest agreement among them as to what, in any sense of the word, it means.[2]

Lewis's sleight of hand is so quick and deft that we may not at first glance detect a piece of thimble rigging. I admit that the symposium smacks of the cobwebbed logomachy which Bacon ridiculed in his *Advancement of Learning*; but it is illegitimate to compare the far-fetched conjectures of Eliot's commentators with the inside information which we might have winkled out of Donne. One could with equal justice stand the argument on its head to prove that Eliot is less obscure than Donne, and produce some such sophistry as the following: there is one correct interpretation of *A Cooking Egg* and Eliot could have told it to you. For the three hundred-odd years during which the dark conceits of Donne have been before the world, his editors have been so baffled by their difficulty that they cannot even decide which of the variant textual readings to adopt, still less agree among themselves as to what, in any sense of the word, Donne means.

Yet I think it must be allowed that there is considerable force in Lewis's main contention and that contemporary verse at least appears to be more obscure than the bulk of older poetry, just as modern totalitarianism, for all that its origins can be traced back to Plato, is more ferocious and all-pervasive than any other system of tyranny in recorded history.

It may therefore be useful to investigate the nature of obscurity in poetry or, to put the matter less pretentiously, to find out some of the reasons why certain poems are obscure; to discover whether every conceivable kind of obscure poetry has always flourished, or whether new species have sprouted in recent times; to ask ourselves if every variety of obscure poetry is equally undesirable; and, finally, to inquire whether

---

[1] *Essays in Criticism*, III, 3 (July 1953), pp. 345–57.
[2] *De Descriptione Temporum*, pp. 13–14.

or not an element of obscurity is almost invariably found in poetry of the highest order.

Sir Herbert Read, in his essay on 'Obscurity in Poetry', did not find it necessary to quote any lines of verse except two from Rilke and two which occur in a passage from Warton's essay on *Paradise Lost*. There seems to me a place for another essay on the same theme, with numerous quotations to support any general principles that may be hazarded. Those who find my method and my argument intolerably pedestrian may care to recall that the lines which I have chosen as the epigraph for this book were placed by Alexander Pope in the mouth of Dullness, that Black Goddess who holds sway over the more arid regions of literary criticism.

1

Vocabulary and Syntax

I sabotage the sentence! With me is the naked word.
I spike the verb—all parts of speech are pushed over on their backs.
I am the master of all that is half uttered and imperfectly heard.
Return with me where I am crying out with the gorilla and the bird.
                                        WYNDHAM LEWIS, *One Way Song, VIII*

HENRY: 'Despised and forgotten by some you may be
               But the spot that contains you is sacred to we'.
MRS. JORDAN: That'll never do. You don't say 'Sacred to we'.
HENRY: It's in the paper.
MRS. SLATER: You wouldn't say it if you were speaking properly, but
               it's different in poetry.
                                        STANLEY HOUGHTON, *The Dear Departed*

NEARLY a hundred years ago Burckhardt declared that 'the greatest innovation in the world is the demand for education as a right of man; it is a disguised demand for comfort',[1] and today in Britain, as a result of this vehement cry for universal, compulsory education, we have a population which is, if not educated, or even fully literate, at least able to read and write. The masses desire to be literate, because that way lies the prospect of material advancement and the mirage of political power; bureaucratic governments encourage the spread of education in order to facilitate their task of ruling a terrifyingly complex society; and those who, on religious and philosophical grounds, proclaim that it is the nature of man to seek knowledge and to develop all his faculties can but applaud the provision of free education for every child, however much they may criticize the soggy futility of our popular art and entertainment.

Apart from incoherent protests from selfish members of the upper classes who rightly foresaw the diminution of their privileges, the only criticisms of this revolutionary process

[1] J. Burckhardt, *Reflections on History*, p. 65.

have come from those whose perennial concern it is to maintain the purity and the vigour of our language. W. B. Yeats lamented the spread of compulsory education because it destroyed the traditional belief of the Irish peasantry in their myths and legends, just as T. S. Eliot sighed for an audience that, unable to read or write, would react more spontaneously to his celebration of the primeval triad of birth, copulation, and death. It is unhappily true that a smattering of education destroys the child-like imagination of the untutored mind without awakening the deeper, passionate imagination of the full man, and deadens the quick, eager response to poetic truth which the poet seeks to awaken. The rich folklore of the countryside, the nutty flavour of regional dialect and the highly sophisticated language of the poet are linked together by an instinctive sympathy for, as Logan Pearsall Smith remarked, 'both the peasant and the literary artist employ, after all, much the same kind of language; both are concerned more with life and idiom than with dictionaries and the rules of grammar'.[1] Anyone who has performed the melancholy task of censoring soldiers' mail will remember that whereas the letters of some game-keepers and miners contained a few vivid phrases and moved, at times, with a curiously beautiful rhythm, the sentences of the slick, half-educated clerks and shop-keepers were stale and flabby, even the genuine emotions being drenched in the cheap perfume of half-remembered clichés from a dozen lachrymose dance-tunes.

In the ordinary transactions of daily life it does not matter very much that men use a restricted, impoverished vocabulary and a monotonously simple grammatical structure. This ironing out of all individual turns of phrase, this flattening of texture and dehydration of flavour enable us to digest speedily a mass of useful information. Demands from income-tax authorities, leading articles, and the views of Her Majesty's Judges can be read and understood at a glance, because the mind need not dwell on the individual words of which they are composed. But poets are not content to use language as if it were a succession of vaguely emotive noises intended to prod the listener into taking some kind of action. They must,

[1] *Words and Idioms*, pp. 155–6.

8

by their very nature, refuse to confine themselves to a standardized vocabulary and a conventional grammar which, adequate for the business of day-to-day living, are clumsy instruments for the delicate and difficult tasks that poets are called upon to perform. The average reader of poetry soon finds himself perplexed by the way in which a poet handles words and syntax, by the range of vocabulary and by the flexibility of grammatical construction; one of the prime reasons for many readers' failure to understand a poem is that they have not begun to grasp the mere mechanics of its structure, the simplest articulation of its components.

Some older poetry is obscure solely because the plain prose meaning is beyond our powers to decipher. Medieval poetry needs a glossary before the modern reader can understand it, and even Skelton, writing as late as the reign of Henry VIII, is often barely intelligible. One of the most obscure poets in the language is Shakespeare, whose vocabulary and grammar are so complex and exuberant that, after three hundred years of editorial labours, whole passages of his verse inspire the most elaborate and mutually contradictory explanations of what he wrote and of what he meant. Sometimes, we are baffled by one or two words only, either because they are now obsolete or because Shakespeare's tremendous inventive power has twisted words out of their normal shape and impressed upon them the unmistakable stamp of his genius. How difficult a single word may prove can be illustrated by a quotation from Macbeth:

> Light thickens, and the crow
> Makes Wing to th' Rookie Wood

William Empson[1] has drawn attention to a note on these lines, in the Arden edition of the play, which is a fine specimen of the minute, pedantic care that has been lavished upon the text of all Shakespeare's plays:

This somewhat obscure epithet, however spelt (and it should be spelt *rouky*), does NOT mean 'murky' or 'dusky' (Roderick, quoted by Edward's *Canons of Criticism*, 1765): NOR 'damp', 'misty', 'steamy with exhalations' (Steevens, also Craig); NOR

[1] *Seven Types of Ambiguity*, p. 81.

9

'misty', 'gloomy' (Clar. Edd.); NOR 'where its fellows are already assembled' (Mitford), and has NOTHING to do with the dialect word 'roke' meaning 'mist', 'stream', etc. . . . the meaning here . . . I THINK, is simply the 'rouking' or perching wood, i.e. where the rook (or crow) perches for the night.

The uncertainty of the Arden editor may remind us that it is often impossible to say precisely what it is that Shakespeare means by a given word or phrase; aided by the lack of standardized spelling in Elizabethan English, he was able to exploit to the full the ambiguity inherent in all language and to attract into the orbit of his chosen words a great variety of associated meanings.

More typical of the obscurity which characterizes Shakespeare's vocabulary is a passage from *Antony and Cleopatra*:

> O! then we bring forth weeds
> When our quick winds lie still, and our ills told us
> Is as our earing.

Even when we are told that *earing* means 'ploughing' the sense of these lines is not easy to grasp. Steevens believed that *winds* meant the ridges made by the plough, whereas other commentators assert that this is a reference to the March winds that must not lie still if there is to be a good harvest. Certain editors, unable to understand Shakespeare until they have simplified him, alter the awkward word to *minds*, thereby breaking the sequence of agricultural metaphors and destroying the alliteration of *weeds* and *winds*.

Curiously enough, many of those who condemn living poets for obscurity would be astonished to be told that Shakespeare can be indicted upon so grave a charge. They fail to recognize this quality in him, partly because his verse moves at such a pace on the swift tide of dramatic action that there is no time to pause at the individual peculiarities of language displayed there, but mainly because they placidly accept as normal and straightforward the wildest distortions of conventional language, the most startling neologisms and the most extravagant tropes in which Shakespeare may care to revel. The horror which Pope felt when confronted by the licentious diction of the plays is the tribute paid by a highly civilized artist to one who transcends both civilization and barbarism in the elemental fury and darkness of his imagination. We smile at his conviction that the word *incarnadine* was an interpolation by a poet even more unlettered than Shakespeare, but he at least was aware that such a use of language was a violation of all commonly accepted standards.

It is precisely this departure from the commonplace language of daily speech that lays a poet open to the charge of being wilfully obscure. A great many of the so-called oddities and eccentricities in Gerard Manley Hopkins spring from the unusual range and remarkable exactness of his vocabulary as well as from his gift of coining new words or of reinvigorating commonplace words. Geoffrey Grigson has given two examples of 'obscurity' in Hopkins which become crystal-clear as soon as the reader has grasped the botanical meaning of certain phrases.[1] The word *bugle* in the line 'Cluster of bugle blue eggs thin' has been taken to mean 'like big blue beads' whereas *bugle* is *Ajuga reptans*, a common plant blossoming in May with a shiny blue surface. In 'The Starlit Night' the phrase *wind-beat whitebeam* has nothing to do with the appearance of moonlight, but is a singularly beautiful image referring to *sorbus aria* which tosses its delicate white underleaves back to front, enabling the wind to beat the whole tree white.

The sestet of the sonnet which begins 'My own heart let me have more pity on' contains two striking examples of the way in which Hopkins delighted to coin new words, hoping that the reader would have the flexibility to accept them:

> Soul, self; come, poor Jackself, I do advise
> You, jaded, let be; call off thoughts awhile
> Elsewhere; leave comfort root-room; let joy size
> At God knows when to God knows what; whose smile
> 's not wrung, see you; unforeseen times rather—as skies
> Betweenpie mountains—lights a lovely mile.

Jackself, formed on the analogy of steeple-jack, jack-knife, and similar words, is a brilliant piece of poetic shorthand for the

---

[1] See his British Book News Supplement, *Gerard Manley Hopkins*, pp. 25–26. W. H. Gardner had anticipated Grigson in this interpretation of *wind-beat whitebeam*.

honest-to-goodness workaday self; *betweenpie* is rather more obscure. Bridges correctly explains its meaning, but coldly remarks that the verb *to pie* 'seems not to exist, and to be forbidden by homophonic absurdities'; Robert Graves pays a just tribute to the skill which enabled Hopkins to invent precisely the word that clinches the entire emotional argument of the sonnet:

Besides being again, the sort of homely kitchen language which the Jackself uses to describe how the sky seems pressed between two mountains, it is also the neatest possible way of combining the patching effect of light—as in the word 'pied', or in 'magpie'— with the way that this light is introduced between the mountains.[1]

The highly idiosyncratic use of language that we find in Hopkins is almost always successful, for even his most baffling obscurities are caused by an excess of burning poetic intensity which lends a glow to the darkest utterance. The employment of a recondite vocabulary is a vicious trick when prompted by a modish desire to be clever:

> When once proleptic of the kiss
> Their parted lips stood poised in air
> No stellar parallax could tear
> Heart from heart in hendiadys.

This is wit writing of the worst kind, a calculated euphuism parading in scientific plumage, frigid fancy masquerading as elegant precision. It illustrates the dangers that beset any poet who, departing from the commonly accepted speech of his own day, adopts an arcane vocabulary drawn from a remote age or from an unfamiliar branch of learning.[2] Unless he commands sufficient poetic authority to compel the general acceptance of his minted coinage his work will inevitably be judged rebarbative and obscure, for although one may dis-

---

[1] *The Common Asphodel*, p. 100.
[2] The Metaphysical poets of the seventeenth century delighted in extraordinary words. Among their choicest discoveries were: esloygne, mastix, and methridate (Donne); angelance and chamleted (Benlowes); antiperistasis (Cowley); panpharmacon (Chamberlayne); and aldisboronifuscophonio (John Hall). See R. L. Sharp, *From Donne to Dryden*, pp. 45–46.

cover its meaning with the aid of a dictionary, it will be a dictionary, not a poetic, meaning.[1]

Modernism and archaism are both to be avoided, although the latter is the more common pitfall, since human laziness and mediocrity tend to lead a poet into an imitation of the past rather than into an exhausting and ill-conceived attempt to anticipate the future. The advice given by Hopkins on this theme needs to be constantly re-emphasized: poetic language, he says, 'should be current language heightened, to any degree heightened and unlike itself, but not an obsolete one'.[2] Verse that ignores this canon is likely to be both obscure and slightly ludicrous, though seldom as outrageously comic as the line from an English opera, 'Hence ho, you bawdy toss-pots', or as weird as the quatrain rescued from oblivion by Daniel George:[3]

> The sand soft-clung about the feet a-bared,
> That still should trod 'pon stones a-sharped
> Yes, Earth e'en then did hold the greened tree
> That burst the sod for upping of the Cross. . . .

John Holloway has recently argued that common speech is not invariably the best medium of poetic communication, although it is the most suitable medium for the majority of poets.[4] He maintains that, even if we dislike Doughty's language, we cannot condemn it as affected, since it is neither literary cliché nor the kind of feeble archaism which Hopkins censured, but a means whereby he can communicate his highly individual perceptions. Yet Doughty's poetry is generally regarded as obscure, the common verdict resembling the judgement passed upon Spenser by Ben Jonson: 'in affecting the Ancients, [he] writ no language'. T. Sturge Moore

---

[1] Lycophron was a great coiner of neologisms. It has been calculated that his poem *Alexandra* contains 518 words which are found nowhere else but in this poem, and 117 which appear there for the first time (F. L. Lucas, *Style*, p. 74). It is not surprising that he is regarded as an exceptionally obscure poet, and that detractors of modern verse like to exhibit him as a dreadful warning against the perils of intellectualism.

[2] *Letters*, vol. i, p. 89.

[3] *Lonely Pleasures*, p. 23.

[4] 'Poetry and Plain Language: The Verse of C. M. Doughty', *Essays in Criticism*, vol. iv, No. 1 (January 1954), pp. 58–70.

dismissed his verse with contemptuous terseness: 'Doughty wrote an epic in eight volumes, not English, but a concrete of all the jargons spoken since before Chaucer.'[1]

Is Doughty as obscure as Sturge Moore makes out and, if so, wherein does his obscurity lie? In an attempt to answer this question I propose to glance at a short passage cited by John Holloway as a typical example of Doughty's epic style:

> Were some, which entered in a temple court,
> Helvetians: there they marvel see one sit,
> Old reverend sire, on throne of ivory!
> Whose eyes like coal under his frozen brows;
> Them seems some ancient purpled magistrate
> Of Rome's forsaken city. Ingenuous Gauls,
> Such deeming, gin salute him in their guise.

This reads to me like an extract from a Latin epic put into English by an intelligent and scholarly foreigner whose knowledge of versification is greater than his acquaintance with our native idiom. It is obscure, less because of its vocabulary than because the entire movement of the syntax is rheumatic and muscle-bound, with neither the flexibility and suppleness of our language, nor the monumental gravity of Latin. Reading this passage may remind us that a poet's syntax is almost more important than his vocabulary, and that one of the most common causes of obscurity in poetry is weak, defective, ambiguous or unusual punctuation, typography, and grammar.

We have grown so accustomed to certain conventions of typography and of punctuation that any flouting of them is apt to baffle us completely. The printing of a poem in such a way that each stanza assumes the form of a diamond or of a geometrical figure irritates most readers (unless the poem is avowedly comic) to such an extent that they look for any excuse to condemn it as obscure. Some readers are prejudiced against English poetry unless each line begins with a capital letter, although these same people demand precisely the opposite convention in the printing of Latin verse. The

[1] *W. B. Yeats and T. Sturge Moore: Their Correspondence 1901–1937*, ed. Ursula Bridge, p. 20.

mere physical shape of some poems by Hopkins upset certain of the few contemporaries who read his verse, and he himself realized that the marking of the stresses in 'The Wreck of the Deutschland' weighed heavily against the poem's chance of acceptance by *The Month*, especially as he admitted that there were 'a great many more oddnesses (which) could not but dismay an editor's eye'. He was aware that such marks were objectionable, yet held them to be necessary to guard his metre and his grammar from misinterpretation, and hoped that he would not be condemned literally at a glance:

When . . . I read some lines (of 'The Loss of the Eurydice') . . . it struck me aghast with a kind of raw nakedness and unmitigated violence I was unprepared for: but take breath and read it with the ears, as I always wish to be read, and my verse becomes all right.[1]

Although Hopkins contemplated inventing a notation so that his poetry could be read as though it were music, he shrank from so revolutionary a step, and the nearest approach to such a system is to be found in the typographical eccentricities of E. E. Cummings, which Robert Graves has defended on the grounds that Cummings has thereby attained a new degree of poetic accuracy, as well as ensuring that no future editors or printers shall tamper with his text.[2] Other poets have taken less drastic measures, Doughty contenting himself with devising a new system of punctuation, and W. H. Auden reverting to the Elizabethan habit of employing stops as a guide to breathing, instead of punctuating his sentences according to the rules of the grammarians. Whatever may be the rights and wrongs of such innovations they have undoubtedly exposed their users to the charge of wilful obscurity.

The fundamental importance of syntax in poetry has seldom been understood or even discussed by the majority of critics, who have preferred to meander through the more picturesque byways of poetic diction, although poets themselves have

[1] *Letters*, vol. i, p. 79. It is possible that Hopkins read Coleridge's Note Books which contain highly individual punctuation. See Humphry House, *Coleridge*, p. 10.
[2] *The Common Asphodel*, pp. 84–86, 95–99.

given due emphasis to this difficult aspect of their craft.[1] T. S. Eliot has reminded us that Milton's consummate skill in controlling the long periods, the intricate sentences and the elaborate paragraphs which abound in *Paradise Lost* is the most conclusive proof of his remarkable intellectual ability,[2] and W. B. Yeats in his letter to H. J. C. Grierson, 21 February 1926, makes an equally pregnant comment:

> The over-childish or over-pretty or feminine element in some good Wordsworth and in much poetry up to our date comes from the lack of natural momentum in the syntax. This momentum underlies almost every Elizabethan and Jacobean lyric and is far more important than simplicity of vocabulary.[3]

Grammatical feebleness, which is usually a token of poetic debility, may sink to such a degree of teetering incompetence that a poem becomes obscured by a misty vagueness, all clarity of outline hopelessly smudged. A lazy poet, shrinking from the intellectual labour involved in making the grammatical structure of his verse firm and coherent, will allow it to drag itself along limply and flabbily, excusing its amorphous shape by a plea of poetic licence. One of the worst examples of this slackness is to be found in an extract from *Pharonnida* by the seventeenth-century writer Chamberlayne:

> . . . the soft breath
> Of Zephyrus sung calm anthems at the death
> Of palsy-shaken Winter, whose large grave,
> The earth, whilst they in fruitful tears did lave,
> Their pious grief turned into smiles, they throw
> Over the hearse a vale of flowers . . .

A curious example of almost impenetrable obscurity, caused by defective grammar as well as by a grotesque vocabulary, occurs in the translation of the hymn *Urbs Beata Hierusalem* by the energetic Victorian ecclesiologist, J. M. Neale, who, it

---

[1] G. Rostrevor Hamilton, *The Tell-Tale Article*, and Donald Davie, *Articulate Energy*, contain many valuable observations on this subject.

[2] See his lecture on Milton delivered to the British Academy in 1947, reprinted in *T. S. Eliot: Selected Prose*, ed. John Hayward, pp. 131–49.

[3] *The Letters of W. B. Yeats*, ed. Allan Wade, p. 710. Cf. 'I only understood vaguely and occasionally that I must for my special purpose use nothing but the common syntax'. W. B. Yeats, *Autobiographies*, p. 155.

may be remembered, would have liked to pull down Peter-borough Cathedral and to replace it by a 'Middle Pointed' building of equal merit.[1] His architectural metaphors were as infelicitous as his architectural projects, judging by his description of the Heavenly City, which presents a formidable linguistic and grammatical puzzle:

> Many a blow and biting sculpture
> Polish'd well those stones elect,
> In their places now compacted
> By the heavenly Architect . . .

This kind of high-flown nonsense should be distinguished from the type of syntactical ambiguity which envelops poetry in a pleasant haze. The final four lines of the first stanza of Ben Jonson's most famous lyric appear to contradict the mean-ing which he presumably intended and, despite William Empson's ingenious explanation of the passage, I still do not know whether Jonson is being remarkably subtle or unusually careless:[2]

> The thirst that from the soul doth rise
> Doth ask a drink divine;
> But might I of Jove's nectar sup
> I would not change for thine.

Humphry House points out the grammatical obscurity into which Coleridge falls when he writes in *The Ancient Mariner*

> Nor dim nor red, like God's own head,
> The glorious sun uprist . . .

for, as the passage stands, it is impossible to tell whether God's head is supposed to be dim and red or not. The first line appeared in the *Lyrical Ballads* (1800) text as:

> Nor dim nor red, like an Angel's head,

which suggests that Coleridge was thinking of the common pictorial representation of an angel as a being whose head is encircled with a glowing halo.[3] A more important example of

---

[1] Reginald Turnor, *Nineteenth Century Architecture in Britain*, p. 68.
[2] *Seven Types of Ambiguity*, pp. 306–7.
[3] *Coleridge*, pp. 99–100.

grammatical uncertainty occurs in 'Kubla Khan', when the poet cries:

> Could I revive within me
> Her symphony and song . . .

Emphasized strongly, the *could*, like the *once* of the line

> In a vision once I saw . . .

becomes a despairing admission of utter inability to recapture a vanished ecstasy, and 'Kubla Khan' must be read as Coleridge's farewell to his creative genius.[1] Most people will agree with House's judgement that the ambiguity here is the invention of over-subtle reading rather than the product of careless writing: it is grammatically possible to lay a heavy emphasis on the two words, but the rhythmical speed and lightness of the passage forbid us to do so, and when we read poetry a feeling for tone and texture is of greater help than an ability to grasp every conceivable permutation of meanings.

The deliberate violation of normal grammar, which merits far more attention that it commonly receives, has been practised by numerous poets for widely differing reasons and with varying degrees of success; and although it is a perfectly legitimate device, it fills a great many readers with impotent rage or baffled incomprehension, unless they are mollified by the sensuous charm of the resulting poem, as in the following stanza from 'The Grasse-hopper', by Richard Lovelace:

> Night as cleare *Hesper* shall our Tapers whip
> From the light Casements where we play,
> And the darke Hagge from her black mantle strip,
> And sticke there everlasting Day.

H. J. C. Grierson, justly remarking that the order of words is obscure, proceeds to paraphrase the lines: 'Our tapers, clear as Hesperus, shall whip Night from the well-lit Casements where we sport ourselves, and strip her black mantle from the dark Hag and stick in its place everlasting Day.'[2] Logically

---

[1] Humphry House, *Coleridge*, pp. 115–16.
[2] *Metaphysical Lyrics and Poems of the Seventeenth Century: Donne to Butler*, p. 238.

18

indefensible as this odd syntax may be, it lends the stanza a peculiar elegance and formal beauty which a more normal grammatical structure could not produce; and a living poet, Charles Causley, in 'The Prisoners of Love' manages to combine a similar obscurity of expression with a comparable poetic exactness:

> Night, on my truckle bed your ease of slumber
> Sleep in salt arms the steering night away.

A desire to improve the texture of their verse is not the only reason why poets have deliberately broken the text-book rules of grammar. Rossetti, in attempting to recapture in English the sonorous, massive, architectural splendour of Latin verse, tried to emulate the density of classical syntax, placing each word with the utmost care so that the complex thought of his verse should move with a measured gravity. The following sestet of a famous sonnet illustrates the intricate magnificence which Rossetti often attains in his best work, but the final two-and-a-half lines spin a web of grammatical ambiguity into which it would be rash to venture:

> Mark me, how still I am! But should there dart
> One moment through thy soul the soft surprise
> Of that winged Peace which lulls the breath of sighs,—
> Then shalt thou see me smile, and turn apart
> Thy visage to mine ambush at thy heart
> Sleepless with cold commemorative eyes.[1]

Browning is said to have been so badly hurt by the reception accorded to his *Paracelsus*, which was criticized for its verbose and involuted style, that he determined upon a surgical excision of connecting words, whose very ruthlessness led to worse confusion than before. Although Betty Miller has disproved this legend[2] it is undeniable that Browning's cavalier way with syntax, coupled with his abrupt transitions, is a prime source of his verbal obscurity. Elizabeth Barrett summed up this stylistic defect in one neat sentence: 'You

---

[1] *The House of Life*, xcvii—'A Superscription'.
[2] *Robert Browning: A Portrait*, p. 63.

sometimes make a dust, a dark dust, by sweeping away your little words.'[1]

His example was followed deliberately and systematically by Mallarmé and by Hopkins, each of whom outraged the placid normality of conventional grammar, Mallarmé by refining it to a quintessential drop, Hopkins by rending it into tatters with the ferocity of his passion. 'It is', says Aldous Huxley of a sonnet by Mallarmé, 'a grammatical apocalypse. A whole world of ideas is miraculously concentrated by means of the syntax into what is almost a point.'[2]

The grammatical obscurity in Mallarmé springs from his concept of a poem as an immaculate, labyrinthine work of art to be fashioned with elaborate, daedalian contrivance, whereas all too often in reading Hopkins one is conscious that his eccentricities of construction proceed from a chafing at conventional restraint, an impatient determination to brush aside the meaningless, neutral words that impeded the impassioned movement of his verse. Bridges was fully justified in holding that the omission of the relatives in

> Squander the hell-rook ranks sally to molest him

and in

> Save my hero, O Hero savest

results in a needless confusion. The abrupt, dramatic opening of 'Henry Purcell', on the other hand, is not seriously flawed by the defiance of commonplace syntax which it displays, because the intricacy of the thought accords with the complexity of the grammar:

> Have fair fallen, O fair, fair have fallen, so dear
> To me, so arch-especial a spirit as heaves in Henry Purcell,
> An age is now since passed, since parted; with the reversal
> Of the outward sentence low lays him, listed to a heresy, here.

Even so, Hopkins seems to have been a shade uneasy about the queerness of his usage, defending himself by claiming that ' Have is the sing. imperative (or optative if you like) of the past, a thing possible and actual both in logic and grammar,

---

[1] Quoted by Phyllis Bartlett, *Poems in Process*, p. 49.
[2] *Texts and Pretexts*, p. 228.

but naturally a rare one.' One feels that Mallarmé would not have condescended to grub among the recondite usages of grammar in an attempt to find a pedantic excuse for his enigmas.

The occasional jerkiness in which Hopkins indulged was erected into a system by W. H. Auden in some of his early poems. Poker-faced, and immensely assured, the medicine-man utters a few clipped, oracular sentences with a disturbing economy of words and gestures:

> Is first baby, warm in mother,
> Before born, and is still mother,
> Time passes and now is other,
> Is knowledge in him now of other,
> Cries in cold air, himself no friend.
> In grown man also, may see in face
> In his day-thinking and in his night-thinking
> Is wareness and is fear of other,
> Alone in flesh, himself no friend.[1]

This is comparatively straightforward, but in *Paid On Both Sides* the laconic simplicity has become tangled, the hypnotic rhythm grown less compelling, the meaning less coherent:

> Can speak of trouble, pressure on men
> Born all the time, brought forward into light
> For warm dark moan.
> Though heart fears all heart cries for, rebuffs
> With mortal beat
> Skyfall, the legs sucked under, adder's bite.

The inappropriateness of this telegraphese, as it has been called, becomes apparent in the following passage, which reads as though Mr. Jingle had inadvertently strayed from *The Pickwick Papers* into the world of the Icelandic sagas:

> Then watchers saw they were attacked
> Shouted in fear A night alarm
> To men asleep Doomed men awoke
> Felt for their guns Ran to the doors
> Would wake their master Who lay with woman
> Upstairs together Tired after love.

[1] *Poems*, XVI. Entitled '1929' in *Collected Shorter Poems*.

Auden's early poems are obscure for a variety of reasons, chief among them being the excessively-mannered pidgin English which he employs with prodigious skill, setting his unfamiliar concepts to a disturbingly original tune. However eccentric his use of grammar may be it is seldom purposeless or uncontrolled, for Auden is a virtuoso ring-master determined to put his syntax through the hoops, compelling it to execute all kinds of tricky manœuvres. Dylan Thomas looks at grammar with a more benevolent eye, content if he can charm it and change it into a species of incantation:

> I see the boys of summer in their ruin
> Lay the gold tithings barren,
> Setting no store by harvest, freeze the soils;
> There in their heat the winter floods
> Of frozen loves they fetch their girls,
> And drown the cargoed apples in their tides.
>
> .   .   .
>
> How soon the servant sun,
> (Sir morrow mark),
> Can time unriddle, and the cupboard stone,
> (Fog has a bone
> He'll trumpet into meat),
> Unshelve that all my gristles have a gown
> And the naked egg stand straight.
>
> .   .   .
>
> Never until the mankind making
> Bird beast and flower
> Fathering and all humbling darkness
> Tells with silence the last light breaking
> And the still hour
> Is come of the sea tumbling in harness . . .

It is idle to pretend that the sole cause of obscurity in Auden and in Thomas is their distortion of, or their indifference to, the orthodox rules of grammar, but if their syntax were more conventional their meaning would be easier to unravel.

I have said enough to show that the poet who makes use of a recondite vocabulary, an individual typography or punctuation, and a grammar which departs from the common run of speech lays himself open to the charge of wilful obscurity. In his desire to attain a high degree of poetic intensity he may so baffle his readers that they will remain bogged down in the task of interpreting the elementary meaning of his words: intent upon destroying prosaic verbiage, he may mortally wound poetic reason.

Yet the risk must be taken, for even on the level of vocabulary, punctuation, and syntax the poet must be for ever breaking new ground and seeking fresh modes of precise usage. At the end of his examination of the sonnet 'Th' expence of Spirit in a waste of shame' in its original punctuation, Robert Graves indicates how obscure a poet Shakespeare frequently is:

Shakespeare's punctuation allows the variety of meanings he actually intends; if we must choose any one meaning, then we owe it to Shakespeare to choose at least one he intended and one embracing as many meanings as possible, that is, the most difficult meaning. It is always the most difficult meaning which is the most nearly final. No prose interpretation of poetry can have complete finality, can be difficult enough. . . . Thus far does a study of Shakespeare's typography take one: to the difficulties of a poet with readers to whom his meanings are mysteries and for the most part must remain mysteries.[1]

This is a dark saying, designed to infuriate those who demand that a poem should be as immediately comprehensible as a piece of straightforward prose, and who pretend that Shakespeare's poetry is not in the least obscure. The truth is that all poets whose apprehension of the world is peculiarly complex or passionate are likely to employ an unusual vocabulary or an uncommon syntax, or both, in order to convey with the utmost exactitude the unique quality of their vision. To grumble that a poet is not using language plainly is to forget that there are times when for him to do so would be insincere, as T. S. Eliot remarked in his essay on the Metaphysical poets, observing that although their language is perfectly clear and pure, 'the *structure* of the sentences . . . is sometimes far from simple, but this is not a vice; it is a fidelity to thought and feeling'.[2] This fidelity, this attempt to reveal with unremitting clarity and force the pattern and the range of his

---

[1] *The Common Asphodel*, pp. 91–93.   [2] *Selected Essays*, p. 285.

sensibility, is one of the hardest tasks of the poet, and one which inevitably exposes him to peril, as Hopkins knew: 'Now it is the virtue of design, pattern or inscape to be distinctive and it is the vice of distinctiveness to become queer.'[1]

Much fine poetry is bound to be condemned as obscure, if only because a poet, whose first loyalty is to his daimon, will intuitively reject the slackness, the low tension and the generalities of everyday prose, the thin, greasy coinage of lazy thought and tepid feeling. He will not hesitate to go beyond the confines of a commonplace vocabulary, or to break the codified rules of grammar which are devised to simplify the business of living. In doing so, he will outrage the prejudices of those who resent any violation of their intellectual and emotional routine for, as T. S. Eliot has pointed out, new poetry tends to disturb the conventional consciousness 'by its syntax more than by its sentiments', and all versification 'is essentially a disturbance of the conventional language'.[2]

Poetry is less a means of communication than a way of communion, more intense, more profound and more personal than the casual intercourse of our social life. Those who desire to share in this communion must learn to accept the strangeness and even the obscurity of a world in which the syntax and the vocabulary of the analytical reason have been transformed into the grammar of assent and the language of the heart.

[1] *Letters*, vol. i, p. 66.
[2] See F. O. Matthiessen, *The Achievement of T. S. Eliot*, p. 86.

2

Thought

Plainly if it is possible to express a subtle and recondite thought on
a subtle and recondite subject in a subtle and recondite way and with
great felicity and perfection, in the end, something must be sacrificed,
with so trying a task, in the process, and this may be the being at once,
nay perhaps even the being without explanation at all, intelligible.
GERARD MANLEY HOPKINS, *Letters*, vol. i, pp. 265–6

THE belief that the intellectual content of poetry is negligible
is not confined to its detractors, for a great many of those who
love it, assuming that the true nature of poetry is lyrical,
valuing it for its power to set the nerves tingling, and judging that its main purpose is to give emotional satisfaction by
its music and its imagery, look upon hard thinking in poetry
as an unwelcome intruder. Yet English poets of the first
order, while scrupulously respecting the medium of their art,
have incorporated in their verse a view of life which, if less
highly systematized than the doctrines of philosophers, is
equally coherent and profound. Wordsworth desired to be
regarded as a teacher or as nothing; Milton expounded and
Blake invented a divine cosmogony; Shelley laboured cease-
lessly to free men from their mental prison by revealing to
them the lineaments of intellectual beauty. That a high degree
of intellectual difficulty characterizes much of our finest
poetry is a truth scarcely realized by the casual reader of
popular anthologies carefully chosen to conceal the tremendous range of thought to which English poets have devoted
their whole strength and passion.

Poetry which is expressing a complex philosophical doctrine or system is likely to be obscure, unless the poet is
falsifying and weakening the content of his message. A great
deal of Donne's obscurity springs from his complete fidelity
to the intricate nature of his chosen themes, his determination

that the most delicate nuances of every subtle concept shall be revealed in all their bewildering variety. He will not hesitate to introduce a highly abstruse theological argument in the middle of a love poem, since only so can he convey the exact quality of his passion:

> What ever dyes, was not mixt equally;
> If our two loves be one, or, thou and I
> Love so alike, that none doe slacken, none can die.

Grierson, explaining this passage by a quotation from Aquinas, provides a gloss upon it: 'What is simple, as God or the soul, cannot be dissolved; nor compounds, e.g. the heavenly bodies, between whose elements there is no contrariety.'[1] Even more ingenious and obscure is the conclusion of Donne's poem, 'The Primrose':

> Live Primrose then and thrive
> With thy true number five;
> And women, whom this flower doth represent,
> With this mysterious number be content;
> Ten is the farthest number; if halfe ten
> Belonge unto each woman, then
> Each woman may take halfe us men;
> Or if this will not serve their turne, Since all
> Numbers are odde, or even, and they fall
> First into this, five, women may take us all.

Once again Grierson comes to the rescue with his interpretation of the passage:

The perfect primrose has apparently five petals. . . . Let woman be content to be herself. Since five is half ten, united with man she will be half of a perfect life; or (and the cynical humour breaks out again) if she is not content with that, since five is the first number which includes an even number (2) and an odd (3) it may claim to be the perfect number, and she to be the whole in which we men are included and absorbed . . . the poem is probably addressed to Mrs. Herbert and is a half mystical, half cynical description of Platonic passion.[2]

[1] *Metaphysical Lyrics and Poems of the Seventeenth Century: Donne to Butler*, p. 217.

[2] *The Poems of John Donne*, vol. ii, p. 49 (1912).

Those readers who dislike the poetry of the Metaphysicals, with its outrageous conceits, its sudden changes of tone, its fusion of passionate tenderness and insolent wit, may complain that the obscurity of their verse is a sign of its essential hollowness and falsity. Such dazzling cleverness, such verbal trickery, such intellectual arrogance, prove (it may be argued) that genuine poetry, the poetry of the soul, is distinguished by its perfect simplicity of utterance, by the absence of cerebral posturing. The most eloquent short refutation of this shallow and misleading theory is to be found in a letter which W. B. Yeats wrote to Grierson on 14 November 1912, acknowledging the debt which he and indeed all lovers of poetry owe to a great scholar and editor:

Poems that I could not understand or could but understand are now clear and I notice that the more precise and learned the thought the greater the beauty, the passion; the intricacy and subtleties of his imagination are the length and depths of the furrow made by his passion. His pedantry and his obscenity—the rock and loam of his Eden—but make me the more certain that one who is but a man like us all has seen God.[1]

It is worth noting at this point that the obscurity of a poet's thought may be caused less by its intrinsic difficulty than by its comparative unfamiliarity. Most readers would be gravelled by the lines of Donne which I have quoted unless a commentator were at hand to expound the tenets of scholastic philosophy and to initiate them into Pythagorean mysticism. The following extract from Chapman, though no less subtle and exact than the meditations of Donne, presents almost no difficulty to the reader:

> A man to join himself with th' Universe
> In his main sway, and make (in all things fit)
> One with that All, and go on, round as it:
> Not plucking from the whole his wretched part,
> And into straits, or into nought revert,
> Wishing the complete Universe might be
> Subject to such a rag of it as he;
> But to consider great Necessity,

[1] *The Letters of W. B. Yeats*, ed. Allan Wade, p. 570.

All things refract as well as voluntary
Reduceth to the prime celestial cause
Which he that yields to with a man's applause,
And cheek by cheek goes, crossing it no breath,
But like God's image, follows to the death,
That man is truly wise.[1]

This passage is perhaps the finest celebration in our language of the philosophy of Stoicism which, softened by Christian sentiment and tinged with Christian morality, remains the natural religion of the English. We need no interpreter to explain the precise philosophical implications of the lines because their poetic meaning is clear and acceptable to us, their import is familiar and unmistakable.

A poet whose philosophy has grown outmoded or unintelligible through the passage of time may be rescued from oblivion and defended from accusations of obscurity by the labour of devoted scholars. It is much easier for them to elucidate the difficulties of a philosophy which was once the common property of a great many thinkers than to piece together the fragments of a system peculiar to one man. Stanzas xxx–xxxviii of *A Song to David* continue to baffle the most resolute commentators, mainly because Christopher Smart is apparently using a symbolism to which he alone has the key. The main theme of the section, as summarized by Smart himself, is that 'the pillars of knowledge are the monuments of God's works in the first week', an orthodox commentary upon the Book of Genesis, but nobody knows why Smart has chosen to designate these pillars by the Greek letters Alpha, Gamma, Eta, Theta, Iota, Sigma, and Omega.[2]

This minor obscurity is a mere speck upon the coherent splendour of a masterpiece whose main design is firm and luminous. The other great mystical writer of the latter half of the eighteenth century, William Blake, is frequently and systematically obscure, an inventor of cosmogonies and mythologies which few readers can hope to understand without the aid of specialists who have immersed themselves in the

---

[1] *The Revenge of Bussy D'Ambois*, Act IV, sc. 1.
[2] *Poems by Christopher Smart*, ed. Robert Brittain, pp. 309–10.

thought of Blake. His cosmogony is a product of his geometrical imagination which gives birth to such involved
speculations as these:

> The nature of infinity is this: That every thing has its
> Own Vortex, and when once a traveller thro' Eternity
> Has pass'd that Vortex, he perceives it roll backward behind
> His path into a globe itself infolding.

> . . .

> The Vegetative Universe opens like a flower from the Earth's
>   center
> In which is Eternity. It expands in Stars to the Mundane Shell
> And there it meets Eternity again, both within and without.

> . .

> The Mundane Shell is a vast Concave Earth, an immense
> Harden'd shadow of all things upon our Vegetated Earth,
> Enlarg'd into dimension and deform'd into indefinite space.[1]

The sonorous deliberation of the language matches the grandeur of the theme, reinforcing the impression of majestic
obscurity with which Blake has clothed his thought, but often
he uses the most limpid and melodious images and cadences in
poems that are even more baffling than his oracular Prophecies:

> Hear the voice of the Bard,
> Who present, past and future, sees;
> Whose ears have heard
> The Holy Word
> That walked among the ancient trees,

> Calling the lapsèd soul
> And weeping in the evening dew;
> That might control
> The starry pole,
> And fallen, fallen light renew!

> O Earth, O Earth, return!
> Arise from out the dewy grass!
> Night is worn,
> And the morn
> Rises from the slumberous mass.

[1] These quotations are taken from the 2nd edition of the Nonesuch *Poetry and
Prose of William Blake*, pp. 490, 571, 492.

'Turn away no more;
Why wilt thou turn away?
The starry floor,
The wat'ry shore
Is giv'n thee till the break of day.'

Unless, like A. E. Housman, we are content to regard this poem as virtually devoid of meaning, as a mysterious incantation which would shed its grandeur if suggestion were to condense itself into thought, its obscurity is likely to form an almost palpable barrier between us and a full understanding of Blake's vision. Before we can hope to grasp its import we shall have to consider its sequel, 'Earth's Answer', and then go on to study the Prophetic Books in an effort to discover the significance of the trees, the stars, and the shore that loom so large in this song. Moreover, while it is clear that Blake is dwelling on the traditional myths of the Bible, on the fall of Adam and of Lucifer, we shall misconstrue his meaning unless we bear in mind his original and unorthodox interpretation of both the Old and the New Testaments, his railing at the repressive, jealous God who binds the winged life of the senses, and his worship of the all-forgiving Christ who leads us to the gates of Paradise.[1]

Most poets, lacking the energy and the audacity of Blake, and deficient in the restless intellectual curiosity which consumed John Donne, are free from the type of obscurity that has occupied our minds in the last few pages, since they are neither constructing a complete metaphysical system, nor expounding an elaborate and traditional philosophy. Their poetry may still be marked by obscurity of thought, either because they are trying to express intricate notions that flash through their brains; or because they are brooding upon an uncommon experience or idea; or because they are struggling to clarify a confused perception of a shadowy truth which cannot be formulated in the standard terms of conventional philosophy. Shakespeare is so alive to every manifestation of existence that he refuses to confine himself within the limits

[1] For three differing interpretations of this poem see A. E. Housman, *The Name and Nature of Poetry*, pp. 41–42; F. R. Leavis, *Revaluation*, pp. 141–2; F. W. Bateson, *English Poetry*, pp. 37–39.

of any set of abstractions, thereby irritating those who desire utter certainty and exact definition, and laying himself open to the accusation that he had no philosophy. It is truer to say that the tide of thought and feeling which flows through his verse seldom congeals into the hard pattern of a philosophical system, although it is clear that Shakespeare's response to the perennial questions that trouble every reflective mind is singularly powerful and passionate. The broken, turbulent movement of the following lines from *Troilus and Cressida*, III, ii, 141–6, is an example of how, for Shakespeare, the obscure, baffling concepts that perplex the philosopher take on the urgency of an emotion:

TROILUS: You cannot shun your selfe.
CRESSIDA: Let me goe and try.
          I have a kind of self resides with you:
          But an unkinde selfe, that it selfe will leave
          To be another's foole. Where is my wit?
          I would be gone. I speake I know not what.

The obscurity that we sometimes find in Shelley's thought is at the opposite pole from the obscurity of Cressida's words. Shakespeare, in complete command of the situation, is dwelling on the torturing paradox of the divided self; Shelley frequently employs a confused imagery in order to express the dim apprehensions of his own troubled mind. In 'Stanzas', composed at Bracknell in April 1814, the mood is one of regret, longing for repose, luxuriant immersion in melancholy reflections:

    Away, away! to thy sad and silent home;
      Pour bitter tears on its desolated hearth;
    Watch the dim shades as like ghosts they go and come,
      And complicate strange webs of melancholy mirth.

Effective as the poem is in communicating an atmosphere of lonely grief, it must be judged obscure, because its exact purport remains shadowy and vague. This diffuseness and uncertainty are found even in poems with an elaborate philosophical framework, of which 'Mont Blanc' is a good example. Beginning with a straightforward assertion:

> The everlasting universe of things
> Flows through the mind . . .

Shelley proceeds to compare the human mind with that dark, deep Ravine

> Where Power in likeness of the Arve comes down
> From the ice-gulfs that gird his secret throne

and then describes how Mont Blanc, dominating the entire scene, stands for some power which controls the universe:

> The secret Strength of things
> Which governs thought, and to the infinite dome
> Of heaven is as a law, inhabits thee!
> And what were thou, and earth, and stars, and sea,
> If to the human mind's imaginings
> Silence and solitude were vacancy?

The poem's main theme is fairly clear, but the accumulation of kaleidoscopic images rushing past us at bewildering speed, while admirably conveying a sense of apocalyptic desolation, makes it extremely difficult to hang on to the thread of coherent argument which runs through the dissolving land-scape of Shelley's imagination. Some passages are too cloudy and involved for comprehension, notably the concluding lines of section II where the poet is addressing the Dizzy Ravine which, like the human mind, holds an unremitting interchange with

> One legion of wild thoughts, whose wandering wings
> Now float about thy darkness, and now rest
> Where that or thou art no unbidden guest,
> In the still cave of the witch Poesy,
> Seeking among the shadows that pass by
> Ghosts of all things that are, some shade of thee,
> Some phantom, some faint image; till the breast
> From which they fled recalls them, thou art there!

Perhaps we are unreasonable in demanding clarity of outline from a poem of which its author says:

It was composed under the immediate impression of the deep and powerful feelings excited by the objects which it attempts to describe; and, as an undisciplined overflowing of the soul, rests its claim to approbation on an attempt to imitate the untamable wildness and inaccessible solemnity from which those feelings sprang.

If Shelley is frequently obscure because his rhapsodic flow of mingled ideas and emotion tends to be cloudy and imprecise, Rossetti occasionally becomes entangled in the thickets of obscurity through his severe compression of thought as well as through his efforts to achieve a marmoreal weight and grandeur and, to baffle us still more completely, he sometimes makes an oracular statement which refuses to yield any precise meaning, despite the impressiveness of its sound:

> How shall my soul stand rapt and awed,
> When, by the new birth borne abroad
>   Throughout the music of the suns,
>   It enters in her soul at once
> And knows the silence there for God.[1]

> .   .   .

> Thy soul I know not from thy body, nor
> Thee from myself, neither our love from God.[2]

Faced by such passages as these, we may well ask with Graham Hough whether we are to regard them as imaginative mythology or as theological truth.[3] The answer may be that even Rossetti did not know or care in what sense these lines were to be interpreted. Shrinking from the labour of rigorous thought (he omitted to translate the more difficult poems of Cavalcanti), he was content to take a striking concept, to let his fancy play upon it, to weave it into the elaborate pattern of his verse in the knowledge that it would lend a strange fascination to the completed work. Thought is not, for Rossetti, a matter of exact definition but rather a means whereby the tone and the colour of a poem can be deepened and enriched. Thus in his sonnet, 'For Our Lady of the Rocks', he conveys most skilfully the mood of awe and of wonder which Leonardo's painting evokes in him, but intellectual clarity has evaporated in the rarefied mystical atmosphere in which he delights to brood:

[1] 'The Portrait'.   [2] *The House of Life*, v.   [3] *The Last Romantics*, p. 80.

Mother of grace, the pass is difficult,
Keen as these rocks, and the bewildered souls
Throng it like echoes, blindly shuddering through.
Thy name, O Lord, each spirit's voice extols,
Whose peace abides in the dark avenue,
Amid the bitterness of things occult.

Only a considerable literary artist could conjure such a music out of words, and none but a man consumed with a tragic uncertainty about the nature of existence would seek to cloak his meaning in this kind of darkness.

Browning's obscurity of thought is notorious, but it is seldom remembered that Tennyson was from time to time charged with a similar fault, even at the height of his fame. The 1832 volume, which was drubbed by the critics, was held to be affected and obscure; *The Times*, reviewing *In Memoriam* on 28 November 1851, censured Tennyson for being 'difficult, not from excess, but from want of meaning'; *The Holy Grail* was adjudged obscure, and in 1889 *The Echo* contended that 'there are long passages in the *Idylls of the King* which are as difficult to understand as the pictures of Mr. G. F. Watts'.[1] These accusations are not so groundless as one might suppose for, despite Tennyson's reputation for perfect clarity of utterance, he is at times a cloudy writer. Leaving aside his fondness for elegant periphrasis, an annoying but minor defect of style, he tends to be obscure, when his emotions are at their most powerful, for one of two reasons. Coleridge's observations in *The Friend* that 'deep feeling has a Tendency to combine with obscure ideas in preference to distinct and clear notions' is certainly true of Tennyson, but there is in his case a more profound and personal source of obscurity than the general tendency which Coleridge noted. He seems to have been shaken to the very depths of his being by a sense of anguish and of emptiness, by a thrilling fear that there was no meaning in the universe, that death was the end of every man as of every human achievement. I suspect that such a conviction, always latent in his nature and flowering inevitably from his black, melancholic temperament, became overwhelmingly powerful after Hallam's

[1] Harold Nicolson, *Tennyson*, pp. 111, 164, 224.

death. Too sensitive to ignore and too honest to falsify his intuitions, he none the less shrank from accepting their full implications, grasping for comfort wherever he could find it, in the promptings of morality, in the Christian message, in the mystery of human affection. The resulting incompleteness, evasiveness and ambiguity of utterance, by virtue of Tennyson's remarkable poetic gifts, lend his verse a unique element of longing tinged with regret which, though it falls short of the finest poetry, is always likely to awaken a responsive chord in the hearts of those who, lacking the conviction of faith or the assurance of despair, have made a precarious truce with their own uncertainty.

This radical doubt and this all-pervading irresolution can be seen in 'Crossing the Bar', with its shift of metaphor, and with its ambiguity about the Pilot's function (ships do not normally require a pilot after crossing the bar) and even about his identity (is he Christ or Hallam?). They are apparent in the closing lines of *In Memoriam*, XXVI, which *The Times* reviewer cited as proof of Tennyson's obscurity, although his charge that they lack meaning is exaggerated. Tennyson, after asserting that 'no lapse of moons can canker Love', goes on to say that if God were to observe in him the decay of love

> Then might I find, ere yet the morn
> Breaks hither over Indian seas,
> That Shadow waiting with the keys,
> To shroud me from my proper scorn.

The Shadow is, of course, 'the Shadow fear'd of man' who bore Hallam away and who awaits Tennyson himself (Section XXII), but the reference to the keys is a little mystifying. It is not clear why Death should keep the keys of all the creeds (Section XXIII) since this implies that Death is the supreme arbiter, whereas in Section XXVI he is envisaged as the servant of God who comes to save Tennyson from spiritual decline. It is this constant elusiveness of attitude that gives Tennyson's verse its peculiar atmosphere of vagueness, its quality of self-contradiction, its power of slipping from doubt to affirmation and back to doubt almost as if the poet himself were unaware of its exquisite modulations. Perhaps the most beautiful example of this characteristic is the close of *In Memoriam*, xv:

> And but for fancies which aver
>   That all thy motions gently pass
>   Athwart a plane of molten glass,
> I scarce could brook the strain and stir
>
> That makes the barren branches loud;
>   And but for fear it is not so,
>   The wild unrest that lives in woe
> Would dote and pour on yonder cloud
>
> That rises upward always higher,
>   And onward drags a labouring breast,
>   And topples round the dreary west,
> A looming bastion fringed with fire.

This kind of luxurious brooding, half reverie, half lamentation, was utterly foreign to the genius of Hopkins who invariably aimed at the most rigorous exactitude, whether of idea or of epithet. Ironically enough, this very determination to leave nothing blurred or imprecise resulted in obscurities more intricately knotted than anything we find in Tennyson. Hopkins was acutely conscious of what he called 'this unspeakable stress of pitch, distinctiveness, and selving, this self-being of my own' and conscious also that every creature of God possessed a uniqueness 'which is more distinctive than the taste of ale or alum, more distinctive than the smell of walnut leaf or camphor'. Despite his knowledge that he was endeavouring to convey the incommunicable, he constantly sought to reveal the multifarious 'inscapes' of the world in verse which is obscure only because of his complete fidelity to his observation, his thought and his vision. The sestet of 'Henry Purcell' is an example of his refusal to simplify a complex thought in the interests of clarity:

> Let him oh! with his air of angels then lift me, lay me! only I'll
> Have an eye to the sakes of him, quaint moonmarks, to his
>   pelted plumage under

Wings: so some great storm fowl, whenever he has walked his
　　while
The thunder-purple seabeach plumèd purple-of-thunder,
If a wuthering of his palmy snow-pinions scatter a colossal
　　smile
Off him, but meaning motion fans fresh our wits with wonder.

Part of the difficulty resides in the curious words *sakes* and
moonmarks, part in the clotted syntax; but the thought is so
heavily compressed that even a gloss upon these two words
and an unravelling of the grammar are not enough to resolve
our perplexity. Hopkins admitted that 'the sestet of the
Purcell sonnet is not so clearly worked out as I could wish',
and without his own explanation the sonnet would present a
formidable problem to all but the most resourceful readers:

The thought is that as the seabird opening his wings with a whiff
of wind in your face means the whirr of the motion, but also unaware gives you a whiff of knowledge about his plumage, the marking of which stamps his species, that he does not mean, so Purcell,
seemingly intent on the thought or feeling he is to express or call
out, incidentally lets you remark the individualising marks of his
own genius.

Robert Bridges and Canon Dixon, for all their sympathy
with Hopkins, were frequently gravelled by the vehemence
and the intensity of his thought no less than by his daring
coinage of words and his reckless disregard for the pro-
prieties of syntax. One can observe in Hopkins a chafing at
the obtuseness of his friends, together with a generous recognition that his art was of a complexity too singular to be
apprehended by even the most receptive and devoted readers.
Nowhere is this irritation, mingled with contrite apology,
more plain and more touching than in the long explanatory
letter of 10 February 1888 which he wrote to Bridges about
'Tom's Garland', a sonnet packed with allegorical meaning,
which testifies to his passionate concern about the brutalized
existence of the industrial proletariat in the great cities of the
north. How deeply he felt about the squalor of their lives can
be judged from another of his letters:

My Liverpool and Glasgow experience laid upon my mind a conviction, a truly crushing conviction, of the misery of town life to the poor and more than to the poor, of the misery of the poor in general, of the degradation even of our race, of the hollowness of this century's civilisation: it made even life a burden to me to have daily thrust upon me the things I saw.[1]

This feeling was so powerful that, in 'Tom's Garland', the turbid onrush of his thought and the abruptness of his emotion overwhelm the clarity of his argument, except in the fine couplet epitomizing the tragedy of the unemployed:

> This, by Despair, bred Hangdog dull; by Rage,
> Manwolf, worse; and their packs infest the age.

Hopkins ruefully confesses as much to Bridges:

I laughed outright and often, but very sardonically, to think you and the Canon could not construe my last sonnet; that he had to write to you for a crib. It is plain I must go no further on this road: if you and he cannot understand me who will?

Then follows an explanation of the sonnet's meaning—'O, once explained, how clear it all is'—and last of all a considered judgement upon his poem, remarkable for its calm appraisal of the sonnet's merits and defects: 'I think that it is a very pregnant sonnet, and in point of execution very highly wrought, too much so, I am afraid.'[2]

It has been reserved for poets of our own time to surpass Hopkins in difficulty and to introduce into poetry new elements of obscurity that can be more easily recognized than defined. Thought, in the traditional sense, has been partially replaced by a curious amalgam of metaphysical conceits, loosely associated ideas and private fantasies held together, more or less successfully, by the unifying mind of the poet. W. H. Auden's early poems, besides their striking delineations of northern landscapes scarred with the marks of industrial development, are remarkable for their laconic, satirical diagnosis of our ills, a diagnosis that is couched in terms drawn

---

[1] *Letters*, vol. ii, p. 97.

[2] *Letters*, vol. i, pp. 272–4. In a letter to Bridges, 3 October 1888, Hopkins says, of his sonnet on St. Alphonsus Rodriguez: 'The sonnet (I say it snorting) aims at being intelligible.' *Letters*, vol. i, p. 293.

from the teaching of Groddeck, Homer Lane, and 'loony Layard'. The riddling, teasing elucidation of a concept in the style of Laura Riding:

> Love by ambition
> Of definition
> Suffers partition
> And cannot go
> From yes to no.[1]

is less in evidence than the attempts to incorporate the symbols of psychoanalysis into the world of a poem:

> For to be held for friend
> By an undeveloped mind
> To be joke for children is
> Death's happiness:
>
> Whose anecdotes betray
> His favourite colour as blue
> Colour of distant bells
> And boy's overalls.
>
> His tales of the bad lands
> Disturb the sewing hands;
> Hard to be superior
> On parting nausea.[2]
>
> .   .   .
>
> For mother's fading hopes become
> Dull wives to his dull spirits
> Soon dulled by nurse's moral thumb,
> That dullard fond betrayer,
> And, childish, he inherits,
> So soon by legal father tricked,
> The tall and gorgeous tower,
> Gorgeous but locked, but locked.[3]

Much of Lawrence Durrell's verse is more obscure than Auden's most irresponsible conjuring-tricks, if only because

[1] *Poems*, X. Entitled 'Too Dear, Too Vague' in *Collected Shorter Poems*.
[2] *Poems*, I. Entitled 'The Questioner Who Sits So Sly' in *Collected Shorter Poems*.
[3] 'As He Is.'

he does not bother to impose a formal, philosophical unity upon the myriad impressions that go shimmering through his mind. Crammed with esoteric learning, and impregnated with the atmosphere of the Mediterranean coast, his poetry, elusive and brilliant as quicksilver, reveals the patterns of a mind that shifts continually like sunlit water reflected in a mirror. At times, his vision is so private that, lacking the key, we find ourselves unable to decipher the vivid cryptograms which lie before us:

> A bleeding egg was the pain of testament,
> Murder of self within murder to reach the Self:
> The grapnel of fury like a husband's razor
> Turned on his daughter in a weird enchantment
> To cut out the iron mask from the iron man,
> His double, the troubled self.[1]

> This prince, this bug, this human,
> Who sleeps under the great cat sleeping,
> Shares with the smiling paranoiac,
> Shares with the baby in the creeping-suit,
> An amniotic balance, the diver's grief,
> Has followed a Roman nose past Mandalay,
> Ladybird on a leaf.[2]

I have said enough in this chapter to show that obscurity of thought in English poetry is far more various, widespread, and pervasive than most people care to admit, and this should be remembered before modern poetry is condemned for being incomprehensible, even although contemporary poets claim more latitude for themselves than critics of the past have been willing to allow:

'Who but Donne', wrote Dr. Johnson, 'would have thought that a good man is a telescope?' Any of us here, since the climate has changed, might think it. For two great taboos have been lifted off the modern poet—the taboo on using his brains and the taboo on so-called free association.[3]

---

[1] 'A Small Scripture.'
[2] 'Five Soliloquies Upon the Tomb of Uncebunke', iv.
[3] Louis MacNeice, 'Experience With Images', *Orpheus*, vol. ii, pp. 126–7.

No poet has revelled more unashamedly in the pleasures of intellectual virtuosity than William Empson who, in a characteristically tart commentary upon his own poetry, explains why he has included so many pages of notes in *The Gathering Storm*:

> Partly they are meant to be like answers to a crossword puzzle; a sort of puzzle interest is part of the pleasure that you are meant to get from the verse. . . . The fashion for obscure poetry . . . came in at about the same time as the fashion for crossword puzzles, and it seems to me that the revival of puzzle interest in poetry, an old-fashioned thing, has got a bad name merely by failing to know itself and refusing to publish the answers.[1]

This is exactly what Aldous Huxley had observed in his essay 'And Wanton Optics Roll the Melting Eye':

> One of the pleasures we derive from poetry is precisely the crossword-puzzler's delight in working out a problem. For certain people the pleasure is peculiarly intense. I have known such people who, too highbrow to indulge in the arduous imbecility of crossword and acrostic, sought satisfaction for an imperious yearning in the sonnets of Mallarmé and the more eccentric verses of Gerard Hopkins.

Empson's powerful and sardonic intelligence has constructed some of the most elaborately obscure poems in the language, nor has he scrupled to pillage both classical mythology and the whole realm of scientific knowledge in his search for images and concepts, which he then proceeds to telescope with a fiendish ingenuity. At its best his verse recalls Pound's observation that poetry is a sort of inspired mathematics and Cocteau's dictum that art is science made flesh; and those who object to the range of his thought on the grounds that it is beyond the compass of his readers are in effect demanding that poetry should not attempt to survey the whole province of human knowledge. Such a demand would have been resisted by every major poet in the language for, if its validity were acknowledged, it would condemn poetry to intellectual debility and expose it to contempt.

[1] *The Gathering Storm*, 'Note on Notes', p. 55.

In Empson's finest achievements we observe a man of very great intellectual power investigating a painful moral and metaphysical problem with the passionate accuracy and detachment of a surgeon. The beautiful exactitude of the verse compels our admiration, and we are moved not only by the formal elegance but by the poetic and imaginative power that can win such elegance from such anguish. The poised complexity of such poems as 'Arachne' and 'To An Old Lady' is proof, if proof were needed, that metaphysical wit and deep feeling are not incompatible, but it is in 'This Last Pain' that his fusion of laconic, dry statement and controlled emotion attains its most memorable expression. After the playful irreverence of the opening stanzas, we get a direct statement of man's predicament, a recognition of his lonely insecurity and, in the final stanza, a triumphant affirmation that to recognize man's tragedy is to win the possibility of exulting in it:

All those large dreams by which men long live well
Are magic-lanterned on the smoke of hell;
    This then is real, I have implied,
    A painted, small, transparent slide.

These the inventive can hand-paint at leisure,
Or most emporia would stock our measure;
    And feasting in their dappled shade
    We should forget how they were made.

Feign then what's by a decent tact believed
And act that state is only so conceived,
    And build an edifice of form
    For house where phantoms may keep warm.

Imagine, then, by miracle with me
(Ambiguous gifts, as what gods give must be)
    What could not possibly be there,
    And learn a style from a despair.

The intellectual difficulty of such writing contributes to the total beauty of the poem, just as, in the best of Donne's poetry, the articulation of the thought assumes the shape and the sensuous quality of a musical theme. Empson's poetry fails when the puzzle-interest becomes so absorbing that neither he nor the reader cares about the poetic meaning, or when Empson appears to be saying 'The poetry is in the puzzle.' 'The Scales' is an example of a poem which seems to display this barren, riddling obscurity:

> The proper scale would pat you on the head
> But Alice showed her pup Ulysses' bough
> Well from behind a thistle, wise with dread;
>
> And though your gulf-sprung mountains I allow
> (Snow-puppy curves, rose-solemn dado band)
> Charming for nurse, I am not nurse just now.

We can, it is true, by looking up the notes, which refer us to Lewis Carroll, Homer, and Rider Haggard, extract a meaning from the poem, just as we can painfully construe the argument of 'Bacchus' by studying the long explanatory note on this poem. The real objection to such poems is that they stir no great desire in us to unravel their knotted meaning, and if we overcome our repugnance we do not always gain a reward commensurate with our efforts. Here are the opening lines of 'Bacchus':

> The laughing god born of a startling answer
> (Cymbal of clash in the divided glancer,
> Forcing from heaven's the force of earth's desire)
> Capped a retort to sublime earth by fire
> And starred round within man its salt and glitter
> (Round goblet, but for star—or whirled-map fitter?
> Earth lost in him is still but earth fulfilled),
> Troubled the water till the spirit 'stilled
> And flowered round tears-of-wine round the dimmed
> flask . . .

In his note Empson tells us that the drink which is being distilled by this mythological chemical operation 'makes you more outgoing and unselfcritical, able to do it more heartily—e.g. both more witty and more sentimental. These two = the salt and water sublimed and distilled over from the retort = the sea from which life arose and to which the proportions of all creatures' blood are still similar. Man is the *goblet* . . .'

Here again we are reminded of Donne, but of the Donne who fashioned chinese-puzzles rather than poems, and who violently yoked together the elaborate speculations of the schoolmen and the new hypotheses of the experimental scientists. Empson's ingenious juggling with alembical mythology recalls the far-fetched conceits which Donne exuberantly imported into his description of 'The Progresse of the Soule':

> And whether by this change she lose or win,
> She comes out next, where the Ape would have gone in.
> *Adam* and *Eve* had mingled bloods, and now
> Like Chimiques equall fires, her temperate wombe
> Had stew'd and form'd it: and part did become
> A spungie liver, that did richly allow,
> Like a free conduit, on a high hils brow,
> Life-keeping moisture unto every part;
> Part hardned it selfe to a thicker heart,
>   Whose busie furnaces lifes spirits do impart.

The most damaging charge against some of Empson's poems is not that they are intellectually difficult, not that they refer to the more abstruse theories of modern science, nor even that they occasionally read like a versified text-book, as in this grotesque passage from 'Plenum and Vacuum':

> From infant screams the eyes' blood-gorged veins
> Called ringed orbiculars to guard their balls;
> These stays squeeze yet eyes no relief ensanguines,
> These frowns, sphincter, void-centre, burst wrinkled,
>   hold-alls.

The worst danger is that Empson's brand of intellectual power may, if it runs wild, or is misapplied, destroy the balance of a poem by substituting a dazzling compression of ideas for the true coherence of poetic thought, and that a metaphysical web may be spun over an abyss of irrationality.[1] It was some such premonition that inspired Coleridge to utter a memorable warning in *Biographia Literaria*:

[1] This has been impressively argued by Thom Gunn in his review of Empson's *Collected Poems* in *The London Magazine*, February 1956, pp. 70–75. For a reply see Kathleen Raine's letter in the March issue, pp. 66–67; Thom Gunn's retort is printed in the April issue, pp. 64–65.

Satisfied that the thoughts, such as they were, could not have been expressed otherwise, or at least more perspicuously, I forgot to enquire whether the thoughts themselves did not demand a degree of attention unsuitable to the nature and objects of poetry.

One answer to Coleridge is that dark and disturbing thoughts have a way of seeping into poetry even without the conscious volition of poets, who may be profoundly affected by the deepest philosophical speculations of their time, although they may not formulate their disquiet in intellectual terms. Keats and Tennyson seem to have been acutely sensitive to the theories of Evolution and of Darwinism even before they had been explicitly stated; the Futurists in the years immediately before 1911 were conscious of the impending disintegration of an old, leisured civilization; the Surrealists, D. H. Lawrence, and W. B. Yeats, dissimilar as they were to one another, all foresaw that an era of irrational violence was about to begin. Lecturing in Zurich in 1922, Valéry spoke of all that had been mortally stricken by the first world war: 'But among all these injured things is the Mind. The Mind has indeed been cruelly wounded; its complaint is heard in the hearts of intellectual men; it passes a mortal judgement on itself. It doubts itself profoundly.'[1] It is certain that the stress of that ordeal has left its marks upon the body of verse written since 1918, and although poetry may seem powerless to assimilate all the recent discoveries in the spheres of anthropology, physics, and psychoanalysis, Lawrence Durrell has argued that the obscurity of much contemporary verse is a reflection of the bewildering concepts which have shattered the jigsaw pattern of the universe so carefully and triumphantly assembled by nineteenth-century scientists:

I do not think that it is stretching a point too far to say that the work of Joyce and Proust, the poetry of Eliot and Rilke, is an attempt to present the material of human and supernatural affairs in the form of poetic continuum, where the language no less than the objects observed are impregnated with the new time. . . . Time and the ego are the two centres of focus for all contemporary poets with any pretensions to message.[2]

[1] Quoted by Hans Kohn in *Time and Tide*, 16 November 1946, p. 1093.
[2] *Key to Modern Poetry*, pp. 31 and 83.

Since it is the nature of poetry to be intensely physical and profoundly metaphysical, even the purest lyric rings with a disturbing and elusive resonance. Poetic thought, more impassioned, subtle, and intricate than ratiocinative prose, will always be obscure to the mind that lingers in the museum-world of classified generalizations, unwilling to explore the heart of darkness where intimations of truth rouse themselves and move slowly towards the light:

> Thought's odour is so pale that in the air
> Nostrils inhale, it disappears like fire
> Put out by water. Drifting through the coils
> Of the involved and sponge-like brain it frets
> The fine-veined walls of secret mental cells,
> Brushing their fragile fibre as with light
> Nostalgic breezes: And it's then we sense
> Remote presentiment of some intensely bright
> Impending spiritual dawn, of which the pure
> Immense illumination seems to pour
> In upon our existence from beyond
> The edge of knowing.[1]

[1] David Gascoyne, 'Odeur de Pensée'.

3

Reference

London Bridge is falling down falling down falling down
Poi s'ascose nel foco che gli affina
Quando fiam uti chelidon—O swallow swallow
Le Prince d'Aquitaine à la tour abolie
These fragments I have shored against my ruins
Why then Ile fit you. Hieronymo's mad againe.
Datta. Dayadhvam. Damyata.
          Shantih shantih shantih.
                                   T. S. ELIOT, *The Waste Land*

　　　　·　　　·　　　·　　　·

Newman, Ciddy, Plato, Fronny, Pascal, Bowdler, Baudelaire,
Doctor Frommer, Mrs. Allom, Freud, the Baron and Flaubert
Lured with their compelling logic, charmed with beauty of
　　their verse,
With their loaded sideboards whispered 'Better join us, life
　　is worse.'
                                   W. H. AUDEN, *Poems*, XXII

ONE of the most famous passages in the 'Ode to a Nightingale' describes how the bird is singing

> Perhaps the self-same song that found a path
> 　Through the sad heart of Ruth, when, sick for home,
> 　She stood in tears amid the alien corn. . . .

Few people would consider these lines difficult, and most readers would find the satire of Robert Graves's 'The Persian Version' immediately comprehensible:

> Truth-loving Persians do not dwell upon
> The trivial skirmish fought near Marathon.

Yet if the Old Testament were to become even more of a closed book than it is at present Keats's image would shed its lustre; and if men were to forget the significance of Marathon the point of Graves's poem would vanish. Poems no more intrinsically difficult than these are often regarded as obscure simply because they contain references which are unfamiliar to the common run of readers. Those who teach English literature in African schools discover that some apparently straightforward poems utterly baffle their pupils, and usually the reason is that the experience described in these poems, while a commonplace to a European child, is alien to the young African. Some fine English poetry, particularly that written since 1900, is beyond the comprehension of a great many adult Englishmen for much the same reason: the poet is taking for granted a whole range of ideas, philosophical concepts, literary allusions and reconstructions of historical events which are meaningless to his readers. East African students of English literature at Makerere College, Uganda, were confronted with Gray's poem 'On a Favourite Cat Drowned in a Tub of Goldfishes':

No one in the class knew what goldfishes were and it took me some time to explain why they should be in a tub. We laboured through the verse, getting to grips with the elegant Augustan circumlocutions of Gray—'Demurest of the tabby kind', 'The Genii of the stream', 'Malignant Fate sat by and smiled'—The Nymphs, Dolphins and Nereids. At the end of the period everyone had understood the meaning of the poem but the elegance and the mock heroic tones had been drowned in the water with the cat.[1]

It was not lack of intelligence that hamstrung these African students, nor is it a sign of stupidity to find the two following passages obscure, beautiful and impressive though they are:

> To the right hand there lies a secret pool
> Alive with speckled trout and fish of gold;
> A hazel overshadows it. Orphion,
> Primaeval serpent straggling in the branches,
> Darts out his tongue. The holy pool is fed
> By dripping water; guardians stand before it.
> Run to this pool, the pool of memory,
> Run to this pool.
>
> ROBERT GRAVES

[1] Alan Warner, 'Teaching English to East African Students: An Interim Report', *English Language Teaching*, vol. x, No. 2 (1956), p. 57.

Before I knocked and flesh let enter,
With liquid hands tapped on the womb,
I who was shapeless as the water
That shaped the Jordan near my home
Was brother to Mnetha's daughter
And sister to the fathering worm.

DYLAN THOMAS

Not until the worship of Jehovah has been generally superseded by the cult of the White Goddess and of the Orphic
mysteries, and the Prophetic Books of William Blake have
grown more familiar than the canon of the Old Testament,
will Orphion and Mnetha's daughter evoke the response that
is awakened by the serpent in the Garden of Eden and by
Ruth amid the alien corn.

The mere lapse of time may obscure the meaning of a passage which can have presented no difficulties to the original
readers. The obscure jokes, the allusions to current events,
the metaphors drawn from country sports, with which Shakespeare's plays are crammed, have to be explained to a modern
reader before he can appreciate them:

If I do prove her haggard
Though that her jesses were my dear heart-strings,
I'd whistle her off and let her down the wind
To prey at Fortune.

What are we to make of that technical metaphor without some
knowledge of falconry, and now that we have rejected all but
the most trivial manifestations of astrology what meaning
resides in an image that must have impressed itself vividly
upon the first readers of Shakespeare's sonnets:

Nativity once in the maine of light
Crawles to maturity?

Obsolete scientific instruments and outmoded scientific concepts derived from the new learning clutter the poems of the
Metaphysicals—the dust lies thick upon such discarded stage
properties—and the two-handed engine at the door in 'Lycidas' is mere lumber, a rusty memento of political hatred.
Satire, like gossip, tends to be almost as ephemeral as the
fashions and the figures that it castigates, the fire of its

indignation petering out, the brightness of the allusions growing ever more tarnished. Dryden's contempt for the folly of his age retains its majesty, and Pope's agony at the impending triumph of Dullness still has power to move us, because their satire is great enough to transcend their grubby material, endowing the gross monsters and the noisome dwarfs who inhabit their worlds with a terrifying and universal import. Yet the details of their portraiture have grown blurred, and some of their gayest quips can be savoured only with the help of an annotated edition:

> A Lady's Face is all you see undress'd,
> (For none but Lady —— shows the Rest)
> But if to Charms more latent you pretend,
> What Lines encompass and what Works defend!
> Dangers on Dangers! obstacles by dozens!
> Spies, Guardians, Guests, old Women, Aunts
>   and Cozens![1]

We shall miss the point of Pope's equivocal jest in the last line unless we realize that Cozens was a stay-maker, just as the full implications of the following couplet will escape us unless we know something about Pulteney, about the early eighteenth-century connotation of Patriotism and about the chemical experiments which were so fashionable and novel:

> Through clouds of Passion Pulteney's views are clear,
> He foams a Patriot to subside a Peer.

Still more puzzling to the majority of readers is the poem which depends for its effect upon their ability to recognize a fine and intricate network of literary allusions. This allusiveness is not a new device, nor did T. S. Eliot invent the practice of weaving into the fabric of a poem a cunningly arranged pattern of quotations, for this method of composition was frequently employed by the poets of Alexandria and of Rome, by Claudian who, though born a Greek, came to live in the Western Empire towards the end of the fourth century A.D., and by numerous English poets from the sixteenth century onwards. The main difference between, let us say, the technique of Milton and of T. S. Eliot is that Milton introduces

[1] *Sober Advice from Horace*, 124–9.

the references to other poets in order to decorate and to en-
rich his verse, whereas a poem such as 'Burbank with a
Baedeker: Bleistein with a Cigar' is composed almost entirely
of quotations, overt, concealed or parodied, and if the reader
is to extract any enjoyment from it he must be aware of these
echoes and admire the skill which the poet has displayed in
prolonging their reverberations and in linking them with a
concise and sardonic running commentary. Ingenious and
witty as such a tessellation of references may be, it is bound to
seem obscure to anybody who happens not to have read the
same authors as the poet, especially when, as in *The Waste
Land*, the connecting passages between the quotations, and all
explanatory matter, have been ruthlessly cut in the interests
of concentration and intensity. W. H. Auden's lines on
Goodness:

> He has a name like Billy and is almost perfect
> But wears a stammer like a decoration

are meaningless unless one is familiar with the story of Billy
Budd; and Lawrence Durrell's potted cultural history merely
baffles the reader who fails to spot the allusions:

> Here St. Augustine took the holy cue
> Of bells in an English valley; and mad Jerome
> Made of his longing half a home from home. . . .

> While those who noted the weather-vane
> In Beatrice's shadow sang
> With the dying Emily: 'We shall never
> Return, never be young again.'

In this same poem, 'Cities, Plains and People', which contains a host of references to a wide diversity of characters,
including Dostoevsky and his wife ('Fëdor and Anna'), the
mythical Yellow Emperor, first exponent of the Tao, Faust,
Hamlet, Rimbaud, Goethe, and Descartes, there is one stanza
which, carrying as a marginal note an extract from *The Ad-
miralty Pilot*: 'All bearings are true', coruscates with dazzling,
cryptic epigrams upon literature old and new, leaving all
except the nimblest-witted and most sophisticated reader
astonished and admiring, but vaguely unsatisfied:

Here however man might botch his way
To God via Valéry, Gide or Rabelais
All rules obtain upon the pilot's plan
So long as man, not manners, makyth man.
Some like the great Victorians of the past
Through old Moll Flanders sailed before the mast,
While savage Chatterleys of the new romance
Get carried off in Sex, the ambulance.
All rules obtain upon the pilot's chart
If governed by the scripture of the heart.

Most of us feel a comforting glow of intellectual pride when we catch an oblique and esoteric allusion and commend the poet for his fine sense of cultural tradition; but should his references fall outside the field of our special interests the temptation is to blame him for clogging his poetry with a mass of recondite knowledge. Old-fashioned critics who solemnly assured their ignorant readers that a full enjoyment of Milton was the rare fruit of a classical education were genuinely disconcerted by the rag-bag of unfamiliar quotations in *The Waste Land*, and experts in English Literature who have learned to hop from one partially submerged tag to another as nimbly as a travel-agent thumbs his way through Bradshaw do not relish William Empson's assured manipulation of scientific concepts, or Pound's long epic so liberally strewn with Chinese ideograms.

Some poets demand that their readers shall be learned not only in literary history but also in mythology, metaphysics, anthropology, and comparative religion. Robert Graves quotes the remarks of what he calls 'a leading English literary columnist' about some lines from *Jerusalem*: 'It is obvious that the imagery of this passage . . . is from Blake's subliminal consciousness of political passions. Albion as a mythical figure may typify Heaven knows what else besides, but that is neither here nor there.' Graves then comments:

It is the function of English popular critics to judge all poetry by gleeman standards. So the clear traditional imagery used by Blake is charactistically dismissed as 'neither here nor there' and he is charged with not knowing what he is writing about. The White Goddess's Starry Wheel here multiplied into the twelve wheeling signs of the zodiac, and the intellectual furnaces of Los (Apollo), and the Tomb of Albion—alias Llew Llaw Gyffes, who also appears as the famished Eagle with his boney wings—are misread as dark, mechanistic images of capitalist oppression.[1]

Much as we may agree with Graves in deploring slapdash literary journalism, can we seriously maintain that Blake's imagery in the Prophetic Books is clear, or that it belongs to a tradition which has been generally accepted by readers of poetry from Blake's day to our own? The poem which begins 'Mock on, Mock on, Voltaire, Rousseau', evokes an instant response with its contrast between the scientific and the religious vision of life, because its imagery is part of our familiar mental furniture:

> The Atoms of Democritus
> And Newton's particles of light
> Are sands upon the Red sea shore,
> Where Israel's tents do shine so bright.

How strange and remote, in comparison, seems the imagery of the Prophetic Books, drawn as it is from Plotinus, Swedenborg, Boehme, the Cabbala, Gnosticism, and from even more curious sources which are still being investigated and uncovered. Moreover, Blake's symbols do not bear a constant meaning: when he employs a given symbol he may be thinking of Druidic lore, or of the Industrial Revolution, or of political events which he dares not allude to openly. Blake's annotations of Bacon's *The Advancement of Learning* and of Bishop Watson's *Apology for the Bible* reveal the violently seditious nature of his opinions in the closing years of the eighteenth century. His preface to the notes on Watson reveals Blake's conviction that 'to defend the Bible in this year 1798 would cost a man his life', and it seems certain that he deliberately cloaked his true opinions in the mantle of an obscure mythology. It is a vulgar mistake to suppose that his reference to dark Satanic mills is a piece of humanitarian rhetoric about factory conditions; it is a more rarefied error, though still an error, to believe that he was exclusively

---

[1] *The White Goddess*, pp. 398–9.

concerned with elaborating a private mythological system
entirely divorced from the industrial scene:

> Here on the banks of the Thames, Los builded Golgonooza,
> Outside the Gates of the Human Heart beneath Beulah
> In the midst of the rocks of the Altars of Albion. In fears
> He builded it, in rage and in fury. It is the Spiritual Four-fold
> London, continually building and continually decaying desolate.
> In eternal labours loud the Furnaces and loud the Anvils
> Of Death thunder incessant.

This is indeed the portrayal of a timeless city, 'the Spiritual
Four-fold London', but is it not also the description of a
terrestrial city at a particular date in recorded history, A.D.
1786, when Boulton and Watt set up their steam-engine in
the Albion flour-mill? Even in passages of arcane symbolism
the shadows of industrial undertakings darken the page:

> These nostrils that Expanded with delight in morning skies
> I have bent downwards with lead molten in my roaring furnaces.
> My soul is seven furnaces, incessant roar the bellows
> Upon my terribly flaming heart, the molten metal runs
> In channels thro' my fiery limbs.

The spiritual tyranny of Locke and of Newton is bodied forth
in imagery derived from the cogs and the wheels that drove
the new industrial machine. W. B. Yeats, looking back over
the desolation which had scarcely begun in Blake's day,
epitomized the whole process in four savage lines:

> Locke sank into a swoon;
> The Garden died;
> God took the spinning-jenny
> Out of his side.

Where Yeats is witty, bitter, and concise, Blake is denuncia-
tory and rhapsodic:

> I turn my eyes to the Schools and Universities of Europe
> And there behold the Loom of Locke, whose Woof rages dire,
> Wash'd by the Water-wheels of Newton: black the cloth
> In heavy wreathes folds over every nation: cruel Works
> Of many Wheels I view, wheel without wheel, with cogs
>   tyrannic

Moving by compulsion each other, not as those in Eden, which,
Wheel within wheel, in freedom revolve in harmony and peace.[1]

To make things more difficult still, Blake's symbols not
only stand for a variety of meanings but may even bear contradictory moral significances. Bernard Blackstone has pointed
out his inconsistent use of mathematical imagery:

When he is thinking of his beloved quaternary, or of Bacon's
denial of it, he makes mathematical proportion an instrument of the
creative Los. When he is thinking of the mechanical world-picture
of Newton, mathematical proportion is seen as devilish.[2]

Newton himself is not invariably a hireling of Satan. Marjorie
Nicolson has shown, in *Newton Demands the Muse*, how Blake
adopted Newton's corpuscular theory of light and his concept
of ether; and Blake seems to have regarded him with something of the reluctant admiration which Milton felt for his
Satan:

Even Newton is not always the single symbol of a narrow
rationalism. . . . He is also the energetic spirit with the compasses in
Blake's colour print of *Newton*, and the spirit who blows the trum-
pet of the Last Judgment in *Europe*. His are the compasses with
which Urizen marks out the Mundane Shell in the greatest of
Blake's designs, which is commonly called *The Ancient of Days*.
They are also the compasses of the child Jesus in Blake's design of
Christ in the Carpenter's Shop.[3]

Shelley's images, like Blake's, have a manifold significance.
In his *Essay on Christianity*, he remarks that 'every human
mind has what Bacon calls *idola specus*—peculiar images which
reside in the inner cave of thought', and it is this type of
image that he employs to suggest the relation of the human
mind to the Universe and of natural phenomena to Platonic
Reality. Nor can we always distinguish between his personal
interpretation of these images and what he borrowed from
his readings in philosophy, mythology, and the scientific
works of Erasmus Darwin, Davy, and a brood of forgotten

[1] These three passages from Blake will be found in the second edition of the
Nonesuch *Poetry and Prose of William Blake*, pp. 630, 410, 574.

[2] *English Blake*, p. 221, n.1.

[3] J. Bronowski, *William Blake: A Man Without a Mask*, p. 95.

minor figures.[1] Shelley's passionate interest in science distinguishes him from most of the early Romantics, who would have gladly joined in the toast which Lamb, Keats, and Wordsworth drank at Haydon's dinner-party on 28 December 1817: 'Newton's health and confusion to mathematics.' Unlike Coleridge, who attended Davy's lectures[2] solely in order to acquire some vivid images, Shelley wished to incorporate the latest scientific theories into his poetry rather than to adorn his verse with stolen plumage. The product is all too often a curious outpouring of highly coloured imagery, which sacrifices mythical grandeur without attaining scientific precision. Thus in *Prometheus Unbound*, Act IV, Ione and Panthea describe how, through two openings in the forest,

> Two visions of strange radiance float upon
> The ocean-like enchantment of strong sound.

Ione sees a chariot driven by an infant of radiant whiteness:

> . . . yet its two eyes are heavens
> Of liquid darkness, which the Deity
> Within seems pouring, as a storm is poured
> From jagged clouds, out of their arrowy lashes,
> Tempering the cold and radiant air around,
> With fire that is not brightness; . . .

That passage is meant to be a depiction of electricity; Panthea then chimes in with her presentation of current scientific theory, telling how

> . . . from the other opening in the wood
> Rushes, with loud and whirlwind harmony,
> A sphere, which is as many thousand spheres,
> Solid as crystal, yet through all its mass
> Flow, as through empty space, music and light:
> Ten thousand orbs involving and involved,
> Purple and azure, white, and green, and golden,
> Sphere within sphere; . . .

This is Davy's theory of the dance of matter raised to a pitch of white-hot intensity and set to an almost incoherent music, the final effect being one of dazzling darkness.

[1] See Peter Butter, *Shelley's Idols of the Cave*, and its review in the *Times Literary Supplement*, 20 August 1954, p. 530.

[2] Wordsworth also admired Davy.

It is no accident that the greatest follower of Blake and of
Shelley should have written some of the most obscure poetry
that even the present century has witnessed. Every new book
on the sources of W. B. Yeats's imagery reveals the extraordinary range and nature of his speculations and illuminates
the fabulous darkness that surrounds so many of the poems
written in the last twenty years of his life. Without the long
commentaries of such critics as Richard Ellmann, Norman
Jeffares, and T. R. Henn, it would be extremely hard to trace
the varying strands of myth and of esoteric doctrines which
interweave so cunningly in the pattern of his verse, and entrap
the reader who ventures there without a guide:

> I saw a staring virgin stand
> Where holy Dionysus died,
> And tear the heart out of his side,
> And lay the heart upon her hand
> And bear that beating heart away;
> And then did all the Muses sing
> Of Magnus Annus at the spring,
> As though God's death were but a play.
>
> Another Troy must rise and set,
> Another lineage feed the crow,
> Another Argo's painted prow
> Drive to a flashier bauble yet.
> The Roman Empire stood appalled:
> It dropped the reins of peace and war
> When that fierce virgin and her Star
> Out of the fabulous darkness called.[1]

This poem remains obscure until we have unravelled the literary, metaphysical, and astrological references which Yeats
has bundled into it; having done this, we are free to admire
not only the energy and the musical richness that irradiate the
poem, even when we do not grasp its full significance, but the
art which has enabled Yeats to amalgamate into the unity of
a song so many complexities of thought.

A full explanation of this poem would entail a discussion of

---

[1] The first of 'Two Songs from a Play'. The play is *The Resurrection* and the
songs are fully discussed by R. Ellmann, *The Identity of Yeats*, pp. 260–3.

the abstruse philosophical system which forms the substance of *A Vision*, and would lead us to consider the elaborate symbolism that Yeats discerned in the Phases of the Moon, his curious theory of history, and his corresponding theory of psychological types. It is enough for our present purposes if we can trace the leading metaphysical themes which he develops in so ingenious and brilliant a counterpoint. The song begins with a reference to 'holy Dionysus', son of Persephone and Zeus, who was torn to death by the Titans, whereupon Athena carried his heart to Zeus, who swallowed it and rebegot him upon Semele. Obsessed as he was by the idea of recurrence and of cyclical return, Yeats seized upon the fact that both Christ and Dionysus died and were reborn in March when the sun was between the Ram and the Fish, and the moon was beside the constellation Virgo. Yeats emphasizes this coincidence to show that Christ's death and resurrection are not unique but a type of all the deaths and resurrections which have occurred in the universal myths. In the same way, the constellation Virgo, who carries in her hand the star Spica, is also Astraea who, according to Virgil's Fourth Eclogue, will restore the golden age. Moreover, she was in medieval times identified with the Blessed Virgin Mary, and Spica with the Star of Bethlehem. God's death is a play enacted many times, and the curtain comes down with the advent of Magnus Annus, the Platonic Great Year, in which a whole cycle of the stellar system is completed.

The second stanza opens with a bitter parody of Shelley's chorus from *Hellas*, 'The world's great age begins anew,' an example of the savage gaiety with which Yeats derided the idea of progress and contemplated the next turn of the wheel in which terror and injustice would ride to the top. Yeats does not mock Shelley's chorus solely because it is a classic example of cosmic optimism: the chorus is particularly relevant to his argument because it is an adaptation of Virgil's Fourth Eclogue. By a similar device, Yeats makes the last four lines of the second stanza recapitulate one of the themes announced in the first stanza. Their obvious meaning is that Christ's birth shattered the pagan dominion of Greece and Rome; the very term 'fabulous darkness' is derived from Proclus, the neo-Platonist, who used the phrase 'fabulous, formless darkness' to describe Christianity. But for Yeats the Annunciation is merely a type of all violent annunciations foreshadowing those births which usher in a new era, the birth of Christ being one with the birth of Helen of Troy and of the rough beast who slouches across the desert in 'The Second Coming'. The Virgin in this poem is triune, just as Christ is a manifestation of Dionysus, and the song ends, as it begins, with a Virgin staring at the future as it rises from the darkness of the past.

Although this song is a relatively simple example of Yeats's elaborate art, it has involved us in a cumbersome and pedantic explanation; yet unless we are content to ignore the intellectual substance of his verse and to be sucked unresistingly into the vortex of his poetry by its all-compelling music we need some such gloss to elucidate the body of belief which inspires so many of his later poems. Perhaps belief is the wrong word to describe that assortment of esoteric philosophy, gnomic wisdom, historical speculation, sexual mysticism and self-dramatization which glitters so bravely in the poems of his two final decades. Vico, Berkeley, Swedenborg, Blake, Spengler, and Toynbee are ransacked to illuminate his chosen themes; memories of his youthful enthusiasm for Madam Blavatsky, the Cabbala and the Order of the Golden Dawn lend an element of direct personal experience to the cosmic speculations; the image of Byzantium, constructed with such rare artifice, and the revelations vouchsafed him by the messengers who dictated *A Vision* deepen the obscurity. There is no fumbling vagueness in the work of this period, for the diction, the syntax and the articulation of the poetic argument are magnificently clear: it is the references alone that darken counsel.

This obscurity does not greatly trouble those who, having fallen under the spell of Yeats's poetry, permit its energy, fire, and music to whirl them over the shadier patches of oracular wisdom, and to silence the nagging doubt that some of Yeats's philosophy is as pinchbeck as the Order of the Golden Dawn. It is instructive to compare the general acceptance of the later poems of Yeats with the lack of enthusiasm aroused by Charles Williams's two final books of verse, *Taliessin Through Logres* and *The Region of the Summer Stars*, despite the advocacy of C. S. Lewis, who regards them as poetry of a very high order. Lewis admits that these poems are distinguished by obscurity of reference: before we can follow their argument we must be familiar with the Bible, Malory, Dante, Gibbon, the Mabinogion, Church history, and the significance of the Seriphotic tree.[1] This is more intellectually formidable than anything demanded by Yeats or by T. S. Eliot, who require above all else an emotional and imaginative response, but it is not a wholly unreasonable stipulation. Where Williams differs from the two great masters of our time is that he asks us to plod through an extremely complex and systematic allegory which he uses in an endeavour to fuse the Arthurian legend with an elaborate Christian theology. A curious fondness for a relentless physiological symbolism loads the sequence of poems with yet another burden. In the first edition of *Taliessin Through Logres* there is a map of Europe in the days of the Byzantine Empire, upon which is superimposed the drawing of a naked woman, every part of the Empire neatly corresponding with a portion of her body. Hence are derived such passages as the following:

> The milk rises in the breasts of Gaul,
> trigonometrical milk of doctrine.
> Man sucks it; his joints harden,
> sucking logic, learning law,
> drawing on the breasts of *intelligo* and *credo*.

Can we swallow the trigonometrical milk of such poetry? My view is that although the language of these poems is always individual and sometimes impressive, it tends to alternate between a melodramatic intensity and a harsh angularity. Moreover, the tone of the verse is unattractive: such episodes as the clapping of a girl into the stocks in 'The Ascent of the Spear' are strangely disquieting, and the mixture of detailed allegory and anatomical exactitude is both uncouth and rebarbative:

[1] *Arthurian Torso*, p. 189.

the stripped maids laughed for joy of the province,
bearing in themselves the shape of the province
founded in the base of space,
in the rounded bottom of the Emperor's glory.
Spines were strengthened, loves settled;
tossed through aerial gulfs of Empire
the lost name, the fool's shame,
fame and frame of lovers in lowlands of Caucasia,
rang round snowy Elburz.
The organic body sang together . . .

Merlin, time's metre, climbs through prisms and lines;
over near Camelot and far Carbonek,
over the Perilous Sell, the See of union,
the phosphor of Percivale's philosophical star shines.
Lancelot's lion, bewildered by the smell of adoration,
roars round Guinevere's lordly body.

The stripped maids and Guinevere's lordly body never spring
to life; like the phosphor of Percivale's philosophical star and
Lancelot's lion, they are bereft of sensual beauty and yet do
not shine with spiritual glory. The verse lacks that sensuous
and musical vitality which informs the poetry of Eliot and of
Yeats and which alone can breathe poetic life into the dry
bones of doctrine. Charles Williams was, by all accounts, a
man of singular grace and wisdom; as a critic and philosopher
he was highly gifted; but as a poet he remains a very queer
fish in a deep, dark pond.

The verse of the two most generally-admired poets of the
past twenty-five years, W. H. Auden and Dylan Thomas,
bristles with obscurities, few of which can be elucidated
simply by reference to a philosophical system outside the
poetry. Probably the only poems of Dylan Thomas which call
for this type of exegesis are those forming the sonnet-
sequence 'Altarwise By Owl-Light', which are, according to
an American commentator, a mixture of Christian and astro-
nomical symbolism, Christ Himself being portrayed as subject
to the inexorable wheeling of the Constellations.[1]

The early poems of Auden, on the other hand, despite their
lack of philosophical system and coherence, shed part of their

[1] Elder Olson, *The Poetry of Dylan Thomas.*

obscurity when we know something of their physical and intellectual background. They depict a world of doom, in which the Icelandic sagas might have been enacted, a landscape of fortified passes, of 'scars where kestrels hover', remote, hostile, and lonely:

> But ever that man goes
> Through place-keepers, through forest trees,
> A stranger to strangers over undried sea,
> Houses for fishes, suffocating water,
> Or lonely on fell as chat,
> By pot-holed becks
> A bird stone-haunting, an unquiet bird.[1]

Curious figures make cryptic gestures; there are references to Captain Ferguson, to a mysterious Adversary:

> Nights come bringing the snow, and the dead howl
> Under the headlands in their windy dwelling
> Because the Adversary put too easy questions
> On lonely roads.[2]

and to a 'supreme Antagonist' whom the poet invokes:

> . . . Summon
> Those handsome and diseased youngsters, those women
> Your solitary agents in the country parishes;
> And mobilize the powerful forces latent
> In soils that make the farmer brutal
> In the infected sinus, and the eyes of stoats.[3]

Even the conflicts in this world seem purposeless, as in *Paid on Both Sides*, or in these lines which pay tribute to

> The tall unwounded leader
> Of doomed companions, all
> Whose voices in the rock
> Are now perpetual,
> Fighters for no one's sake,
> Who died beyond the border.[4]

[1] *Poems*, II. Entitled 'The Wanderer' in *Collected Shorter Poems*.
[2] *Poems*, XXVI. Entitled 'Taller To-day' in *Collected Shorter Poems*.
[3] *Poems*, XXIX. Entitled 'Consider' in *Collected Shorter Poems*.
[4] *Poems*, XXIV. Entitled 'Missing' in *Collected Shorter Poems*.

Confused and confusing as these passages may be, one feels that they are meant to convey a definite message, even though one lacks the key to the cryptogram. It is clear that Auden's early work owes something to his fondness for Icelandic tales:

> With northern myths my little brain was laden,
>   With deeds of Thor and Loki and such scenes;
> My favourite tale was Andersen's Ice Maiden; . . .[1]

although the next four lines remind us of Auden's early interest in the machines that dominate our society:

> But better far than any kings or queens
> I liked to see and know about machines:
> And from my sixth until my sixteenth year
> I thought myself a mining engineer.

Auden seems to have been fascinated by the calm power of machinery, yet horrified by the desolation of men's lives passed in its shadow:

> On your right is the Power House: its chimneys fume gently
>   above us like rifles recently fired.
> Look through the grating at the vast machinery; at the
>   dynamos and turbines
> Grave, giving no sign of the hurricane of steam within their
>   huge steam bottles,
> At the Diesel engines like howdahed elephants: at the dials
>   with their flickering pointers:
> Power to the city: where loyalties are not those of the family . . .
>
> Full as a theatre is the foul thoroughfare: some sitting like
>   sacks, some slackly standing,
> Their faces grey in the glimmering gaslight: their eyeballs
>   drugged like a dead rabbit's,
> From a window a child is looking, by want so fretted his face
>   has assumed the features of a tortoise:
> A human forest; all by one infection cancelled.[2]

The answer to the disease that was destroying society was a surgical operation, with Karl Marx as the surgeon. Marxism

---

[1] *Letter to Lord Byron*, Part IV.
[2] Chorus from *The Dog Beneath the Skin*.

appealed to Auden because of its apocalyptic violence, which seemed in his imagination to take on the heroic quality of a Norse legend; it promised also to use machinery boldly and rationally, unlike the decadent capitalist world of the early 1930s where

> Man is changed by his living; but not fast enough.
> His concern to-day is for that which yesterday did not occur.
> In the hour of the Blue Bird and the Bristol Bomber, his thoughts are appropriate to the years of the Penny Farthing.

Finally, it appeared to give hope and dignity to those who lived in 'the byres of poverty', wretched, degraded, unwanted. So, with a kind of grim relish, Auden warns the financier:

> The game is up for you and for the others,
> Who, thinking, pace in slippers on the lawns
> Of College Quad or Cathedral Close,
> Who are born nurses, who live in shorts
> Sleeping with people and playing fives.[1]

The last two lines introduce a new element into what seems to be a straightforward piece of political ranting, and they are typical of the fourth, and the most baffling, type of reference in the early poems of Auden—his employment of concepts derived from psychoanalytical theories, and in particular from the works of Groddeck, whose writings are not easy to come by, and whose doctrines are extremely curious. Moreover, Auden picks and chooses only what pleases his nimble imagination, without attempting to present Groddeck's theories logically or systematically. Disease in the body politic, as in the human body, is the manifestation of a neurosis; we *will* cancer, war, even the form of our death, because of what we are; there is indeed a common wish for death, in each one of us and in our society. Now it is clear that, in this mood, Auden cannot simply look to a Marxist revolution as the answer to our deep-seated discontents: he must postulate a saviour, or a healer, whom he addresses in one poem, 'Petition', much as Hopkins addressed the God whom he worshipped:

---

[1] *Poems*, XXIX. These lines are omitted in the version of the poem printed in *Collected Shorter Poems*, and given the title of 'Consider'.

Sir, no man's enemy, forgiving all
But will its negative inversion, be prodigal:
Send to us power and light, a sovereign touch
Curing the intolerable neural itch,
The exhaustion of weaning, the liar's quinsy,
And the distortions of ingrown virginity.

Why the liar should suffer from quinsy is not made clear: the answer may be available in Groddeck, or the conjunction may have tickled the poet's fancy.

Much of the obscurity in Auden's early work comes from his fondness for ringing the changes upon his four main themes—the world of saga, the world of machinery, and of social engineering, the impending Marxist catastrophe, and the clinical analysis of Groddeck. He swings from one level of reality to another with the agility of a trapeze-artist, blinding the audience with science; one feels as bewildered as poor Miss Tray when she asks Captain Mallet which theory he believes in, and receives the answer:

As they are one and all infallible, despite being utterly different, there's little point in describing the differences. What does it matter to you, after all, whether you are diagnosed on a principle of ancestry, heredity, environment, instinct, the lavatory, or genetics? Nothing you can say is going to make the slightest difference to the outcome.[1]

The effect upon his first readers of Auden's original set of references has been best described by Christopher Isherwood in his portrait of 'Weston':

For Eliot's Dante-quotations and classical learning, he sub-stituted oddments of scientific, medical and psycho-analytical jar-gon: his magpie brain was a hoard of curious and suggestive phrases from Jung, Rivers, Kretschner and Freud. He peppered his work liberally with such terms as 'eutectic', 'sigmoid curve', 'Arch-nomad', 'ligature', 'gastropod'; seeking thereby to produce what he himself described as a 'clinical' effect.[2]

There are other causes of obscurity in Auden's work, apart from the obscurity of his references. I have already spoken of

---

[1] See Nigel Dennis, *Cards of Identity*, pp. 76–77.
[2] *Lions and Shadows*, p. 191.

his fondness for clipped syntax and I shall, in later chapters, remark on his contempt for his readers, his indulgence in private fantasy, and his remarkable use of imagery. Even so, much of the darkness which surrounds his early poems would be dissipated if we were more familiar with the concepts that were occupying his mind in the late 1920s and early 1930s, and could trace more precisely his debts to Freud, Groddeck, and Homer Lane. We lack, for his first group of poems, what he himself provided in *New Year Letter*, a body of notes indicating in some detail the sources from which the ideas and images of the poem were derived.

It will not have escaped notice that Yeats, Eliot, Charles Williams, Empson, and Auden, all highly-educated men living between the two wars in the same country, have no common background of reference, and cannot count on their readers' being able to follow their train of thought. In Shakespeare's day, even in Johnson's day, all men with any pretensions to culture shared a common heritage, a fund of traditional myths, sacred books, accumulated knowledge, and canons of taste which, however limited, were clearly defined. By the end of the nineteenth century, the ancient certainties had been dethroned. We are no longer confident that Greek art of the fifth century B.C., and the art of the Italian Renaissance are the finest sculpture and painting that human beings have achieved; there are other gods in the pantheon of literature besides Homer, Virgil, the Bible, Dante, Shakespeare, and Milton; a glance at Ezra Pound's *How to Read* is enough to show that anarchy is raging in what used to be called the republic of letters. All this is too obvious to dwell on, and it should be equally obvious that poetry is bound to become increasingly obscure as a culture grows more fissiparous:

> We were the last romantics—chose for theme
> Traditional sanctity and loveliness;
> Whatever's written in what poets name
> The book of the people; whatever most can bless
> The mind of man or elevate a rhyme; . . .

The book of the people no longer exists, and in its place we are assailed with a multitude of pamphlets written by specialists for specialists. When poets have lost the sense of responsibility and the exhilarating discipline that come from a joyful observance of common standards and accepted codes, their references will inevitably grow ever more far-fetched and eccentric. It is no accident that *The Waste Land* should be at once a profoundly moving threnody for a lost civilization and the most allusive poem of our age; and that when Yeats laments the passing of the last romantics his elegy should mourn not only a literary tradition but a whole way of life:

> But all is changed, that high horse riderless,
> Though mounted in that saddle Homer rode
> Where the swan drifts upon a darkening flood.[1]

[1] The two final quotations in this chapter are taken from the last stanza of W. B. Yeats's 'Coole and Ballylee, 1931'.

4

Common Readers

Turn what they will to Verse, their toil is vain,
Critics like me shall make it Prose again.
                              POPE, *The Dunciad*

.   .   .

Be subtle, various, ornamental, clever,
And do not listen to those critics ever
Whose crude provincial gullets crave in books
Plain cooking made still plainer by plain cooks.
       W. H. AUDEN,
              'The Truest Poetry is the Most Feigning.'

EVER since Ben Jonson prophesied to William Drummond
that John Donne 'for not being understood, would perish',
one of the favourite charges levelled against poets of true
originality by their contemporaries is that they are obscure.
Although few people have the audacity to blame mathematic-
ians or physicists for being difficult to understand, there is a
general belief that poetry should be immediately comprehensible, even to the meanest intelligence:

When books are written in the prevailing language of the
country, everyone becomes a critic who can read. An author is no
longer tried by his peers. A species of universal suffrage is introduced in letters, which is only applicable to politics. The good old
Latin style of our forefathers, if it concealed the dullness of the
writer, at least was a barrier against the impertinence, flippancy,
and ignorance of the reader.[1]

The truth is that much poetry of the highest quality demands
of its readers a degree of mental alertness and of general
culture which most people do not possess:

[1] Hazlitt, 'On Pedantry'.

68

Among bewildering appliances
For mastering the arts and sciences
    They stroll and run,
And nerves that never flinched at slaughter
Are shot to pieces by the shorter
    Poems of Donne.[1]

This belief was firmly rooted in the minds of good eighteenth-century critics, who expected readers of poetry to use their brains and their critical faculties when confronted with major verse. Jonathan Richardson the Elder made an admirable observation on Milton's obscurity which was quoted by Richardson the Younger in *Explanatory Notes and Remarks on Milton's Paradise Lost* (1734):

> A Reader of *Milton* must be Always upon Duty; he is Surrounded with Sense, it rises in every Line, every Word is to the Purpose; There are no Lazy Intervals, All has been Consider'd, and Demands and Merits Observation . . . if this is call'd obscurity let it be remembered 'tis Such a One as is Complaisant to the Reader . . . not that Vicious Obscurity which proceeds from a Muddled Inaccurate Head.

Boswell records a conversation which shows that Richardson's doctrine was not universally accepted even by men of letters and which helps us to understand the hostile reception of 'The Progress of Poesy' and of 'The Bard', much to Gray's chagrin:

BOSWELL: Well, I admire Gray prodigiously. I have read his odes till I was almost mad.

GOLDSMITH: They are terribly obscure. We must be historians and learned men before we can understand them.

DAVIES: And why not? He is not writing to porters or carmen. He is writing to men of knowledge.[2]

Hostile as Blake was to the polite world of his day, he would have no truck with the doctrine that it is the poet's duty to flatter the weakest intellects among his readers, as this spirited letter to the Rev. John Trusler plainly shows:

[1] W. H. Auden, 'Under Which Lyre, a Reactionary Tract for the Times'.
[2] *Boswell's London Journal* (ed. F. A. Pottle), p. 106.

You say that I want somebody to Elucidate my Ideas. But you ought to Know that What is Grand is necessarily obscure to Weak men. That which can be made Explicit to the Idiot is not worth my care. The wisest of the Ancients consider'd what is not too Explicit as the fittest for Instruction, because it rouzes the faculties to act. I name Moses, Solomon, Esop, Homer, Plato.[1]

The first Romantics were at one with Blake in holding that poetic grandeur may baffle and irritate those who are constitutionally unfit to sustain the exhilarating shock administered by all great art to our torpid spirits. There is a fine passage in De Quincey about Addison's limitations as a critic of poetry: 'The feeble constitution of the poetic faculty as existing in himself forbade his sympathy with Shakespeare; the proportions were too vast for his delicate vision.' De Quincey goes on to explain that a stupid reader may be disturbed by poetry much as an idiot is affected by music:

. . . it alarms, irritates, disturbs, makes him profoundly unhappy, and chiefly by unlocking imperfect glimpses of thoughts and slumbering instincts, which it is for his peace to have entirely obscured because for him they can be revealed only partially, and with the sad effect of throwing a baleful gleam upon his blighted conditions.[2]

If we bear in mind this judgement we may find it less strange that the verse of Wordsworth, Shelley, and Keats was greeted with obloquy by its first readers. Shelley himself, despite his ardent love for mankind, never lost his aristocratic disdain for the common run of humanity, especially for the vulgar-minded who vilified his morals and bespattered his poetry. The 'Advertisement' to *Epipsychidion* contains a lofty avowal of the poet's indifference to those whose ignorance disqualifies them from judging his work:

The present Poem, like the *Vita Nuova* of Dante, is sufficiently intelligible to a certain class of readers without a matter-of-fact history of the circumstances to which it relates; and to a certain other class it must ever remain incomprehensible, from a defect of a common organ of perception for the ideas of which it treats.

[1] Quoted by Mona Wilson, *Blake* (2nd ed.), p. 81.
[2] Quoted by Edith Sitwell, *A Notebook on William Shakespeare*, p. 230.

Acknowledging his presumption in comparing himself with
Dante, Shelley none the less calmly translates Dante's Can-
zone and applies the lines to his own poem. Since there exist
three versions of the 'Advertisement', we may conjecture that
Shelley set great store by this deliberate and reasoned
apologia for his poetry, which is one that all poets who are
derided for obscurity by shallow critics would gladly echo:

> My Song, I fear that thou wilt find but few
> Who fitly shall conceive thy reasoning,
> Of such hard matter dost thou entertain;
> Whence, if by misadventure, chance should bring
> Thee to base company (as chance may do),
> Quite unaware of what thou dost contain,
> I prithee, comfort thy sweet self again,
> My last delight! tell them that they are dull,
> And bid them own that thou art beautiful.[1]

When Lucien de Rubempré read André Chénier's poems at
Mme. de Bargeton's party the guests believed that he was
passing off his own poems under an invented name. Balzac
makes this comment on their boredom: 'Those who would
understand poetry must allow the germ that the author has
put in his verses to unfold in their own minds: but these indifferent auditors, far from aspiring to understand the soul of
poetry, could barely understand the words.'[2] A hundred years
after Lucien's encounter with provincial ignorance, Ezra
Pound discovered that the blockheads who had censured the
Romantics had spawned a worthy progeny, fulfilling to the
letter Dryden's prognostication:

> Fools change in *England*, and new Fools arise;
> For, tho' th' Immortal Species never dies,
> Yet ev'ry Year new Maggots make new Flies.

---

[1] Rymer, in his *Preface to Rapin* (1674), after remarking that 'one of the
greatest faults in discourse is *obscurity*', declared that 'the thoughts of Dante are
so *profound* that much art is requir'd to dive into them'. Nicholas Breton, in
1604, referred to:
> Ariosto's best invention,
> Dante's best obscured intention.

See E. F. Carritt, *A Calendar of British Taste*, p. 95 and p. 6.

[2] Balzac, *Lost Illusions*, translated by Kathleen Raine, p. 98.

In one of his letters Pound virtually repeats Shelley's justification of *Epipsychidion*, in language that is more vigorous
though less elegant:

There is no *intentional* obscurity. There is condensation to maxi-
mum attainable. It is impossible to make the deep as quickly comprehensible as the shallow.

The order of words and sounds *ought* to induce the proper
reading; proper tone of voice, etc., but can *not* redeem fools from
idiocy. If the goddam violin string is not tense, no amount of
bowing will help the player.[1]

This is an appropriate place to remind ourselves that the
judgements passed on new poetry by clever people are frequently distinguished by a reckless stupidity and ignorance
which they would be ashamed of displaying in any other
branch of life except in the criticism of music or of painting.
Now that T. S. Eliot is universally accepted as a distinguished
poet it is difficult to recall that, throughout the 1920s and
even to the middle of the 1930s, he was contemptuously dismissed as a purveyor of obscurity by the majority of academic
critics, and of fashionable reviewers. Writing of Ezra Pound,
Eliot remarks that 'he and I and our colleagues were mentioned by a writer in *The Morning Post* as "literary bol-
sheviks" and by Mr. Arthur Waugh (with a point which has
always escaped me) as "drunken helots"'.[2] The *Manchester
Guardian* consigned his work to oblivion by its pronouncement that 'if Mr. Eliot had been pleased to write in demotic
English *The Waste Land* might not have been, as it just is to
all but anthropologists and literati, so much waste-paper'.
Sir John Squire's pontifical verdict on Eliot's *Poems 1909–
1925* throws a revealing light upon the standards of criticism
prevalent between the wars:

Usually he is obscure, so inconsequent that the kindest thing one
can suppose is that he is experimenting with automatic writing.
Why on earth he bothers to write at all it is difficult to conceive:
Why, since he must write, he writes page after page from which
no human being could derive any more meaning (much less

[1] *The Letters of Ezra Pound*, 1907–1941, ed. D. D. Paige, p. 418.
[2] *The Use of Poetry*, p. 71.

edification or pleasure) than if they were written in Double-Dutch (which parts of them possibly are) is to me beyond conjecture.[1]

As late as 1934 Ivor Brown in his denunciation of modern degeneracy, grandiloquently entitled *I Commit to the Flames*, repeats the farcical charge that Eliot is an incompetent blunderer. Having observed that 'Mr. T. S. Eliot offers the public the balderdash of his *Waste Land*', Brown goes on to describe the poem as 'pretentious bungling with the English language'. Elsewhere in the book he refers to 'Mr. T. S. Eliot's antics' and to 'the dubious truffles of Mr. Eliot's scholarship', and in a pathetic attempt at bluff wit castigates *The Waste Land* (though he does not name the poem) by announcing his refusal to accept as poetry 'the hiccoughs and grunts of the mentally dyspeptic young men who have been peering into Bloomsbury basements and have seen underclothes drying by the fire'.[2]

In the face of such insolent folly we may pause for a while to consider two questions which are intimately related to each other and to the main object of our inquiry. First, how does it come about that highly-intelligent men are so frequently baffled and infuriated by originality in a work of art? Secondly, why do less intelligent people in the next generation find no difficulty in understanding poetry, music and painting that have gravelled their predecessors?

This latter phenomenon is so striking that some theorists have maintained that a quasi-biological mutation occurs which enables young men and women to take in their stride what has proved beyond their parents' capacity to absorb. I see no reason to fall back upon this kind of mysticism when there are more rational explanations at hand. Part of the answer to this problem is that critics, when they are doing their proper job,

[1] I owe this reference to an article by Geoffrey Grigson, 'Notes on Literature as a Career', *Scrutiny*, I, 4 (1933), p. 404.

[2] The phrase about 'balderdash' occurs on p. 10; the references to 'antics' and to 'dubious truffles' on pp. 203–4; the witticism about underclothes on p. 25. Those who are inclined to blame F. R. Leavis and his contributors to *Scrutiny* for their narrow rigour should consult Ivor Brown's book and read what he says about Eliot and Lawrence. They will then understand the kind of superficiality and vulgarity that Leavis has endeavoured to combat in his books, lectures, teaching and editorial labours.

can dissipate the clouds of prejudice which hinder the recognition of unfamiliar excellence and thus act as an intermediary between the artist and his public. Coleridge and De Quincey performed this service for Wordsworth; when the Apostles visited Oxford to debate at the Union they proclaimed the genius of Shelley in the university which had rejected him and all his works; Monckton Milnes rescued Keats from the almost total oblivion into which he had fallen. In our own time the reputation of T. S. Eliot was advanced by those critics who, in the teeth of conservatism and insensibility, continued to assert that he was a great poet. But this is not the whole story: critical commentaries may expound the intellectual content of poetry, explain the references and paraphrase the overt meaning, but they can scarcely attune reluctant ears to discover in it that musical delight which is the life of poetry, any more than criticism of music and of painting can persuade a new generation to enjoy harmonies, melodies, shapes, and colours which an older generation found so hideous and dissonant. This revolution in taste can take place only when the technical experiments of the innovators are imitated so widely that they can be accepted by everybody as a normal and obvious mode of expression. When writers of light music adapt the harmonies of Debussy to their own special purposes, and when a watered-down version of Cubism appears on every hoarding, a generation that has grown up surrounded by this type of popular art will find nothing obscure or outrageous in the music of Debussy or in the painting of the Cubists. Each generation wonders why its predecessors made such a fuss about their revolutionary artists, and proceeds to make a similar fuss about its own. Now, with T. S. Eliot grown respectable, W. H. Auden enthroned in the Chair of Poetry at Oxford and Dylan Thomas canonized, it is time to look for a new scapegoat, who can be denounced for his obscurity and driven into the wilderness.

We have still to answer the first of the two questions that I posed—why are clever men predisposed to condemn original work as obscure? One reason is that they tend to have very firm ideas about the nature of art and to be blind to the merits of any new developments which do not conform to their preconceived notions. I propose to show that this is certainly true in the field of poetry.

Dryden, while recognizing the essential force of Shakespeare's genius, felt bound to make certain reservations about his use of language: 'Let any man, who understands English, read diligently the works of Shakespeare and Fletcher, and I dare undertake that he will find in every page either some solecism of speech, or some notorious flaw of sense.'[1] A typical expression of the early eighteenth-century attitude is to be found in Atterbury's letter to Pope, written in 1721, where he accuses Shakespeare of bombast, 'whatever apology you may have contrived on that head for him', and confesses his inability to understand Shakespeare or to follow his allusions:

I protest to you, in a hundred places I cannot construe him. . . . The hardest part of Chaucer is more intelligible to me than some of those scenes, not merely through the faults of the edition, but the obscurity of the writer, for obscure he is. . . . There are allusions in him to a hundred things of which I know nothing and can guess nothing. . . . Aeschylus does not want a comment to me more than he does.[2]

Pope himself, while admiring Shakespeare's power, is driven by his conception of clarity and propriety to emend some of Shakespeare's most characteristic metaphors, which offend the canons of orthodox Augustan taste. His edition of Shakespeare, like Bentley's edition of Milton, is an endeavour to purify the text of the irregularity, the imprecision and the logical absurdities of language which are presumed to have been interpolated by a malicious or an incompetent editor. Bentley's commentary on Milton is commonly regarded as the *reductio ad absurdum* of stiff-necked pedantry, yet one sometimes cannot help admiring the formidable logic so relentlessly applied to the task of improving the imperfect poetry of a barbarous age; and, dazed by the syllogisms of a supremely great classical scholar whose intellect had been sharpened by textual criticism of the noblest poets of antiquity, we are almost persuaded that both logic and piety

---

[1] *On the Dramatic Poetry of the Last Age* (1672).
[2] Quoted by E. F. Carritt, *A Calendar of British Taste*, p. 187.

constrain us to reject as 'very improper' the two final lines of
Paradise Lost, and to accept Bentley's offer of 'a Distich as
close as may be to the Author's Words, and entirely agreeable
to his Scheme:

> THEN hand in hand with SOCIAL steps their Way
> Through EDEN took, with HEA'NLY COMFORT
>   CHEER'D.'

Later in the century, the poetry of Christopher Smart sorely
perplexed even those who had loved the man and who desired
to honour his memory. His daughter Elizabeth, who 'improved' his *Hymns*, apologetically confessed that *A Song to
David* had been greatly over-estimated; his nephew, and first
editor, Christopher Hunter, omitted it from his collection of
Smart's poems in 1791 because it bore 'melancholy proofs of
the recent estrangement of his mind'; Mason wrote about
Smart to Gray on 28 June 1763 saying: 'I have seen his Song
to David and from thence conclude him as mad as ever';
Boswell, in a letter to Sir Donald Dalrymple, 30 July 1763,
called it 'a strange mixture of *dun obscure* and glowing genius
at times'.[1]

High and admirable as were eighteenth-century standards
of taste, they were fitted neither to measure nor to circum-
scribe poetry whose genius was totally alien to the spirit of
that age. The contempt which Byron felt for Keats was partly
an aristocratic distaste for an upstart, partly a temperamental
antipathy, but still more an avowal of his preference for the
Augustan clarity and force which Keats was dissolving in the
sensuous profusion and confusion of his verse. While admit-
ting that some of the reviewers in *Blackwoods* and the *Quarterly* were actuated by personal and political rancour, we must
remember that even those critics who attempted to judge the
Romantics as impartially as possible genuinely found them
incomprehensible. In the *Edinburgh Review*, August 1820,
Jeffrey, though acknowledging that Keats 'has a very beautiful imagination, a perfect ear for harmony, and a great
familiarity with the finest diction of English poetry', censures
his writings on the grounds that 'they are full of extravagance

---

[1] See *Poems of Christopher Smart*, ed. Robert Brittain.

and irregularity, rash attempts at originality, interminable wanderings and excessive obscurity'.

That intelligent men should be misled by too rigid an adherence to inadequate standards is not particularly blameworthy, although good poetry may thereby be unjustly condemned for obscurity. Unfortunately, a great many clever critics who are more concerned with displaying their intellectual nimbleness than with maintaining any critical standards try to gain a reputation for wit by poking fun at unfamiliar excellence. Worse still are those men whose intellectual arrogance has destroyed the humility and the candour that one must bring to all poetry and, in particular, to poetry written by men younger than oneself. There are few more dangerous enemies of poetry than the man of fairly wide reading who, priding himself on his acuteness and on his ability to smoke out the charlatan, examines a poem as if he were a famous advocate determined to discredit a tissue of fabricated evidence, and to convict the witness of perjury. The obloquy with which reviewers greeted the first Romantics affords the most striking example of this ugly trait, but this episode in literary history is so well known that I propose to say nothing about it, except to record two judgements that sum up the squalid story. The first occurs in one of Landor's *Imaginary Conversations*[1] wherein Southey is made to say:

What a rabble has persecuted my friend! An elephant is born to be consumed by ants in the midst of his unapproachable solitudes: Wordsworth is the prey of Jeffrey. Why repine? Let us rather amuse ourselves with allegories, and recollect that God in the creation left His noblest creature at the mercy of a serpent.

The second is quoted by F. R. Leavis as the epigraph to his *New Bearings in English Poetry*, as though to remind us that Lockhart's analysis of Wordsworth's detractors applies to those critics of our day who are hired by Satan to depress poetry:

What we cannot understand, it is very common and indeed a very natural thing for us to undervalue; and it may be suspected that some of the merriest witticisms which have been uttered against

---

[1] 'Southey and Porson.'

Mr. Wordsworth, have had their origin in the pettishness and dissatisfaction of minds unaccustomed and unwilling to make, either to others or to themselves, any confession of incapacity.

Instead of dwelling upon the notorious misdemeanours of the early nineteenth-century reviewers, we may find it more profitable to glance at some of the criticisms to which Browning was subjected. He certainly laid himself open to the charge of obscurity, but Mrs. Carlyle was clearly trying to raise an easy laugh at his expense when she declared that she had read *Sordello* all the way through without discovering whether Sordello was a city, a man, or a book;[1] and Tennyson was being spiteful when he declared that he had understood only the first and last lines of the poem, and both were lies. Miss Mitford's opinion of Browning, written eight months after his marriage, is a mere indulgence in feminine malice under the disguise of perceptive criticism:

I saw Mr. Browning once and remember thinking how exactly he resembled a girl drest in boy's clothes—and as to his poetry I have just your opinion of it. It is one heap of obscurity, confusion and weakness. . . . I met him once, as I told you, when he had long ringlets and no neckcloth and when he seemed to me about the height and size of a boy of twelve years old. Femmelette is a word made for him.[2]

More interesting and more significant than these pinpricks is the attitude which C. S. Calverley adopted towards Browning's poetry. Calverley's powerful intellect, deep scholarship, and delightful wit made a vivid impression upon his contemporaries, who expected him to achieve far greater things than he accomplished. The most engaging example of his precocious quickness of wit is his reply to the Master of Balliol, Dr. Jenkyns, who, at 'Collections', asked Calverley (then known as Blayds) the following question: 'And with what feelings, Mr. Blayds, ought we to regard the decalogue?' Not knowing what the decalogue was, Calverley gave 'a very proper answer', as Dr. Jenkyns called it:

[1] Betty Miller, *Robert Browning: A Portrait*, pp. 63–64.

[2] This passage occurs in a MS. letter from Miss Mitford to Charles Bonner, 22 February 1847. Quoted by Betty Miller, *Elizabeth Barrett to Miss Mitford*, p. xiii.

'Master, with feelings of devotion, mingled with awe.'[1] His masculine intelligence, his knowledge of the classics, and a remarkable facility in juggling with words, fostered by the exercise of writing Latin verses, combined to make him a formidable parodist. The fatuousness of mechanical ballad-writing, and the decorative feebleness of much pre-Raphaelite verse, so wickedly described by an anonymous wit:

> Long ladies, knights, and earles and choris-
> ters in the most appropriate drapery,
> Samite and silk and spotless napery,
> Sunflowers and apple blossoms and orris,
> Behold the works of William Morris!

have never been more cruelly or justifiably mocked than in the pages of Calverley:

> The farmer's daughter hath frank blue eyes;
>   (*Butter and eggs and a pound of cheese*)
> She hears the rooks caw in the windy skies,
>   As she sits in her lattice and shells her peas.[2]
>
>   *   *   *
>
> Thro' God's own heather we wonn'd together,
>   I and my Willie (O love my love):
> I need hardly remark it was glorious weather,
>   And flitterbats waver'd alow, above . . .
>
> Then we thrid God's cowslips (as erst His heather)
>   That endowed the wan grass with their golden blooms;
> And snapt—(it was perfectly charming weather)—
>   Our fingers at Fate and her goddess-glooms;[3]

Unfortunately, the very gifts that enabled him to pulverize the minor verse of the mid-nineteenth century disqualified him from doing justice to a major poet whose markedly original and subtle art he mistook for wanton eccentricity. As one of his admirers proclaims in his biographical notice,

his own clearness and, so to speak, point-blank directness of mental vision rendered him especially impatient of all the crooked and nebulous antics and vagaries of thought or speech in which writers

---

[1] *The Complete Works of C. S. Calverley*, with a Biographical notice by Sir Walter J. Sendall, G.C.M.G., p. xx.
[2] 'Ballad.'   [3] 'Lovers, and a Reflexion.'

of the modern transcendental school are pleased to indulge; and his parodies of this class may be regarded as a genuine and out-spoken expression of resentment that so much genius should seem to take so much pains to be unintelligible. . . . To such (votaries of the modern school) it may not be amiss to suggest that in matters of literary taste, as well as in graver matters, *securus judicat terrarum orbis*, and that if the common sense of mankind had not long ago delivered judgment upon the affectations and extravagances of style against which Calverley's satire is directed, the word mannerism would either not have been invented or would have acquired a different connotation.[1]

Point-blank directness of mental vision and common sense, however admirable in a minor politician or in a business man, are of very little use to a critic of poetry. It is a healthy exercise to clear one's mind of cant, but the man who gains a reputation as a professional scourge of humbug has a vested interest in smelling out humbug where none may exist: there must be a false sixpence in every Christmas pudding even if he has to put it there himself. Calverley seems to have had such confidence in the sufficiency of his own intellectual powers that he neglected to cultivate that humility and imaginative sympathy which alone can fit us to understand certain types of poetry. Ironically enough, this deficiency weakens his most ambitious attempt at parody, 'The Cock and the Bull':

> You see this pebble-stone? It's a thing I bought
> Of a bit of a chit of a boy i' the mid o' the day—
> I like to dock the smaller parts-o'-speech,
> As we curtail the already cur-tail'd cur
> (You catch the paronomasia, play 'po' words?)
> Did, rather, i' the pre-Landseerian days . . .
> I shoved the timber ope wi' my omoplat;
> And *in vestibulo*, i' the lobby to-wit,
> (Iacobi Facciolati's rendering, Sir,)
> Donn'd galligaskins, antigropeloes,
> And so forth; and, complete with hat and gloves,
> One on and one a-dangle i' my hand,
> And ombrifuge (Lord love you!), case o' rain,
> I flopp'd forth, 'sbuddikins! on my own ten toes . . .

---

[1] *The Complete Works of C. S. Calverley*, p. xxxv.

Although this is a brilliant imitation of Browning's verbal tricks it remains a mere caricature of his surface defects. J. K. Stephen's insight into the true nature of Browning's genius stands in marked contrast to the crudity of Calverley's perceptions, and his parody of the poet whom he admired and revered (as his verses on Browning's death prove beyond all doubt) is far deadlier than Calverley's because its critical discernment is informed by love rather than by arrogant impatience. Stephen grasped the truth that Browning's obscurity, far from being a stylistic excrescence, is part of his poetry's essential nature, just as a turn of speech or an idiosyncratic gesture is inseparable from a man's personality. One would mistake 'Of R.B.'[1] for a genuine poem by Browning, so perfectly does it reproduce not only the very accents of his voice, the exuberant, surging rhythms in which he delighted, but also the true quality of his obscurity—the enigmatic aphorism, the ironic, sidelong glance, the sudden ejaculation, the queer shifts of mood, the swivelling turn that casts an unexpected ray of light upon the chosen theme, the attempt to cram a metaphysical speculation within the compass of a gnomic utterance:

> Birthdays? yes, in a general way;
> For the most if not for the best of men:
> You were born (I suppose) on a certain day:
> So was I: or perhaps in the night: what then?
>
> Only this: or at least, if more,
> You must know, not think it, and learn, not speak:
> There is truth to be found on the unknown shore,
> And many will find where few will seek.
>
> For many are called and few are chosen,
> And the few grow many as ages lapse:
> But when will the many grow few: what dozen
> Is fused into one by Time's hammer-taps?
>
> A bare brown stone in a babbling brook:—
> It was wanton to hurl it there, you say:
> And the moss, which clung in the sheltered nook
> (Yet the stream runs cooler) is washed away.

[1] One of a group of poems entitled 'Sincere Flattery'.

That begs the question: many a frater
Thinks such a suggestion a sound 'stop thief!'
Which, may I ask do you think the greater,
Sergeant-at-arms, or a Robber Chief?

And if it were not so? Still you doubt?
Ah! Yours is a birthday indeed if so.
That were something to write a poem about,
If one thought a little. I only know
     P.S.

There's a Me Society down at Cambridge,
Where my works, *cum notis variorum*
Are talked about; Well I require the same bridge
That Euclid took toll of as *Asinorum*.

And, as they have got through several ditties
I thought were as stiff as a brick-built wall,
I've composed the above, and a stiff one *it* is,
A bridge to stop asses at, once for all.

I have dwelled at some length on Calverley's deficiencies as a critic of poetry because he seems to me a classic example of a man in whom acute intelligence is continually frustrated by wilful obtuseness, and because his spiritual descendants are still flourishing today. It is noteworthy that F. O. Matthiessen, in his study of T. S. Eliot, should single out for particular blame a man who has attained considerable eminence in the academic world and whose intellectual powers, combined with a lawyer-like dexterity of argument, make him a formidable controversialist:

Mr. Sparrow's mind represents English criticism at its most hardened conventional level. He combines considerable knowledge of the past, a certain amount of commonsense in pointing out the excesses of some minor figures in modern art, and an almost complete lack of taste or of ability to discriminate between Eliot and Edith Sitwell. His kind has been familiar, and unchanging, since the Quarterly Reviewers.[1]

[1] *The Achievement of T. S. Eliot*, pp. 150–1. Matthiessen's criticism is directed against John Sparrow's book, *Sense and Poetry*. His implied belittlement of Edith Sitwell was written in 1935, before the publication of *Street Songs* and of her later poetry.

Closely akin to the stultifying cleverness that impedes a fruitful response to poetry is an impatient grasping after certainty and clarity which demands that poetry should yield all its secrets at a first reading. People of this cast of mind are fond of misquoting a hoary old tag from Milton, despite Sir Herbert Read's warning: 'When Milton wrote that poetry should be *more* simple, sensuous, and passionate *than rhetoric*, he did not imply that poetry should necessarily be easy, placid, and platitudinous.'[1] A reader who comes to a poem, convinced that it presents a challenge to his ingenuity, and determined that he will vanquish it, may tear out a few shreds of meaning from the poem, but he will do a lot of damage in the process. C. Day Lewis gives an amusing instance of this inability to accept a poem as a poem:

A year or two ago I wrote a sequence called *From Feathers to Iron* which for me expressed simply my thoughts and feelings during the nine months before the birth of my first child: the critics, almost to a man, took it for a political allegory; the simple, personal meaning evaded them.[2]

T. S. Eliot has warned us that:

. . . difficulty may be caused by the reader's having been told, or having suggested to himself, that the poem is going to prove difficult. The ordinary reader, when warned against the obscurity of a poem, is apt to be thrown into a state of consternation very unfavourable to poetic receptivity. Instead of beginning, as he should, in a state of sensitivity, he obfuscates his senses by the desire to be clever and to look very hard for something, he doesn't know what—or else by the desire not to be taken in. There is such a thing as stage fright, but what such readers have is pit or gallery fright.[3]

Another aspect of this fretful impatience is the frequent insistence by many readers that a poem shall soothe and flatter their emotional and mental habits. When a man says: 'That's not my idea of poetry,' he is usually expressing resentment or disgust, rather than a delighted surprise at having discovered something new. The person who goes to a poem, like the

---

[1] *The Politics of the Unpolitical*, p. 78.   [2] *A Hope for Poetry*, pp. 37–38.
[3] *The Use of Poetry*, pp. 150–1.

person who goes to church, in order to get from it a certain experience or a particular satisfaction, is likely to feel cheated if his hopes are disappointed. Laura Riding explains why readers often feel aggrieved when a poem fails to give them what they claim to be their due: 'When a poem is attacked for obscurity it is . . . because the reader has gone to the poem in order to be put into a poetic mood (not to have reality uncovered for him as it can be uncovered alone in poems).'[1]

Inertia, timidity, the desire to cling to familiar certainties and to nestle in comfortable platitudes, all of which are among the most powerful human emotions, are sufficient to account for the irritated bewilderment that many readers experience when confronted with original poetry. After giving a number of reasons why modern poetry is said to be difficult, T. S. Eliot concludes:

And finally, there is the difficulty caused by the author's having left out something which the reader is used to finding; so that the reader, bewildered, gropes about for what is absent, and puzzles his head for a kind of 'meaning' which is not there, and is not meant to be there.[2]

Coleridge and Wordsworth had reached a similar conclusion almost a hundred and fifty years before. In his series of lectures delivered in 1818, Coleridge, in likening Shakespeare to Nature, attributed to him 'a genial understanding directing self-consciously a power and an implicit wisdom deeper even than our consciousness'. Those who have condemned him for barbaric wildness have made the mistake of 'confounding mechanical regularity with organic form'. Coleridge knows that in permitting organic form to shape itself in his verse, a poet risks being accused of lawless obscurity by obtuse readers who forget that 'no work of true genius dares want its appropriate form, neither indeed is there any danger of this. As it must not, so genius cannot, be lawless; for it is even this that constitutes it genius—the power of acting creatively under laws of its own origination.' In one of the finest passages of the *Essay Supplementary* (1815), Wordsworth explains why new poetry is always

[1] *Collected Poems*, 'To the Reader', p. xix.   [2] *The Use of Poetry*, p. 151.

likely to be resisted by stubborn conservatism, since every author,

as far as he is great and at the same time *original*, has had the task of *creating* the taste by which he is to be enjoyed . . . for what is peculiarly his own, he will be called upon to clear and often to shape his own road:—he will be in the condition of Hannibal among the Alps . . . of genius, in the fine arts, the only infallible sign is the widening the sphere of human sensibility. . . . Remember, also, that the medium through which, in poetry, the heart is to be affected, is language; a thing subject to endless fluctuations and arbitrary associations. The genius of the poet melts these down for his purpose; but they retain their shape and quality to him who is not capable of exerting, within his own mind, a corresponding energy.

Wordsworth's conclusion that 'the poet must reconcile himself for a season to few and scattered hearers', reminds us of Dr. Johnson's melancholy and majestic pronouncement:

The poet must divest himself of the prejudice of his age and country; he must consider right and wrong in their abstracted and invariable state; he must disregard present laws and opinions, and rise to general and transcendental truths, which will always be the same. He must, therefore, content himself with the slow progress of his name, contemn the praise of his own time, and commit his claims to the justice of posterity.

Wordsworth desired, above all, to enlarge the imagination of man, Johnson to preserve the immemorial wisdom of the past: both reckoned as their main enemy the hardened complacency of vulgar opinion. In a gloomy moment, Wordsworth perceived that his youthful dream of arousing men from their benighted condition was incapable of fulfilment:

It is an awful truth, that there neither is, nor can be, any genuine enjoyment of poetry among nineteen out of twenty of those persons who live, or wish to live, in the broad light of the world—among those who either are, or are striving to make themselves, people of consideration in society. This is a truth, and an awful one, because to be incapable of a feeling of poetry, in my sense of the word, is to be without love of human nature and reverence for God.

Wordsworth's judgement remains valid today: it is arguable that the appreciation of poetry at the present time is even feebler than it was a hundred years ago. Victorian statesmen had the leisure and the inclination to read and even to write poetry, Gladstone and Derby producing good translations of the classics, Palmerston and Disraeli carrying on the tradition of light verse in which Canning had excelled. Lord John Russell was an excellent critic of romantic poetry, and Gladstone, who wrote a remarkable review of Tennyson's poetry, was among the first to perceive the merit of Wordsworth's *Peter Bell*.[1] There is no reason to suppose that our contemporary politicians of the front rank have any genuine feeling for poetry,[2] and there is some evidence for holding that poetry in general and modern poetry in particular means nothing to the vast majority of our lesser politicians.[3] Nor do our spiritual leaders disguise their genial contempt for poetry and their total inability to understand it. Archbishop William Temple confessed that he was bored by Milton;[4] Dr. Garbett, when Archbishop of York, declared in the course of a sermon in Ripon Cathedral on 8 May 1954 that 'most of our modern poets, when intelligible, tell of a wasteland which offers little hope or meaning'.[5] As a summary of poetry since 1922, and as a criticism of T. S. Eliot's work, this judgement is so inept that one can account for it only by invoking the ecclesiastical dogma of invincible ignorance.

Those who dislike modern poetry are fond of proclaiming that the ordinary person is fully justified in ignoring the unintelligible verse of today; and, posing as the champions of plain, straightforward men, they quote a passage from Johnson's life of Gray: 'I rejoice to concur with the common reader; for by the common sense of readers, uncorrupted by

[1] See F. W. Bateson, *English Poetry*, p. 262.

[2] Except, probably, Mr. Macmillan.

[3] See J. W. Saunders, 'Poetry in the Managerial Age', *Essays in Criticism*, vol. iv, No. 3 (July 1954), pp. 345–57.

[4] '. . . a later confession runs: "I am not worthy of Milton: I do not know if I ever shall be".' F. A. Iremonger, *William Temple*, p. 47.

[5] Reported in the *Sunday Times*, 9 May 1954. Nor does orthodox Anglican opinion welcome any attempt to enlighten it about literature. Brother George Every's *Christian Discrimination* was dismissed by the *Church Times* as a book dealing with writers who were of little interest to most Anglican readers. The writers in question were Hopkins, Yeats, Joyce, D. H. Lawrence, and T. S. Eliot.

literary prejudices, after all the refinements of subtilty and the dogmatism of learning, must be finally decided all claim to poetical honours.' But whereas the common reader of Johnson's time, however unsystematic and amateurish a critic he might be, was a member of a well-educated minority whose tastes and standards would today be ridiculed by the average man as highbrow and stuffy, his twentieth-century counter-part is a debilitated creature, weaned on what Meredith called the pap and brandy of journalism, accepting his reading-fodder in the same spirit (and often from the same shop) as he buys his aspirin, indifferent to the claims of poetry upon him in a world where picture-papers and television relieve him from the strain of serious thinking or thoughtful reading:

> The 'age demanded' chiefly a mould in plaster,
> Made with no loss of time,
> A prose kinema, not, not assuredly, alabaster
> Or the 'sculpture' of rhyme.[1]

It is true that few lines of contemporary poetry are likely to become part of the familiar currency of speech, and true also that some good poets of the past were able to satisfy the perennial demand for comfortable moralizing or for pithy sayings. Yet the success of Thomas Tusser, Martin Tupper, and Ella Wheeler Wilcox, to name only three popular bards, should remind us that memorability is no criterion of poetic merit; and it is mere self-delusion to pretend that good poems of today, however simple, will become household words in households where the only words studied with in-tensity and care are hints on filling in football coupons, and stereotyped descriptions of sex-crimes in the cheaper Sunday newspapers.

[1] Ezra Pound, 'E.P. Ode Pour L'Election De Son Sepulchre.'

5

Indifferent Writers

Who sayes that fictions onely and false hair
Become a verse? Is there in truth no beautie?
Is all good structure in a winding stair?
May no lines passe, except they do their dutie
    Not to a true, but painted chair?

Is it no verse, except enchanted groves
And sudden arbours shadow course-spunne lines?
Must purling streams refresh a lover's loves,
Must all be vail'd, while he that reades, divines,
    Catching the sense at two removes?

Shepherds are honest people; let them sing:
Riddle who list, for me, and pull for Prime:
I envie no man's nightingale or spring;
Nor let them punish me with losse of ryme,
    Who plainly say, *My God, My King*.
              GEORGE HERBERT, 'Jordan.'

A POET withdraws from the commerce of the world to the solitude of his imagination in order that he may find there a pattern of experience which he can embody in the musical delight of a poem and communicate to his fellow men. We have seen that the ignorance, the stupidity, the arrogance, the impatience, the timidity, and the slothful complacency of his readers may cause a poet to be unjustly condemned for obscurity; but there remains the possibility that he may richly deserve to be censured for being incompetent, muddle-headed, vain, and contemptuous of his readers.

Many of the ferocious onslaughts upon the first Romantic poets were clearly inspired by the prejudice and the malice of the reviewers, but the poets themselves, in their more candid moments, admitted that their verse was tinged with obscurity. Coleridge, in his note to his 'Lines Written at Shurton Bars', after acknowledging that the phrase *green radiance* was

88

copied from Wordsworth's 'An Evening Walk', confesses that Wordsworth is a 'Poet whose versification is occasionally harsh and his diction too frequently obscure'.[1] Moreover, in *Biographia Literaria*, he repeats this judgement about his friend's early poems, referring to 'the occasional obscurities which had arisen from an imperfect control over the resources of his native language'. We so commonly think of Shelley as an uncritical rhapsodist, oblivious to everything but the cascading torrent of his imagination, that we are surprised to encounter a recognition of his technical imperfection in a letter to Hogg about his own poems (1813): 'They are, in a great measure, abrupt and obscure.'[2]

As the nineteenth century wore on, poets became more self-conscious about obscurity in their own verse, and more critical of that vice in others. Hopkins, far from wilfully indulging in obscurity, was always pained when his correspondents were unable to construe his poetry and he severely rebukes his friends when they have not taken pains to clarify their meaning. He writes of Patmore: 'The faults I see in him are bad rhymes; continued obscurity; and, the most serious, a certain frigidity, when, as often, the feeling does not flush and fuse the language.'[3] He criticizes R. W. Dixon on similar grounds: 'The obscurity is a great fault: from remarkably clear speaking he will lapse into gibberish,'[4] and elsewhere he amplifies this judgement in a characteristically acute and penetrating observation: 'He is faulty by a certain vagueness of form, some unpleasing rhymes, and most by an obscurity— partly of thought, partly of expression—suggesting a deeper meaning behind the text, without leaving the reader any decisive clue to find it.'[5]

It must be confessed that the blemishes which Hopkins detected in the verse of R. W. Dixon vitiate much contemporary poetry. Louis MacNeice has candidly avowed his failure in some of his early writings to subdue his thoughts and his emotions into the ordered discipline of poetic coherence:

[1] Quoted by Malcolm Elwin, *The First Romantics*, p. 154.
[2] Quoted by Herbert Read, *The True Voice of Feeling*, p. 218.
[3] *Letters*, vol. i, p. 82.
[4] *Letters*, vol. i, p. 74.
[5] *Letters*, vol. ii, p. 177.

Blind Fireworks (published 1929) is full of images such as I have described from my childhood but it is also full of mythological tags, half-digested new ideas and conceits put in for the hell of it. Thus in one poem coal, thought of as a black panther (which might just pass?), must needs have been petrified by Circe and, when the panther (which is also a sphinx) comes to life in the fire-place, it is discovered (a) to have horns (biblical reminiscence?) and (b) to be 'sprung in the stirrups of life'; this is too much. As for mythology, I was in those days only too happy mixing up Greek, Biblical and Nordic; in one poem called *Twilight of the Gods*, a factory chimney 'skewering the consciousness out of mental distance' is equated first with a totem pole throwing a shadow across Enna, the meadow where Persephone was raped, and then with the tree Ygdrasil, famous in Norse legend; round this the dead gods go dancing while Pythagoras (become a sort of cosmic timekeeper) plays tunes on an abacus until it breaks and the universe has to end—beneath 'the snow-flakes of Nirvana'. This sort of thing was not, in the ordinary sense, fake; it sprang from an only too genuine emotion and was indeed poured out 'as the bird sings'. The fault of such a poem lies not in its feeling but in its technique. For technique begins in the junkshop, in a process—conscious or unconscious—of sorting out. Free association, when it makes literature, isn't as free as it may look.[1]

The misapplied ingenuity of an intelligent man may betray him into writing poems more obscure and confused than the verse of a feeble hack; but there is more than one kind of vicious obscurity into which even highly gifted poets may plunge. In his essay on 'Swinburne Versus His Biographers', Ezra Pound analyses the insidious temptations which lie always ready to engulf those writers who, like the author of *Dolores*, voraciously respond to the sensuous properties of words:

There is an emotional fusion of the perceptions, and a certain kind of verbal confusion has an emotive value in writing; but this is of all sorts of writing the most dangerous to an author, and the unconscious collapse into this sort of writing has wrecked more poets in our time than perhaps all other faults put together.[2]

But what of a poet who deliberately wills this kind of collapse, who erects the negation of clarity into a system, to the

---

[1] 'Experience with Images', *Orpheus*, vol. ii, pp. 129–30.
[2] *The Literary Essays of Ezra Pound*, ed. T. S. Eliot, p. 294.

accompaniment of hypnotic music? Robert Graves's judgement on Dylan Thomas, though only part of the story, cannot be dismissed as mere irresponsible critical malice:

> He kept musical control of the reader without troubling about the sense. I do not mean that he aimed deliberately off-target, as the later Yeats did. Thomas seems to have decided that there was no need to aim at all, so long as the explosion sounded loud enough. The fumes of cordite would drift across the target and a confederate in the butts would signal bull after bull.[1]

The best comment on this passage comes from the lips of Dylan Thomas himself. In the spring of 1953, at a conference in the University of Utah, he was asked by a student: 'Is it ever fair deliberately to confuse the reader?' His reply was given after a long pause for consideration:

> No—it is a deliberate avowal of your own inefficiency. It is impossible to be too clear. . . . I am trying for more clarity now. At first I thought it enough to leave an impression of sound and feeling and let the meaning seep in later, but since I've been giving these broadcasts and reading other men's poetry as well as my own, I find it better to have more meaning at first reading.[2]

The very form of the student's question implies that obscurity in poetry is a matter of morality no less than of style, if indeed one can distinguish sharply between them. It may appear far-fetched to trace moral significance in Wordsworth's verbal uncouthness, in Dixon's muzziness or in MacNeice's technical immaturity; but there are types of obscurity which seem to have their roots buried in the very depths of the poet's nature. We cannot, for example, attribute Browning's obscurity solely to his cavalier treatment of syntax, still less to his technical incompetency, for his superficial roughness frequently conceals a considerable mastery of poetic technique which, at its best, seems to me as remarkable as Tennyson's. A recent biographer has divined in Browning a morbid reticence about himself which sprang from the fact that he felt a keen remorse at his failure to

---

[1] *The Crowning Privilege*, p. 133.
[2] Marjorie Adix, 'Dylan Thomas: Memories and Appreciations', *Encounter*, January 1954, pp. 13–14.

reveal his innermost convictions. Believing that a poet was commissioned by God to speak the truth, Browning nevertheless jettisoned the doctrines inspired by his love of Shelley in order not to wound his mother's susceptibilities:

This truth, this 'imprisoned splendour', Browning had at a moment of crisis chosen to obscure; and it was the consciousness of having done so, of delivering falsely or imperfectly the message with which he had been entrusted, that was the primary inspiration of the poet's life-long obsession with the psychology of the charlatan, the quack, the second-rater and the 'apparent failure'.[1]

On this view, his obscurity, 'after the inadvertent self-exposure of *Pauline*', was dictated by the promptings of his nature which drove him into

the search for a denser, a more adhesive disguise, the adoption of the dramatic form, in collusion with which he was enabled for so many years effectively to outwit the proctors of society. The most successful disguise of all, of course, was language itself: there can be little doubt that much of the obscurity of Robert Browning was an involuntary form of self-protection. (Browning himself put it otherwise: I write 'ugly things', he said, 'in order to warn the uncongenial and the timorous off my grounds at once.')[2]

Such a radical, tortuous, and imperfectly recognized motive for obscurity is rare, if only because few poets have equalled Browning in the power of their moral feelings or in the scrupulous intensity of their self-examination. Far more common in a poet is a mixture of vanity, insecurity, and affectation, a half-conscious resolve to inflate his talent and to hide his weaknesses by taking refuge beneath a billowing cloak of obscurity. A poem is justly attacked if the poet is concerned 'only with enjoying the display of his own faculties. The poem that has the reason of flattering the author's vanity deserves to be called something more than obscure; and when people use the term they generally mean something worse— vain, arrogant, snobbish.'[3]

Poets may speak in riddles for a variety of reasons. There

---

[1] Betty Miller, *Robert Browning: A Portrait*, pp. 11–12.
[2] Betty Miller, ibid., p. 105.
[3] Laura Riding, *Collected Poems*, 'To the Reader', p. xix.

is in all poetry an element of mystery, because the poet is a hierophant as well as a craftsman, but there is a constant danger that the celebration of a mystery may degenerate into a slick exhibition of mystery-mongering, and that the hierophant, throwing all craftsmanship overboard, may be transformed into a mountebank. It is often hard to tell which of the two is in the ascendant at any given moment—even the poet may not know, for who can infallibly discern whether a man is play-acting to deceive an audience, or putting on a mask that he may reveal unsuspected truths to himself?

Occasionally, a poet will admit that he has indulged in a bit of showmanship for the sheer delight of fooling the public, rather as if Moses, though smiting the rock primarily in order to display God's power, had revelled in the discomfiture of those who got an unexpected wetting. According to William Drummond, Donne told Ben Jonson that he wrote his 'Epitaph on Prince Henry, *Look to me, Faith,* to match Sir Ed: Herbert in obscurenesse'. Jonson believed that the fondness of the influential wits of the day for knotted conceits was dictated by a desire to be smart and modish: 'That which is writhed and tortured is counted the more exquisite. . . . Nothing is fashionable till it be deform'd; and this is to write like a gentleman.'

Poets, like other men of letters, have in them a streak of vanity which exposes them to two closely allied temptations —the desire to be up to date and the craving to win applause for their elegance. Mallarmé was clearly adopting the insolent pose of the dandy when he said to his friend Hérédia: 'I have just written a superb poem, but I do not quite know what it means, and I have come to see you that you should explain it to me.'[1] Such playing to the gallery would clearly be unprofitable if the gallery did not enjoy it, and some readers obviously derive from poetry which they do not comprehend a peculiar, ambivalent pleasure. Many people, as Anatole France once remarked, are deeply moved by obscurities of utterance, and what is vague is particularly delightful to the young. Moreover, their genuine liking for the imprecise

---

[1] This anecdote is quoted by Joseph Bard, *Transactions of the Royal Society of Literature,* vol. xxvi, Introduction, p. vi.

and the suggestive may be reinforced by the desire to be in the intellectual fashion, by a feeling of comfortable superiority to the vulgar mass of philistines who are sweating with perplexed anger at this difficult manifestation of art, and by a dread of revealing that even they, with their delicacy of perception, are completely stumped by what they profess to admire. Thus the vanity of the poet and the snobbishness of his readers perpetually nourish each other.

Many admirers of advanced poetry in Australia were hoaxed into accepting as authentic the parodies concocted by Ern Malley (the pseudonym of Douglas Stewart and J. P. McAuley). This kind of gullibility, this unwillingness to condemn the nonsensical, the pretentious and the bogus for fear of being derided as reactionary blockheads who cannot perceive the exquisite fineness of the Emperor's new clothes, has paralysed the judgement of some contemporary readers. A characteristic anecdote about Dr. Johnson suggests that there were devotees of poetry in the eighteenth century who suffered from a similar affliction. When a certain admirer of Thomson's verse denied that it was obscure Johnson pulled down a volume of his poems from the shelf, chose a passage, read it aloud and questioned Thomson's champion, who stubbornly maintained that it was perfectly clear, whereupon Johnson triumphantly proclaimed that he had omitted every other line.

This was one of those occasions when a vigorous, straightforward man, laying about him with a cheerful brutality of speech, can administer a salutary buffet to conceit and humbug, even though a person who prides himself on clearing his mind of cant may in the process blunt his sensibility and, benumbing his faculty of generous sympathy, debar himself from exploring a whole range of subtle and invigorating experience. Those critics whose tastes were formed by the Scientific Movement of the later seventeenth century, and by the climate of opinion which prevailed after the Restoration, were blind to the strength and the suppleness of the Metaphysical poets, and constitutionally incapable of responding to the intellectual and emotional resonance of their finest verse. Yet the coarse-minded commonsense of such critics must command a measure of respect, and one cannot but applaud their bludgeoning assaults upon affectation, which deservedly gave a number of coxcombs their quietus.

In his *Answer to Davenant*, Hobbes lays his finger upon the weakness of so much poetry of his day and of our own when he singles out for condemnation 'the ambitious obscurity of expressing more than is perfectly conceived, or perfect conception in fewer words than it requires. Which expressions, though they have had the honour to be called strong lines, are indeed no better than Riddles.' Hobbes is a formidable writer because the unsmiling penetration of his gaze and the relentless, sardonic ferocity of his intellectual power expose in all its nakedness the reality that we seek to conceal beneath conventional veils. Nor does he care if, in the process, he tears asunder the delicacy of the imagination and the decent reticence of the heart. The narrow acuteness of his mind reveals its glint in one of his most trenchant sentences, which is aimed at those disturbers of civil and of literary peace whom he castigates for 'working on mean minds with words and distinctions that of themselves signifie nothing, but bewray (by their obscurity) that there walketh . . . another kingdome, as it were a kingdome of Fayries, in the dark'. How shallow and inadequate a theory it is that would condemn the plays of Shakespeare no less than the poems of Donne (to say nothing of the Romantic poets); yet one is forced to admire his firm grasp of the fact that poetic obscurity, far from being a mere stylistic blemish, has political, moral, and even metaphysical implications.

Compared with the disconcerting force of Hobbes's criticism, Flecknoe's belabouring of a luckless poet is little more than rowdy abuse, though he gets in one or two shrewd blows at a type of versifier who is always with us: 'His *Muse* is none of the *Nine*, but a *Mungril* or *By-Blow* of *Parnassus*. . . . His high-sounding Words and Verses are but like empty Tunns or Hog-heads, which make the greater sound the emptier they are. A long while, some admir'd him because they understood him not; and for the same reason he admir'd himself.'[1] Locke makes a similar point, though with more philosophical

[1] *Enigmaticall Characters* (1658): '*Of a Chymerical Poet*'.

subtlety, when he defines the relationship of obscurity to absurdity:

> There is no such way to gain Admittance, or give Defence to strange and absurd Doctrines, as to guard them round about with Legions of obscure, doubtful and undefined Words. . . . For untruth being unacceptable to the Mind of Man, there is no other Defence left for Absurdity, but Obscurity.[1]

Eighteenth-century critics, priding themselves on their plain, blunt commonsense, were largely indifferent to the suggestiveness of poetry, to the latent meanings, to the musical overtones, that seem of the utmost significance to critics of our day. Fielding can even place in Shakespeare's mouth a condemnation of all poetry whose meaning is not immediately plain:

> Shakespeare in Elysium questioned about the meaning of a passage: 'I marvel nothing so much as that men will gird themselves at discovering obscure beauties in an author. Certes the great and most pregnant beauties are ever the plainest and most evidently striking; and when two meanings of a passage can in the least balance our judgments which to prefer I hold it a matter of unquestionable certainty that neither of them is worth a farthing.'[2]

Defoe is equally emphatic on the desirability of a clear mode of expression:

> If any man were to ask me what I would suppose to be a perfect style of language, I would answer, that in which a man speaking to five hundred people, of all common and various capacities, idiots or lunatics excepted, should be understood by them all, and in the same sense which the speaker intended to be understood.

We have grown so practised in analysing the meaning of meaning, so adept in subdividing types of ambiguity into seventy times seven, that such a crude philosophy of language seems beneath contempt. It is certainly deficient in delicacy and in depth; it completely fails to apprehend the subtlety, the mystery or the majesty of much great poetry; yet it is certainly not without merit. In the first place, it may help us to

[1] *An Essay Concerning Human Understanding.*

[2] *A Journey from this World to the Next.* Roger Fry used this passage as an epigraph to his translation of Mallarmé.

recall that the greatest poets, ancient and modern, for all their profundity and difficulty, are distinguished by a certain directness of utterance, by an ability to invest the most commonplace truths with a memorable grandeur. Secondly, it reminds us that those poets who are notoriously obscure, Lycophron, Timotheus, Bacchylides, Callimachus, Lucan, Hyperides, Gongora, Donne, and the lesser Metaphysicals, Browning, and Hopkins, are usually held to be inferior to the greatest masters, partly because they lack the universal appeal of those whose concern is for the unchanging passions of the heart rather than for the most intricate refinements of language, and the most curious labyrinthine ways of the speculative intelligence. Finally, it helps to guard us against the affectation of the poet who adopts an eccentric mode of expression in the belief that he can bluff his readers into accepting a farrago of nonsense. When Eliot and Pound insist that poetry must be at least as well written as prose they are merely restating an eighteenth-century commonplace:[1]

Imagining that the more their writings are unlike prose, the more they resemble poetry, they have adopted a language of their own, and call upon mankind for admiration. All those who do not understand them are silent, and those who make out their meaning are willing to praise, to show they understand.[2]

Twentieth-century critics of poetry are kinder than their eighteenth-century counterparts towards obscure verse, and less severe even than Coleridge, who describes the style of the Metaphysical poets as 'the reverse of that which distinguishes too many of our recent versifiers; the one conveying the most fantastic thoughts in the most correct language, the other in the most fantastic language conveying the most trivial thoughts'. There are various reasons for our modern tenderness: we are in some ways more generous and less cocksure than our predecessors; now that the Metaphysicals are more highly valued than at any time since the middle of the seventeenth century we find it easier than would critics

---

[1] One of the marks of a good critic is the ability to restate valuable commonplaces which have fallen into undeserved neglect.

[2] Goldsmith, in his life of Parnell.

brought up in the Romantic tradition to forgive our contemporaries for being arid, abstruse, ingenious, and fantastic; we have become slower to condemn verse on the score of obscurity for fear of making fools of ourselves in the eyes of posterity; a cynic might add that a great many critics have a certain vested interest in the production of obscure poetry, since without a steady supply they would have to shut up shop. Thus a mixture of timidity, wisdom, and self-interest has prevented a number of intelligent critics from denouncing the worst caprices of modern verse.

Goaded into an extravagant frenzy by this placid acceptance of charlatanism, Robert Graves has attempted to redress the balance by a diatribe against the obscurity of contemporary poets. In his Clark Lectures he analyses and arraigns what he calls the Impressionist, Expressionist, Futurist, Surrealist, and Lycophronic techniques,[1] having contended in an earlier book that poets, deprived of a common myth, no longer possessing an honoured place in society, and driven into the wilderness,

rave on like Elizabethan Abraham-men, until raving becomes a professional affectation; until the bulk of modern poetry ceases to make poetic, prosaic, or even pathological sense. . . . It is not as though the so-called surrealists, impressionists, expressionists and neo-romantics were concealing a grand secret by pretended folly, in the style of Gwion; on the contrary, they are concealing their unhappy lack of a secret.[2]

The final word may be left to Oscar Wilde—'Nowadays to be intelligible is to be found out'—and to Aldous Huxley, who re-echoes the opinion of Locke that obscurity is the praetorian guard of nonsense:

Almost all the contents of the 'advanced' reviews are just 'Mary had a little lamb' translated into Hebrew and written in cipher. Re-Englished and decoded, they astonish the reader by their silliness. Catching the sense at two removes, or ten, he is annoyed to find that it is either nonsense or platitude.[3]

---

[1] *The Crowning Privilege*, pp. 95–98.
[2] *The White Goddess*, pp. 400–1.
[3] *Texts and Pretexts*, p. 220.

More deep-rooted and pervasive than the kind of vanity we have been considering is a form of pride that leads a poet to ignore or to despise his readers, sometimes from sheer indifference, sometimes as a deliberate act of policy. Not that one wants a poet to be servile, or even to clip his wings so that he may not soar beyond the range of his dimmest-sighted readers. Somerset Maugham's remark that the finest compliment he ever received was a letter saying: 'I read your novel without having to look up a single word in the dictionary' could never have been made by any great poet, ancient or modern. Goethe speaks for almost every true poet when he says: 'The author whom a lexicon can keep up with is worth nothing.'[1] Indeed the only poet of any merit who would have sympathized with Maugham is Jonathan Swift, whom Maugham has recommended as a model for aspiring writers:

> It was his practice, we are told, to have two of his men-servants brought in to listen to his poems being read, 'which, if they did not comprehend, he would alter and amend, until they understood it perfectly well, and then would say, *This will do, for I write to the vulgar more than to the learned.*'[2]

Perhaps the servants were unusually intelligent, or exceptionally tactful: one feels that even Swift would not have made himself an intellectual eunuch to gratify the readers of the *News of the World*.

There are poets, however, who go to the other extreme and appear to take a malicious delight in baffling their readers. Even Blake, one feels, occasionally makes his poems needlessly cryptic, partly because he dares not speak openly, for political reasons, but still more because he intends his verse to be a stumbling-block for the polite world which he so cordially despises. It was typical of Blake that of all the passages in Wordsworth's *Ode on the Intimations of Immortality*, he should particularly admire that which begins: 'But there's a tree, of many, one', upon which Crabb Robinson

---

[1] Maugham and Goethe are quoted by Randall Jarrell, *Poetry and the Age*, in the essay called 'The Obscurity of the Poet', p. 28.

[2] James Sutherland, *A Preface to Eighteenth Century Poetry*, p. 48. The passage in quotation marks is from Swift's *Works* (1762), vol. i. 'To The Reader.'

comments: 'The parts of Wordsworth's Ode which he most enjoyed were the most obscure and those I the least like and comprehend.'[1] Crabb Robinson seems to have been unlucky in his encounters with poets, for he got short shrift from Wordsworth when trying to persuade him to consider the effect of his verse on the public. It embarrassed him, said Robinson, to read aloud in company two lines from *The Thorn*:

> I've measured it from side to side
> 'Tis three feet long and two feet wide.

Wordsworth merely replied: 'They ought to be liked', but in the 1820 edition of his poems wisely altered the lines to read:

> Though but of compass small, and bare
> To thirsty suns and parching air.

Some poets look upon any concession to the public as a violation of their poetic integrity, and since they regard intelligibility as the most disgraceful concession of all, it is not surprising that their verse should be obscure. The most rigorous and deliberate challenge to the notion that art is a means of communication among men is to be found in the Surrealist Manifesto, which proclaims that 'any work of art that can be understood is the work of a journalist'. This kind of mettlesome arrogance, when allied with great talent, endows poetry with a certain devilish energy and because, like all the most corrosive and deadly sins, it may disguise itself as a rare, high-minded nobility, those who are most proud of singing

> high and aloofe,
> Safe from the wolves black jaw, and the dull Asses hoofe[2]

are most in danger of being corrupted by it.

W. B. Yeats's temperament, no less than his philosophical and political beliefs, perpetually exposed him to the lure of this form of pride. In his youth he detested the rationalism of Huxley, the flatulent moralizing of Tennyson, the didacticism of George Eliot, everything that smacked of journalism,

---

[1] Quoted by Bernard Blackstone, *English Blake*, p. 185.
[2] Ben Jonson, 'An Ode to Himself'.

as much as the Surrealists despised all attempts at rational communication, and for much the same reasons. He plunged into a study of Blake, of Theosophy, and of the occult, all of which reinforced his contemptuous indifference to 'the old bitter world where they marry in churches'. So many critics have questioned the sincerity of Yeats's early preoccupations with magic that one must in fairness remember his avowal to John O'Leary in a letter written in late July 1893: 'If I had not made magic my constant study I could not have written a single word of my Blake book, nor would *The Countess Cathleen* have ever come to exist. The mystical life is the centre of all that I do and all that I think and all that I write.'[1] As he grew older, personal unhappiness, the strain of endless controversy with his fellow-countrymen, and a deepening scorn for the pettiness of the mob, coupled with a grateful admiration for the tradition of the great houses, led him to exalt whatever was proud and solitary. In one of his poems written in honour of Lady Gregory, 'To A Friend Whose Work Has Come to Nothing', he counsels the friend to practise, in solitude, whatever is most difficult:

> Amid a place of stone,
> Be secret and exult,
> Because of all things known
> That is most difficult.

In the poems of his old age this note of triumph and of solitude is struck again and again. One of his favourite symbols, the tower, is, among many other things, an emblem of the poetic imagination which rises above the muddle and the mire of common existence:

> Blessed be this place,
> More blessed still this tower;
> A bloody, arrogant power
> Rose out of the race
> Uttering, mastering it . . .[2]

The revelations vouchsafed to him by the heavenly messengers and expounded in *A Vision*, a savage hatred for democracy,

[1] *The Letters of W. B. Yeats*, ed. Allan Wade, p. 211.
[2] 'Blood and the Moon.'

and a belief in a new, violent annunciation that would usher in a terrifying age of exultant cruelty, all confirmed his innate conviction that the poet is a guardian of sacred mysteries which he must preserve from the profanation of the vulgar. Thus a genuine mysticism, a lofty disdain for everything base, a considered belief in ceremony and in social inequality, a touch of arrogance and, it must be admitted, a tincture of charlatanism, made it inevitable that Yeats should favour an arcane mode of expression which occasionally degenerates into mumbo-jumbo. We can discern this fondness for mystification in a letter to Katharine Tynan, which was probably written some few days after 6 September 1888:

> In the second part of 'Oisin' under disguise of symbolism I have said several things to which I only have the key. The romance is for my readers. They must not even know there is a symbol anywhere. They will not find out. If they did, it would spoil the art.[1]

It is amusing and touching to observe the youthful poet's delight in hugging a secret to himself, but most readers will be merely irritated by the solemnity with which the older Yeats enunciates a very dubious principle:

> The arts are very conservative, and have a great respect for those wanderers who still stitch into their carpets among the Mongolian plains religious symbols so old that they have not even a meaning.[2]

What prevented Yeats from dwindling into a minor poet, ever more deeply immersed in a quagmire of eccentric nonsense? And why, despite his agreement with the Surrealists in their detestation of what he once called 'an ever-growing burden of noble attitudes and literary words . . . imposed upon the poet by papers like the *Spectator*',[3] was he less influenced by their example than any other major poet of his time?

Yeats had, in the first place, a hard-headed streak which enabled him to boast that he had sometimes failed as a poet

---

[1] *The Letters of W. B. Yeats*, ed. Allan Wade, p. 86.
[2] Quoted by Graham Hough, *The Last Romantics*, p. 228, with no indication of the source from which it is taken.
[3] Letter to J. B. Yeats, 16 February 1910. *The Letters of W. B. Yeats*, ed. Allan Wade, p. 548.

but never as a business man;[1] nor in his pursuit of mystical enlightenment did he forget the wisdom of the body: 'As you know, all my art theories depend upon just this—rooting of mythology in the earth.'[2] Hostile as he might be to the deification of abstract reason, he had an unfailing respect for the great works of the human intellect, and though in one of his last letters he wrote: 'You can refute Hegel but not the Saint or the Song of Sixpence',[3] he had studied not only Hegel but Plato, Vico, Berkeley, Nietzsche, and Spengler, together with a mass of other historical and philosophical writing. Even his rejection of scientific rationalism— 'Europe belongs to Dante and the witches' sabbath, not to Newton'[4]—was inspired by hard thinking as well as by a passionate intuitive certainty. Finally, however scornful he may have felt towards the common run of humanity, his devotion to the art of poetry, his determination to hammer his thoughts into unity, forbade him the luxury of slack or clumsy workmanship. He was, in short, too proud a poet to indulge in the vanity of despising his audience. That is why even his most difficult poems move with an unfaltering precision of imagery and of music, as if to assure the reader that their complexity is a sign of respect for his intelligence.

When lesser poets dispense with this kind of respect we have every justification for losing our temper, because few things are more irritating than the combination of insolence and incompetence which so many poets are not ashamed to exhibit. Finding it beyond their capacity to express an intricate or an unusual thought with clarity, they excuse their failure by pretending that their readers lack the perception to appreciate their subtlety, and complacently retreat into an impenetrable thicket of obscurity. Thus an unhealthy mixture of self-mistrust and self-satisfaction gives rise to those curious

[1] The *Daily Express* headline on the death of Yeats read 'Scoffed At Fairies, But They Made His Living'. This curious tribute at least did justice to Yeats's financial acumen.

[2] *W. B. Yeats and T. Sturge Moore: Their Correspondence 1901–1937*, ed. Ursula Bridge, p. 114.

[3] Letter to Lady Elizabeth Pelham, 4 January 1939. *The Letters of W. B. Yeats*, ed. Allan Wade, p. 922.

[4] Letter to Olivia Shakespear, 9 March 1933. Ibid., p. 807.

piebald poems, irregularly stippled with commonplace reflections, halting intimations and extravagant fantasies, before which the reader can only pause and recall the judgement of the King of Hearts:

'If there's no meaning in it', said the King, 'that saves a world of trouble, you know, as we needn't try to find any. And yet I don't know,' he went on, spreading out the verses on his knee, and looking at them with one eye, 'I seem to see some meaning in them, after all.'

It is difficult to acquit W. H. Auden, in his early poems, of a jaunty indifference to the susceptibilities of his readers. The first two lines of 'Journey to Iceland' provide an illuminating example of the casual, slap-happy technique of poetic revision which he was content to adopt:

And the traveller hopes: 'Let me be far from any
Physician'; and the ports have names for the sea.

A letter to Christopher Isherwood reveals how the lines attained their final form: 'No, you were wrong. I did not write: "the *ports* have names for the sea" but "the *poets* have names for the sea". However, as so often before, the mistake seems better than the original idea, so I'll leave it.'[1] Isherwood himself has explained how 'Weston' compiled some of his youthful work. He would jot down isolated lines of various poems which Isherwood had chanced to admire, 'until a poem had been evolved which was a little anthology of my favourite lines strung together without even an attempt to make connected sense'.[2] In *Paid on Both Sides*, aptly subtitled *A Charade*, one can sense both an inner uncertainty about the purport of this playlet and a contemptuous amusement at the perplexity of the audience. To quote Isherwood once more: 'Weston produced a short verse play in which the two worlds are so confused that it is almost impossible to say whether the characters are epic heroes or members of a school O.T.C.' Worse still, the tone of the play is varied so often

[1] W. H. Auden and Louis MacNeice, *Letters from Iceland*, p. 27.
[2] *Lions and Shadows*, p. 191. See also Isherwood's article, 'Some Notes on Auden's Early Poetry', in *New Verse*, Double Number 26–27 (November 1937), pp. 4–9.

and so clumsily that its mixture of symbolism, knockabout farce, sophistication, and epic doom remains unalluring and indigestible. A Spy is captured, and there follows this stage direction:

> Lights. A trial. John as the accuser. The Spy as accused. Joan as his warder with a gigantic feeding bottle. Xmas as president, the rest as jury, wearing school caps.

When the Spy has been shot, we pass from the Icelandic saga to the Edwardian music-hall, and are introduced to a doctor who takes circular saws, bicycle pumps, etc., from his bag, and swings into a routine dialogue with his Boy:

> B. Tickle your arse with a feather, sir.
> D. What's that?
> B. Particularly nasty weather, sir.

It would be pointless to dwell on the faults that vitiate some (but by no means all) of his early work, if only because Auden himself has admitted his failings:

> For I relapse into my crimes:
> Time and again have slubbered through
> With slip and slapdash what I do.[1]

It is enough to note that there are worse offenders who are unlikely to make so frank a recantation and who are still rather proud of not being understood or unmasked by their readers.

There remains one type of poet who is genuinely indifferent to the opinion of his readers, because his verse is not addressed primarily to them. In a letter to Woodhouse written in October 1818, Keats reveals that he has become obsessed with the pursuit of beauty to the exclusion of everything else: 'I feel assured I should write from the mere yearning and fondness I have for the beautiful even if my night's labours should be burnt every morning, and no eye ever shine upon them.'

If a poet is to have no audience but himself it does not matter very much whether he comprehends what he is saying, and even if he speaks to God as well as to himself, God will

[1] *New Year Letter*, lines 218–20.

doubtless understand him. Browning found consolation in this belief: 'Do you think poetry was ever generally understood— or can be? . . . A poet's affair is with God—to whom he is accountable and of whom is his reward.'

On such a theory, poetry is either a self-communing or a murmured prayer to God which the reader is permitted to overhear rather than to hear, and since the poem is not meant for him he has no right to complain if he fails to make out its meaning. A poet who argues on these lines is deliberately violating the implicit bargain that is struck between an author and his readers: admirable as it is to meditate in private and to pray in secret, the mere act of publication implies the desire to communicate with other people, and one can scarcely pocket a man's money in return for making a speech and then dismiss him as an eavesdropper.

'The right of being obscure', says Ruskin, 'is not to be lightly claimed; it can only be founded on long effort to be intelligible.' It is never easy to decide whether a contemporary writer has made the effort required of him, whether he is a true poet misunderstood by the impatient, arrogant Philistine, or a vain charlatan given the benefit of the doubt by a long-suffering, gullible public. Time has a way of settling such questions for us, or rather for our descendants, who can scarcely conceive why we were in any doubt about the answer. It is tempting, when faced with much dark and difficult poetry of our day, to be scornful and witty, to echo François Maynard's judgement on an obscure poet of his time:

> Ce que ta plume produit
> Est couvert de trop de voiles;
> Ton Discours est une Nuit
> Vesve de Lune et d'Estoiles
>
> Mon Amy, chasse bien loin
> Cette Noire Rhetorique.
> Tes Ouvrages ont besoin
> D'un Devin qui les explique.
>
> Si ton Esprit veut cacher
> Les belles choses qu'il pense,

Dy-moi, qui peut t'empescher
De te servir du Silence ?[1]

To yield to such a temptation would be less than just to good poets who feel that they must speak obscurely in order that they may express with patient fidelity their sense of the world's complexity and of their own bewilderment, yet although we must admire them for their honesty we may still regret that so many of our most talented contemporaries are likely to suffer the fate which Elizabeth Barrett prophesied for Robert Browning:

He will not die, because the principle of life is in him, but he will not live the warm summer life which is permitted to many of very inferior faculty, because he does not come out into the sun.[2]

[1] Quoted by Daniel George, *Alphabetical Order*, p. 66.
[2] Letter to Thomas Westwood, April 1845. *The Letters of Elizabeth Barrett Browning*, ed. Frederic G. Kenyon, vol. i, p. 255.

6

Public Worlds

Things fall apart; the centre cannot hold;
Mere anarchy is loosed upon the world,
The blood-dimmed tide is loosed, and everywhere
The ceremony of innocence is drowned;
The best lack all conviction, while the worst
Are full of passionate intensity.
W. B. YEATS, 'The Second Coming'

I can connect
Nothing with nothing.
T. S. ELIOT, *The Waste Land*

IT has been said that the medieval world begins with St.
Augustine, the modern world with Alexander the Great, and
certainly the Alexandrian epoch, with its vague humanitarian-
ism, its gropings towards a cosmopolitan philosophy, its
scientific achievements and its abandonment of traditional
religion, presents some striking parallels with the present age.
In literature, the Alexandrian age witnessed the perfection
and the refinement of an erudite, top-heavy scholarship, a
flowering of subtle and exact literary criticism, and the cult
of a poetry notorious for its sophistication and its obscurity.
Dangerous as it is to make sweeping generalizations about
the relationship between poetry and the society in which it
is written, it seems likely that a civilization which is complex, individualistic, restless, sceptical, and deeply aware of
its fundamental insecurity will give rise to verse that is
subtle, highly-wrought and difficult. It seems to me undeniable
that, from the early seventeenth century onwards, our poets
have found the world growing more bewildering, unfriendly
and disordered; and that they have become correspondingly
more and more self-conscious about the weight and the intricacy of their task. The obscurity of much contemporary
verse, far from being willed by the arrogant caprice of the

individual poet, faithfully mirrors the turbulent uncertainty of a whole age.

When, precisely, English poets began to be visited by that kind of self-consciousness, to sense the fissure in the order of society, to feel the strain of living in a world of innumerable tensions, is impossible to determine. Shakespeare is the last poet in whose writings we can discern a deep, whole-hearted acceptance of the universe and of the social order. We know that the medieval portrayal of the world revealed, or invented, a coherence, a meaning, in the pattern of existence, and we know also that, despite the impact of the Renaissance and of the Reformation, medieval ideas persisted throughout the sixteenth century. Thomas à Kempis was far more widely read in England than Machiavelli from 1500 to 1630, and the religious works of Robert Southwell, whom Elizabeth executed for treason in 1595, went into edition after edition in the years following his death. The first disquieting intimations of profound uncertainty belong to the years after the turn of the century, when Puritanism, the new philosophy, and an intensification of economic activity began to threaten the solidity and the harmonious unity of the world that Shakespeare celebrated. The nature of the Shakespearean universe has been delineated by Aldous Huxley in a remarkably eloquent passage:

In practically any comedy or tragedy of Shakespeare one cannot read twenty lines without being made aware that, behind the clowns, the criminals, the heroes, behind the flirts and the weeping queens, beyond all that is agonizingly or farcically human, and yet symbiotic with man, immanent in his consciousness and consubstantial with his being, there lie the everlasting data, the given facts of planetary and cosmic existence on every level, animate and inanimate, mindless and purposively conscious.[1]

Herrick's world, although on a much smaller scale, and with the tragic figures banished, has something of that same fullness, that acceptance of ordered freedom, that sense of the indissoluble relation between man and nature. Yet by 1648, when *Hesperides* was published, Herrick had become unfashionable, and Bishop Corbet's lament for the exiled fairies

[1] *The Devils of Loudun*, pp. 96–97.

was a recognition that a whole world of myth had passed away:

> Witness those rings and roundelays
> Of theirs, which yet remain,
> Were footed in Queen Mary's days
> On many a grassy plain;
> But since of late, Elizabeth,
> And later, James came in,
> They never danced on any heath
> As when the time hath been.

In Donne, more than in any other poet of the age, we can trace the uneasy premonitions of a preternaturally keen intelligence which loves the elaborate splendour of a traditional mode of life, yet knows that it will soon be destroyed by the raging flux in the mind of man:

> And new Philosophy calls all in doubt,
> The Element of fire is quite put out;
> The Sun is lost, and th' earth, and no man's wit
> Can well direct him where to looke for it.
> And freely men confesse that this world's spent,
> When in the Planets, and the Firmament
> They seeke so many new; they see that this
> Is crumbled out againe to his Atomies.
> 'Tis all in peeces, all cohaerence gone;
> All just supply and all Relation.[1]

By the end of the century the new philosophy had swept away almost every familiar assumption that had nourished the minds of English poets from Chaucer to Shakespeare. The world had indeed crumbled out to his atomies, and even the force of Milton's intellect could barely clamp the fragments into a coherent whole. After him no poet could hope to fashion a Divine Comedy out of the bewildering array of new facts and concepts which threatened to overwhelm him. Men tacitly admitted that even the pretence of aspiring to universal knowledge was futile when they began to compile encyclopedias alphabetically, to parcel out knowledge into neat little segments and to breed a new race of specialists, each of whom was trained to cultivate his own tiny island, like a

---

[1] *An Anatomie of the World: The First Anniversary*, lines 205–14.

marooned Robinson Crusoe, that perfect symbol of an epoch in which economic man had dethroned royal man, as imagined by George Chapman in the full pride of the Renaissance, and elbowed aside man the pilgrim who, in the pages of Dante, Bunyan, and Milton, followed the divine promptings in his way through the world.

By the end of the eighteenth century we hear for the first time a note that was to become more plangent and more familiar in the next hundred and fifty years—disquiet at the ever-growing complexity of life, a fear that the individual was doomed to lose his stature and his significance in a world of huge, impersonal, mechanical processes, a pathetic desire to recapture the sense of organic unity with nature which less sophisticated civilizations had enjoyed as their birthright. Sir Richard Livingstone, quoting a passage by von Humboldt on this very theme, remarks that 'it is curious to find him attributing these modern weaknesses to the eighteenth century':[1]

The study of a character like the Greek must have a specially salutary effect on an age, in which, from numerous circumstances, the attention is drawn more to things than to men, more to masses of men than to individuals, more to external values and use than to inner merit and enjoyment, and where high and many-sided culture has led us far from primal simplicity.

An English poet, bred in the eighteenth-century tradition, experienced even more profoundly and passionately the sense of decaying order in all things. Wordsworth included in the notes to his poems an extract from the foundation charter of the Abbey of St. Mary's Furness:

Considering every day the uncertainty of life, that the roses and flowers of Kings, Emperors and Dukes, and the crowns and palms of all the great wither and decay; and that all things, with an uninterrupted course, tend to dissolution and death . . .

The melancholy which suffuses much of his finest poetry is deeper and more poignant than a mere rehearsal of the commonplace that men are mortal. It springs from his recognition that man's harmony with nature, no less than the finest

[1] *Greek Ideals and Modern Life*, p. 43.

works of his hands and the most satisfying of his myths, is at the mercy of time and chance. In the less familiar of his sonnets about King's College Chapel he envies the assurance of the men who raised such a monument to God's glory:

> They dreamed not of a perishable home
> Who thus could build . . .

and in one of his finest sonnets, 'Mutability', he faces the knowledge that the outward forms of truth (which are all that we can discern)

> drop like the tower sublime
> Of yesterday, which royally did wear
> His crown of weeds, but could not even sustain
> Some casual shout that broke the silent air,
> Or the unimaginable touch of Time.

Wordsworth saw this cosmic insecurity mirrored in the shifting pattern of the social order. His mistrust of the new, sprawling industrial cities may be partially explained by reference to his social origins and to his admiration for the yeomen of his native dales who were fast becoming anachronistic, just as his detestation of the amorphous, pullulating metropolis may have been dictated by his consciousness that, however remarkable a prodigy of learning he might have seemed to the admiring smallholders of the Lake District, he was a gawky nobody in the polished literary and social world of London. But local patriotism and wounded vanity alone do not explain the strength and the consistency of his feelings, which sprang from a steady, visionary insight into the true import of the bewildering agrarian and industrial revolutions. Even his lonely figures, placed on the very edge of being, are victims of man's inhumanity to man, waifs and strays reduced to misery and to destitution by social as well as by natural calamities. The vagrants, widows, and discharged soldiers who wander through his desolate landscapes are creatures for whom society has no use, the forerunners of our displaced persons, and they are unwanted nuisances because society has ceased to be an organic whole, having broken down into warring atomies. Wordsworth could endure to gaze on

London only when sleep had linked its inhabitants together in the unity of repose, when its mighty heart was, uncharacteristically, lying still. His description of the view from Westminster Bridge:

> Ships, towers, domes, theatres, and temples lie
> Open unto the fields, and to the sky;
> All bright and glittering in the smokeless air . . .

conjures up a classical city rather than the great wen of early nineteenth-century England, and his feeling for the balance, the poised simplicity, of Mediterranean antiquity is strangely touching. Unlike Swinburne, who lashed himself into the delusion that Venus might resume her reign in Hampstead and enable him to enjoy the lilies and languors of vice, Wordsworth knew that he and his contemporaries could never hope to experience the natural piety of a pagan, or to

> Have sight of Proteus rising from the sea;
> Or hear old Triton blow his wreathèd horn.

In a characteristic phrase Wordsworth refers to

> the heavy and the weary weight
> Of all this unintelligible world . . .

and the world is unintelligible to the poet because it has grown mysteriously hostile:

> For a multitude of causes, unknown to former times, are now acting with a combined force to blunt the discriminating powers of the mind, and, unfitting it for all voluntary exertion, to reduce it to a state of almost savage torpor. The most effective of these causes are the great national events which are daily taking place, and the increasing accumulation of men in cities.

It is not only the tide of events that overwhelms the poet's ability to speak coherently to his fellows: even the deep, wonderful currents of human thought are flowing in an unfamiliar direction. I know of few passages in Wordsworth so candid and so revealing as the sentences in which he admits that, for the time being, there is a world of knowledge which the poet is powerless to explore:

The remotest discoveries of the chemist, the botanist, or mineral-ogist, will be as proper objects of the poet's art as any upon which it can be employed, if the time should ever come when these things shall be familiar to us, and the relations under which they are contemplated by the followers of these respective sciences shall be manifestly and palpably material to us as enjoying and suffering beings. If the time should ever come when what is now called science, thus familiarized to men, shall be ready to put on, as it were, a form of flesh and blood, the poet will lend his divine spirit to aid the transfiguration, and will welcome the Being thus produced as a dear and genuine inmate of the household of man.[1]

Wordsworth was free to ignore what he could not absorb, but since his day the depredations of industrialism and of science into the traditional provinces of poetry have grown more widespread and ruthless. Nor can the poet remain indifferent to those other forces which, in the past hundred years, have transformed the world in which he lives and which he must try to assimilate, unless he is content to whimper in a corner. He is forced to transfigure the discoveries of Darwin, Marx, and Freud, to contemplate the turmoil of democracy's frustrated longings and devouring fears, to interpret the semi-articulate desires of men and women whose vocabulary is pitiably thin and imprecise, and with whom he can barely communicate.

A hundred years ago the most perceptive minds of the day had already begun to appreciate the strenuous nature of the poet's task. In his essay on 'The Function of Criticism at the Present Time', Matthew Arnold laid his finger upon the strain and the effort necessarily involved in the writing of contemporary poetry:

Every one can see that a poet, for instance, ought to know life and the world before dealing with them in poetry; and life and the world being in modern times very complex things, the creation of a modern poet, to be worth much, implies a great critical effort behind it; else it must be a comparatively poor, barren, and short-lived affair.

Life and the world, it may be retorted, always have been very complex things; but Arnold's observation is valid, if only

[1] *Preface to Lyrical Ballads* (1802).

because he stressed the new self-consciousness that was hence-forth to weigh upon the heart of every poet. The first major English poet to become fully aware of this modern complex-ity and to face, however imperfectly, the problems which it posed was Tennyson. It is true that Browning may, on the surface, appear more modern than Tennyson, and undeniable that he enjoyed showing his awareness of new inventions and fresh social habits—he was probably the first poet to refer to photography, to use the word 'cocktail',[1] and to mention, in 'Meeting At Night' (1845), the phosphorous matches which had been imported from Germany in 1833:[2]

> . . . the quick, sharp scratch
> And blue spurt of a lighted match.

The depths of his nature, however, were almost untouched by the anxieties and the perplexities that weighed so oppres-sively upon his eminent contemporaries, and if he chose to adorn his dramatic presentations with a few modish stage properties it was in the spirit of a producer who dresses a Shakespearean production in modern costumes. The sensuous opulence of his temperament, his omnivorous response to the hot colours and strong scents of the Mediterranean, his fascinated brooding upon evil, the cool detachment with which he delighted to scrutinize the tortuous subtleties of human passions show that he was, essentially, a man of the Renaissance who, by some accident of chronology, had wan-dered into the wrong century and the wrong country, an error which he hastened to repair by emigrating and by concentra-ting his imagination upon a more congenial epoch. Tennyson, on the other hand, was rightly acclaimed by the Victorians as the representative poet of the age because he experienced, though with uncharacteristic acuteness and intensity, the doubts and aspirations peculiar to the period in which he lived. Browning would have sensed the evil that is incarnate in the world had he flourished in the cheerfully optimistic days of Sir Robert Walpole; Tennyson's desperate longing to believe in the Christian revelation, his dogged, earnest study

[1] Raymond Mortimer, *Channel Packet*, p. 9.
[2] E. L. Woodward, *The Age of Reform*, p. 601, n. 2.

of the whole body of contemporary knowledge, and the painful honesty which forbade him to ignore the discoveries of the geologists and of Darwin help to explain why he became so faithful an interpreter of the Victorian temper. James Smetham recognized the magnitude and the difficulty of the task which Tennyson had set himself. In a letter dated 10 August 1855 he comments on *Maud*:

> The poetic power which can swallow newspapers full of business, bankruptcy courts, sanitary commissions, wars, murders, and medical reports on the adulteration of food, and then reproduce them, as the conjuror brings out his coloured horn from his mouth after a meal of shavings, *is* poetic power.[1]

It is scarcely necessary to enumerate the revolutionary changes in our civilization since 1855 which have intensified the strain to which poets are subjected and made it increasingly hard for them to impose a coherent design upon the turbulent flood that threatens to engulf them. In 1855, when men could still contemplate the rapidly changing pattern with hopeful eagerness as well as with a faint tremor of apprehension, Smetham could describe *Maud* as 'an episode of life with the commonest romance-plot and the paltriest moral, but wrought out with the lyrical changefulness of the life of this our time'. For the past fifty years most intelligent men and almost all poets have regarded the process of change with a half-despairing, uncomprehending nausea, the lyricism grown mute beneath the crescendos of brutality and terror that have stormed across the world. Nor is it merely the complexity of our social organization that makes it so difficult for poets to speak clearly to their fellow-men: language itself has become a barrier rather than a means of communication.

When the majority of Englishmen lived in small towns and villages there flourished a genuinely popular culture which, for all its crudities and limitations, unified and enriched the lives of those who grew up beneath its shade. Attendance at church attuned men's minds to the cadences of the Bible and the Prayer Book; the pastoral images of these sacred books

[1] *Letters of James Smetham* (1891). Quoted by G. Grigson, *The Victorians*, p. 84.

were in perfect accord with the lives of the villagers; the flowering of local dialects redolent with exact, vivid words and the handing down of a fruitful body of myth, legend, folk-songs, and ballads from one generation to another kept alive a racy, idiomatic language which poets could use as the staple of their verse. The herding of a rapidly-increasing population into the enormous, hideous barrack-like towns of the industrial regions destroyed irreparably the older ways of life, substituting for the varied nourishment of the soil the meagre, processed diet of hard facts which Mr. Gradgrind prescribed for the inhabitants of Coketown. At the same time as the emotional life of the masses was being steadily impoverished, their response to the imaginative use of words becoming ever more sluggish, the resources of language at the disposal of the more sophisticated poets grew richer and more elaborate than ever before, thanks to the scores of new words invented during the nineteenth century and to the hitherto uncharted modes of expression which were explored by the first Romantics and their followers. At the end of the nineteenth century there stretched an enormous gulf between the greasy, threadbare speech of the lower-middle classes and the highly specialized, self-conscious language of poetry, a gulf which has widened during the present century. For, in the past fifty years, a multitude of professional entertainers, journalists, advertisers, song-writers, script-writers, scenario-writers, and other peddlers of anodynes have made their living by providing millions of people with the emotional sustenance which they can no longer find for themselves. They have discovered that the easiest way to satisfy their clients is to arouse their passions and play on their feelings by exploiting the most obvious associations of words which the imperfectly educated regard as romantic and beautiful, thereby exemplifying the melancholy truth of W. B. Yeats's adage: 'Every country likes good art till it produces its own form of vulgarity and after that will have nothing else.'[1] In the face of such cynical debasement of the poetic currency the best poets of our time have grown more vigorous and critical in their

[1] Letter to Olivia Shakespear, 15 April 1926. *The Letters of W. B. Yeats*, ed. Allan Wade, p. 713.

choice of language, eschewing all that awakens an easy response, seeking an ever more exacting precision of phrase, desperately trying to preserve their poetry from the taint of shallow emotionalism.

Herrick's poetry moves with an enviable assurance and clarity because he unquestioningly accepts the order of society as natural and meaningful and because he speaks in his verse as unconstrainedly as he might chat with his parishioners. He defines the scope of his art in 'The Argument of his Book':

> I sing of *Brooks*, of *Blossoms*, *Birds*, and *Bowers*:
> Of *April*, *May*, of *June* and *July*-Flowers.
> I sing of *May-poles*, *Hock-carts*, *Wassails*, *Wakes*,
> Of *Bride-grooms*, *Brides*, and of their *Bridall-cakes*.
> I write of *Youth*, of *Love*, and have Accesse
> By these, to sing of cleanly-*Wantonnesse*.
> I sing of *Dewes*, of *Raines*, and piece by piece
> Of *Balme*, of *Oyle*, of *Spice*, and *Amber-Greece*.
> I sing of *Times trans-shifting*; and I write
> How *Roses* first came *Red*, and *Lillies White*.
> I write of *Groves*, of *Twilights*, and I sing
> The Court of *Mab*, and of the *Fairie-King*.
> I write of *Hell*; I sing (and ever shall)
> Of *Heaven*, and hope to have it after all.

When men feel that civilization has grown purposeless and incoherent their verse will tend to reflect their perturbation, to show signs of the inner stress which accompanies their efforts to make sense of a disjointed pattern. It is instructive to compare Herrick's introductory lines with a poem by Ronald Bottrall, 'The Thyrsus Retipped', to notice how the older poet walks in a world that has not entirely lost the glory and the wholeness of Eden, whereas the poet of our day looks blankly at an indifferent, neutral world of unrelated objects:

> Nightingales, Anangke, a sunset or the meanest flower
> Were formerly the potentialities of poetry,
> But now what have they to do with one another,
> With Dionysius or with me?
>
> Microscopic anatomy of ephemerides,
> Power-house stacks, girder-ribs, provide a crude base;

But man is what he eats, and they are not bred
Flesh of our flesh, being unrelated
Experientially, fused in no emotive furnace.

We can hear, in the powerful, grinding sound of these lines
the incessant, nerve-wracking clamour of our machine-age,
just as in Herrick we are ravished with the music appropriate
to his mood of serenity.

The harshness and the difficulty of so much contemporary
verse will no longer seem inexplicable to us when we understand that, for many poets, our culture is a vast junk-shop to
preserve the contents of which we are expected to sacrifice
our children every twenty-five years:

> There died a myriad,
> And of the best, among them,
> For an old bitch gone in the teeth,
> For a botched civilization,
>
> Charm, smiling at the good mouth,
> Quick eyes gone under earth's lid,
>
> For two gross of broken statues,
> For a few thousand battered books.[1]

Nor ought we to find it strange that so much of our best
modern poetry should be distinguished by the excessive
violence of its imagery and by the strained virtuosity of its
language, for only by a tremendous exertion of the imagination and of the intellect can a poet hope to counter-balance the
unrelenting pressure of the modern world which threatens to
shatter the poem that he is trying to fashion.

De Tocqueville foresaw that the advent of democracy would
unleash a destructive frenzy upon the world and that poetic
images would become charged with an uncontrollable energy.
W. H. Auden, in his introduction to Henry James's *The
American Scene*, quotes De Tocqueville's prophecy:

Poets living in democratic times will prefer the delineation of
passions and ideas to that of persons and achievements. . . . The
destinies of mankind, man himself taken aloof from his country and

[1] Ezra Pound, 'E.P. Ode pour l'Election de son Sepulchre'.

his age and standing in the presence of Nature and God, with his passions, his doubts, his rare prosperities and inconceivable wretchedness, will become the chief, if not the sole, theme of poetry. . . . I do not fear that the poetry of democratic nations will prove insipid or that it will fly too near the ground. I rather apprehend that it will be forever losing itself in the clouds, and that it will range at last to purely imaginary regions. I fear that the productions of democratic poets may be surcharged with immense and incoherent imagery, with exaggerated descriptions and strange creations; and that the fantastic beings of their brain may sometimes make us regret the world of reality.

That is only half the story, for while it is true that the wildness of much contemporary imagery points to a loss of poetic control it is equally true that some poets have deliberately employed images of concentrated violence in order to impose a momentary stability and order upon the raging fury of modern life. C. Day Lewis argues that only by some such device can a poet of our time both convey the complexity of life in the present century and yet illuminate the meaningful pattern which lies beneath what Matthew Arnold called 'an immense, moving, confused spectacle which, while it perpetually excites our curiosity, perpetually baffles our comprehension':

I believe that his preoccupation with images is a sign of the modern poet's effort to elucidate and control the modern situation. Metaphor is the natural language of tension, of excitement, because it enables man by a compressed violence of expression to rise to the level of the violent situation which provokes it. Images are, as it were, a breaking down of the high tension of life so that it can be safely used to light and warm the individual heart.[1]

Yet even if the poet avoids the incoherence which De Tocqueville singled out as the probable hallmark of poetry in a democratic age, and achieves the precarious discipline that Day Lewis believes to be within his power, the resulting poem is likely to seem bafflingly difficult, for original modes of complex order are not easily distinguishable from aimless disorder, and for every reader of *The Waste Land* who recognized its technical mastery there were a dozen who saw in it the nonsensical outpourings of a charlatan.

[1] *The Poetic Image*, p. 99.

There is another way in which the peculiar character of our civilization may be reflected in the complex obscurity of our poetry. George Whalley has claimed that the difficulties confronting poets of the past hundred years proved too much for the Victorians and have forced poets of the twentieth century to adopt a desperate remedy:

The Victorians failed to react away from contemporary abstractions into rediscovering the metaphysical nature of poetry; this is the mark of their debility. But Hopkins achieved it and is therefore the most characteristic (though most individual) figure of his time. In this century the force of arrogant rationalism in a fragmented society has encouraged a conceited and allusive verse; and at the same time an unparalleled erosion of language has occurred through vulgarised education, propaganda, and calculated imprecision.[1]

The rediscovery of this lost metaphysical tradition and the perfection of an allusive and highly concentrated poetic style have been among T. S. Eliot's major achievements: if we can ascertain what drove him to adopt this particular mode of expression, what impelled him to look for sustenance outside the Romantic tradition, some light may be shed upon the main theme of this chapter.

We know that he desired to assimilate into poetry the grubby incoherence, the raucous complexity of our modern cities, to make sense of what he observed, yet to exclude nothing and to falsify nothing. It was, he tells us, from Baudelaire and Laforgue that he first learned 'the possibility of fusion between the sordidly realistic and the phantasmagoric, the possibility of the juxtaposition of the matter-of-fact and the fantastic'.[2] There were other masters to whom he turned for guidance. He was influenced by the Symbolists, who had utterly rejected what seemed to them the booming platitudes of official Victorian poetry; by those who, like Ezra Pound and T. E. Hulme, believed that the whole Romantic tradition had gone soggy; by his study of the Jacobean dramatists, of Donne, of the Augustans, and of Johnson—

---

[1] *Poetic Process*, p. 144, n. 1.
[2] 'Talk on Dante', *The Adelphi*, First Quarter 1951, p. 107.

poets whose compact, subtle, and ironical use of language might serve him as a model. By about 1920 he had fashioned a technique that enabled him to translate into poetry every aspect of our multifarious civilization, a technique designed to meet the challenge of the age and to prove that poetry might be fashioned out of the most intractable material. In his essay on 'The Metaphysical Poets' (1921) which, like so much of the finest criticism written by poets, is in part an apology for the poet's own practice, he delineates the kind of poetry which the age demands:

> We can only say that it appears likely that poets in our civilization, as it exists at present, must be *difficult*. Our civilization comprehends great variety and complexity, and this variety and complexity, playing upon a refined sensibility, must produce various and complex results. The poet must become more and more comprehensive, more allusive, more indirect, in order to force, to dislocate if necessary, language into his meaning.[1]

Some of his poems written at this period are so tightly crammed with references and suggestions that their meaning suffers the same kind of fracture as their language. In 'Burbank with a Baedeker: Bleistein with a Cigar', the ingenious concatenation of oblique literary allusions, the ironical, enigmatic observations and the capricious shifts of mood are designed to convey an impression of the fascinating, tortuous complexities of a sophisticated and corrupt civilization. The brilliant compression of several themes into thirty-two lines, the masterly weaving of Shakespearean *motifs* into the melodic texture of the poem, the evocation of Venice in its glowing decay, the portrayal of a meretricious Princess, the satirical references to Jewish financiers make this one of Eliot's most remarkable minor poems, and indicate the precision of the poetic instrument which he had devised. In *The Waste Land* (1922), published two years after 'Burbank', the same devices are used as in the earlier poem, but with a fiercer intensity and for a deeper purpose. Instead of contemplating a city still beautiful, despite its decline, we stare at a nightmarish, shadowed city:

[1] *Selected Essays*, p. 289.

Unreal City,
Under the brown fog of a winter dawn,
A crowd flowed over London Bridge, so many,
I had not thought death had undone so many . . .
There I saw one I knew, and stopped him, crying:
    'Stetson!
'You who were with me in the ships at Mylae!
'That corpse you planted last year in your garden,
'Has it begun to sprout? Will it bloom this year?
'Or has the sudden frost disturbed its bed?
'Oh keep the Dog far hence, that's friend to men,
'Or with his nails he'll dig it up again!
'You! hypocrite lecteur!—mon semblable,—mon
    frère!'

What had been, in 'Burbank', an amused, sardonic comment
upon an amorous intrigue, becomes an agonized rehearsal of
the brevity, the vulgarity, and the cruelty of sexual desire in
the face of death and eternity:

White bones naked on the low damp ground
And bones cast in a little low dry garret,
Rattled by the rat's foot only, year to year.
But at my back from time to time I hear
The sound of horns and motors, which shall bring
Sweeney to Mrs. Porter in the spring.
O the moon shone bright on Mrs. Porter
And on her daughter
They wash their feet in soda water
Et O ces voix d'enfants, chantant dans la coupole!

Twit twit twit
Jug jug jug jug jug jug
So rudely forc'd.
Tereu.

It seems that only by cryptic utterances, oblique hints and
carefully modulated gestures can the poet convey every
nuance of his meaning and, at the same time, make us aware
of the terrifying chaos of modern life. In primitive societies
where men fear the daimonic powers that mysteriously control the universe, it is dangerous to speak openly of these dark
forces: in Eliot one senses an inner compulsion to disguise

123

emotions and thoughts which, uttered directly, would shatter the unity of his poem, and disintegrate his world into jagged fragments, but which can be glanced at in the oracular music of his verse.

Ten years after the publication of *The Waste Land* a group of younger poets abandoned the difficult, metaphysical style of the previous decade, only to produce verse that rivalled Eliot's in obscurity. The reasons for their rejection of Eliot's practice and for their plunge into a new kind of obscurity are not easy to summarize, if only because, contrary to popular belief, the 'poets of the 'thirties' were never a highly organized clique, and never issued a poetic manifesto. It is, however, possible to discern what they were trying to achieve, by reading their verse and by studying the literary criticism of such writers as Louis MacNeice and Michael Roberts.

One reason for their reaction against Eliot was that he had perfected a mode of writing and had thereby exhausted its possibilities for the time being. Any poet following at the heels of a great master must either swerve from his path or have his teeth kicked out: original poets change direction before it is too late, their instinct of poetic self-preservation being highly developed. Even if W. H. Auden's vision of the world had been akin to Eliot's he could not have expressed it in the technique of *The Waste Land* without becoming a writer of pastiche. So, despite his passionate admiration for Eliot in his undergraduate days, he turned for his models to Edward Thomas and to Thomas Hardy.

Moreover, Auden and his fellow-poets who were introduced to the public by Michael Roberts in *New Signatures* and *New Country* did not share Eliot's religious and political beliefs. The title of Eliot's first volume of poems, *Prufrock and other Observations*, is significant. Eliot is an observer, a man who contemplates the world with pity, with irony, with horror, but who does not strive to change it. The desolate world that he portrays in *The Waste Land* is inhabited by men and women who have been corrupted by human depravity and unredeemed by Grace. The Bradford millionaire and the loitering heirs of city directors are, like the rich neurotic woman and the girls in the pub, examples of Eliot's power to study contemporary social types with the merciless accuracy of a revolutionary satirist, but he does not delude himself with the belief that if you shoot the war profiteers and liquidate those who live on unearned incomes the waste land will blossom like a rose. Sin would walk the earth, incarnate in other forms, in any conceivable order of society, and the counsel of the Thunder is repentance and resignation: give, sympathize, control.

The poets of the 'thirties held that the muddle and the degeneration of contemporary society were the product of human folly, of political insanity, and that it was possible to restore to men their human dignity by sweeping away the out-moded, irrational way of life which the ruling classes had established. 'The poems in this book', wrote Michael Roberts in his introduction to *New Signatures*, 'represent a clear reaction against esoteric poetry in which it is necessary for the reader to catch each recondite allusion.' I have suggested that it would have been, aesthetically, disastrous for the younger poets to have imitated the metaphysical allusiveness which attained perfect expression in *The Waste Land*: by a happy coincidence the dictates of prudence were reinforced by a moral imperative:

These new poets, in fact, were boiling down Eliot's 'variety and complexity' and finding that it left them with certain comparatively clear-cut issues. Instead, therefore, of attempting an impressionist survey of the contemporary world—a world which impinges on one but which one cannot deal with, they were deliberately simplifying it, distorting it perhaps (as the man of action also has to distort it) into a world where one gambles upon practical ideals, a world in which one takes sides.[1]

Despite this deliberate rejection of esoteric verse, the elimination of literary allusions, the plunge into partisan commentary upon the political and social conflicts of the day, the poetry of the 'thirties is no less obscure than the poetry which it superseded. If Eliot's ironical despair at the spectacle of human futility bred an oblique, introspective, enigmatical verse, the embittered indignation, the helpless frustration, of

[1] Louis MacNeice, *Modern Poetry*, p. 15.

left-wing intellectuals resulted in a tirade which, at times, became incoherent with fury or tailed off into a cryptic, satirical muttering. When Byron and Shelley desired to express their hatred of the established order they concentrated their fury on a few individuals in whom all evil seemed to be incarnate. A hundred years later no intelligent man could delude himself that the wickedness of a single person or even a single group was responsible for the misery of the world. The phantasmagorical nature of life in the 1930s, the impossibility of making sense of history, became almost an obsession in the years immediately before 1939:

> Ten thousand of the desperate marching by
> Five feet, six feet, seven feet high:
> Hitler and Mussolini in their wooing poses
> Churchill acknowledging the voter's greeting
> Roosevelt at the microphone, Van Lubbe laughing
> And our first meeting.[1]

Stephen Spender, in a poem characteristically entitled 'The Uncreating Chaos', portrays the nightmarish quality of the epoch:

> Meagre men shoot up. Like Verey Light
> A corporal's wagging tongue burns above burning
> parliament.
> There flows in the tide of killers, the whip masters,
> Breeches and gaiters camouflage blood,
> Gangsters shooting from hips, pathics with rubber
> truncheons,
> Spontaneous joy in the padded cell.
>
> Centrifugal movements of a will
> Invent these violent patterns.
> History rushes. The crowds in towns,
> Cerebral boundaries of nations over mountains,
> Actors in flesh and death and material nature,
> Dance to a gripless private stammer of shouting,
> Like thoughts in a minister's dying brain.

The impotent fury of these poets in the face of an apparently meaningless, though horrifying, sequence of events and

[1] W. H. Auden, 'A Bride in the '30s'.

agglomeration of social habits is everywhere apparent in their verse. Whitman pours out lists of objects, like a child recounting with wonder its Christmas presents, or Traherne numbering the jewels of the world, or Adam naming the creatures. The poets of the 'thirties reel off their catalogues to demonstrate their disgust at the cheap multiple store into which they have wandered:

> You say that our civilisation is Willesden Green; is Beaverbrook; Lyons'; halitosis advertisements; cancer and pyorrhoea; prize-day, the cheers and avuncular tips for the prudent cheaters; pearl-divers diving their lungs out; tin-workers breathing in tin.[1]

In 'A Happy New Year'[2] W. H. Auden speaks of his feelings dying away,

> Leaving the mind to moralise
> Upon these blurring images
> Of the dingy difficult life of our generation.

The images that follow are a compound of high-spirited buffoonery and irreverent wit, but underneath the mockery there spreads a despairing nausea brought on by the contemplation of a society from which all virtue and all sense have been drained away:

> Churchill[3] was speaking of a battleship:
> It was some little time before I had guessed
> He wasn't describing a woman's breast . . .
> Lord Baden-Powell with a piece of string
> Was proving that reef-knots honour the King . . .
> In the middle distance a titled whore
> Was distributing trusses to the ruptured poor.

Then the last attempt of the poet's conscious mind to interpret the disorder of society is abandoned, the final pretence of rationality disappears, and the poem collapses into a sequence

---

[1] A. J. Tessimond, 'Steel April'.

[2] Printed in *New Country* and not reprinted.

[3] It is worth noting that, in two poems, Auden regards Churchill as a symbolic figure, and this at a time when he was in the wilderness, with no hope of regaining power. In a review of Churchill's *Thoughts and Adventures*, Auden proclaims a reluctant admiration for that great amateur: 'Mr. Churchill cannot candidly be said to know anything, but he has his talent. He could have been, and indeed, to a certain extent he is, a great writer. . . . The old humbug can write.' *Scrutiny*, I, 4 (March 1933), pp. 410–13.

of dissolving images which appear to have strayed from a
Freudian dissertation or a Marx Brothers film:

> Orders were shouted, a hubbub arose
> 'Look out. A deserter. We want that man.
> Gup Vexer, Bramble, Verse out of Prose!'
> Waving rattles the healers ran.
> Dr. Ernest Jones was well in the van.
> And panting and pounding after the rest
> My old headmaster in a little pink vest.

A similar recognition that the times were muddled and evil
occurs again and again in the early poems of Louis MacNeice,
particularly in 'An Eclogue for Christmas':

> The jaded calendar revolves,
> Its nuts need oil, carbon chokes the valves,
> The excess sugar of a diabetic culture
> Rotting the nerve of life and literature . . .
> I who was Harlequin in the childhood of the century,
> Posed by Picasso beside an endless opaque sea,
> Have seen myself sifted and splintered in broken facets,
> Tentative pencillings, endless liabilities, no assets,
> Abstractions scalpelled with a palette-knife
> Without reference to this particular life.

The recognition of complexity in all things left its mark upon
the most characteristic poetry of that decade, making it impossible for its poets to write with the untroubled simplicity
that comes of certainty and acceptance. Even the past, which
for many poets has been a cool, translucent, and refreshing
stream, had grown turbid, and for MacNeice, a classical
scholar, the golden purity and radiant health of ancient Greece
were infected by the unease of the present. The simplicity
that scholars find in classical times is a reflection of the Don's
well-fed tranquillity; then, as now, chaos is come again:

> So the humanist in his room with Jacobean panels
> Chewing his pipe and looking on a lazy quad
> Chops the Ancient World to turn a sermon
> To the greater glory of God.
> But I can do nothing so useful or so simple;
> These dead are dead

And when I should remember the paragons of Hellas
    I think instead
Of the crooks, the adventurers, the opportunists,
    The careless athletes and the fancy-boys,
The hair-splitters, the pedants, the hard-boiled sceptics
    And the Agora and the noise
Of the demagogues and the quacks; and the women pouring
    Libations over graves
And the trimmers at Delphi and the dummies at Sparta
      and lastly
    I think of the slaves.
And how one can imagine oneself among them
    I do not know;
It was all so unimaginably different
    And all so long ago.[1]

It seems as if Eliot's compassionate, sidelong glance at the sordid incoherence of modern life, and the helpless fury of Auden and his contemporaries in the face of its murderous insanity have led alike to a bafflingly obscure poetry. Some poets, notably W. B. Yeats, have tried to assimilate the violence and the perplexities of our times by leading their dark, turbulent images to the deep pool of myth, in the hope that they may plunge into the waters and rise more lucid and less strange. I shall endeavour to show that contemporary poets develop their mythopoeic faculties partly as a measure of self-protection, in order that the emotional pressure of the world shall not become intolerable. Yet, as T. S. Eliot saw in 1923, the impulse that drives writers to employ myths is primarily aesthetic:

In using the myth, Mr. Joyce is pursuing a method which others must pursue after him. . . . It is simply a way of controlling, of ordering, of giving a shape and a significance to the immense panorama of futility and anarchy which is contemporary history. It is a method already adumbrated by Mr. Yeats . . . for which the horoscope is auspicious. . . . It is, I seriously believe, a step towards making the modern world possible for art, towards order and form.[2]

---

[1] *Autumn Journal*, ix.
[2] 'Ulysses, Order and Myth', in *The Dial*, November 1923; reprinted in *James Joyce: Two Decades of Criticism*, ed. Seon Givens. Quoted by G. Melchiori, *The Tightrope Walkers*, p. 131.

When a poet can adopt one of the great religious myths, his verse is likely to be generally acceptable and comprehensible. David Gascoyne's sequence *Miserere* makes an immediate and profound impression even on those who normally shy at modern poetry, because he employs the symbols of the Christian faith to elucidate the darkness of our world:

> Amid the plain beneath His transfixed hands,
> Exuding darkness as indelible
> As guilty stains, fanned by funereal
> And lurid airs, besieged by drifting sands
> And clefted landslides our about-to-be
> Bombed and abandoned cities stand . . .
> Not from a monstrance silver-wrought
> But from the tree of human pain
> Redeem our sterile misery,
> Christ of Revolution and of Poetry,
> That man's long journey through the night
> May not have been in vain.

The verse in the section of his *Poems 1937–1942* entitled *Metaphysical* is, though equally fine, far more obscure, since the images of violence which reflect the shattering terror of our epoch refer to no commonly accepted corpus of fact or of legend, and the beauty of these poems is too strange and remote to console

> Our weak hearts dulled by the intolerably loud
> Commotion of this tragic century.

It is sometimes asserted that Yeats was so obsessed by the fascination of esoteric mysticism that he became indifferent to the condition of the world. The best answer to such a charge is a letter to Ethel Mannin, postmarked 8 April 1936:

. . . as my sense of reality deepens, and I think it does with age, my horror at the cruelty of governments grows greater . . . Communist, Fascist, nationalist, clerical, anti-clerical, are all responsible according to the number of their victims. I have not been silent; I have used the only vehicle I possess—verse. If you have my poems by you, look up a poem called 'The Second Coming'. It was written some sixteen or seventeen years ago and foretold what is happening. I have written of the same thing again and again since . . . I am not callous, every nerve trembles with horror at what is happening in Europe, 'the ceremony of innocence is drowned'.[1]

Yeats felt the cruelty and the meaningless horror of the modern world with such intensity that he could endure to contemplate them only by setting them in the perspective of a timeless myth. It is impossible to explain the precise significance of the image out of *Spiritus Mundi* which, first glimpsed by Yeats in the 1880s under the tutelage of MacGregor Mathers, rose again forty years later as a symbol of destruction in his poem 'The Second Coming':

> . . . somewhere in sands of the desert
> A shape with lion body and the head of a man,
> A gaze blank and pitiless as the sun,
> Is moving its slow thighs, while all about it
> Reel shadows of the indignant desert birds.
> The darkness drops again; but now I know
> That twenty centuries of stony sleep
> Were vexed to nightmare by a rocking cradle,
> And what rough beast, its hour come round at last,
> Slouches towards Bethlehem to be born?

We can, however, be certain that it was the nightmarish, dragon-ridden days in which Yeats lived that moulded the lineaments of this fabulous creature, just as it is the ghastly pink light of the hydrogen bomb that reveals in a flash to D. J. Enright the daimon which animates Hokusai's laughing hyena, with 'a face like a bomb-burst':

Between the raised talons of the right hand
    rests an object—
At rest like a pale island in a savage sea—
    a child's head,
Immobile, authentic, torn and bloody—
The point of repose in the picture, the point
    of movement in us.

Terrible enough this demon. Yet it is present and perfect,
Firm as its horns, curling among its thick
    and handsome hair.
I find it an honest visitant, even consoling, after all

---

[1] *The Letters of W. B. Yeats*, ed. Allan Wade, p. 851.

Those sententious phantoms, choked with rage and uncertainty,
Who grimace from contemporary pages. It, at least,
Knows exactly why it laughs.

If our poets knew precisely why they grieved it is likely
that their verse would shed much of its obscurity and attain
the agonized simplicity of despair. Our age is probably not
more cruel or harsh than most epochs but it is incomparably
more confused and inchoate. It is, as W. H. Auden has
reminded us, an age of anxiety and because anxiety is a product of uncertainty, sophistication, brooding premonitions,
and undefined sensations, the poetry to which it gives rise will
tend to lack the precision of more violent emotions. When, in
'Tom's Garland', Hopkins attempts to convey the dis-
membered ugliness of an industrial society he becomes almost
incoherent, but in contemplating the certainty of his own
anguish he achieves a terrible crystalline purity:

> See, banks and brakes
> Now, leavèd how thick! lacèd they are again
> With fretty chervil, look, and fresh wind shakes
> Them; birds build—but not I build; no, but strain,
> Time's eunuch, and not breed one work that wakes.
> Mine, O thou lord of life, send my roots rain.

There is, in the intensity of extreme suffering, no place for
doubt or anxiety or bewilderment at the complicated nature
of the modern world. That is why the poetry of Wilfred Owen
has passed beyond the borders of obscurity, why Milton's
Satan can say, with lacerating simplicity:

> I would be at my worst; worst is my port,
> My harbour, and my ultimate repose,

and why René Char can write to André Breton: 'Ce n'est pas
moi qui a simplifié les choses, mais les choses horribles qui
m'ont rendu simple.'

Edwin Muir has expressed one of the central paradoxes of
contemporary poetry:

The more a writer tries to render his vision of the world in its
completeness, the more irrevocably he turns it into his private

world. The more carefully he connects everything with everything, the less is his reader able to connect anything with anything.[1]

It is scarcely to be wondered at if, in the face of such discouragement, some poets have given up the struggle to interpret the dingy and difficult life of our generation, and have retreated into poetic monasteries, exclusive clubs or private asylums; or if the bustling, oppressive world seems to them as desolate as the gravel-pit field where David Gascoyne stood at sunset in the spring of 1941:

> As I stand musing, overhead
> The zenith's stark light thrusts a ray
> Down through dusk's rolling vapours, casts
> A last lucidity of day
>
> Across the scene: and in a flash
> Of insight I behold the field's
> Apotheosis: No-man's-land
> Between this world and the beyond,
> Remote from men and yet more real
> Than any human dwelling-place:
> A tabernacle where one stands
> As though within the empty space
> Round which revolves the Sage's Wheel.[2]

[1] A review, 'Correspondences', *The Observer*, 2 November 1952. Quoted by Bonamy Dobrée, *The Broken Cistern*, p. 141.
[2] 'The Gravel-Pit Field.'

7

Private Countries

Alas, it is an undeniable fact that the more a poet becomes a poet, the more he expresses feelings that are only known to poets, the more does the crowd round him dwindle and at last becomes so small that he can count his true admirers on the fingers of his hand.

GOGOL, *A Few Words about Pushkin*

Retire into yourself and probe the depths from which your life springs up. . . . For the creative artist must be a world unto himself and find everything in himself and in Nature of which he is part and parcel. . . . Love your loneliness and endure the pain it causes you with harmonious lamentations.

RILKE, *Letters to a Young Poet*

Pour moi le cas d'un poète en cette société qui ne le permet pas de vivre, c'est le cas d'un homme qui s'isole pour sculpter son propre tombeau.

MALLARMÉ

JOHN CLARE's first book of poems sold more than three thousand copies within two years of publication, a happy contrast to the fate of Keats's volume *Lamia* which, published in 1820, had by March 1822 sold less than five hundred copies. It was not until Clare's subsequent volumes had been received with general indifference that the insanity which had lain dormant within him since 1819, when he was twenty-six, took complete possession of him.[1] When Dr. Skrimshire, who certified him in 1841, was asked to state whether Clare's insanity had been 'preceded by any severe or long-continued mental emotion or exertion', he answered, with decisive brevity: 'After years addicted to Poetical prosing.' Having finally

---

[1] His literary failure was not the sole cause of his insanity. Apart from the fact that there may have been insanity in his family his life after his childhood was one of poverty and deprivations. As Geoffrey Grigson puts it in his Introduction to the selection of Clare's poetry which he made for *The Muses' Library* (p. 14), 'Clare is deprived of the happiness of childhood; he is deprived, by enclosure, of the actual scenery and objects of that happiness . . . he is deprived of love and freedom by a marriage which on the whole he did not desire, and against which he developed the fantasy of his ideal wife, Mary Joyce.'

rejected and been rejected by a society where there was no room for him, Clare severed the tenuous links which tethered him to the world of daily realities, wandering from one century to another, his mind totally unhinged. He believed that he had witnessed the execution of Charles I, that he was a prize-fighter, or Byron or Nelson for, as he explained to G. J. de Wilde: 'I'm John Clare now. I was Byron and Shakespeare formerly. At different times you know I'm different persons—that is the same person with different names.' This last qualification is important, for it indicates the desperation with which Clare strove to preserve some contact with the normal, rational mode of being: 'As schizophrenics do so often, Clare had fought, and still fought for some years more, to hold on to the central portion of his own spiritual identity (hence the lucidity of his verse, the disorder of his prose and his conversation).'[1] The lucidity of his verse was as precarious as his hold upon his one remaining certainty, and when Clare at last became isolated even from himself the darkness of total obscurity enveloped whatever poetic impulses may have crowded into his mind.

In Clare's deepening loneliness, in his ability to make poetry out of that loneliness and in organized society's laconic diagnosis of his malady, we can discern an image of the modern poet's place in a world which regards him with a mixture of envy, hostility, suspicion, amusement, and contempt. Clare was not, of course, the first victim of society's ambivalent feeling towards poets: it is arguable that the degradation of poetry had begun in the reign of Charles II when a new economic class helped to foster and to direct a scientific revolution. Fifty years later, in *The Dunciad*, Pope revealed his dread that poetry, which for him was a symbol of the whole tradition of western culture, even of God's creative *logos*, was destined to be swamped in a flood of shapeless mediocrity; and emphasized that the Hanoverian court, by succumbing to the debased values of the City, had abandoned its duty to protect the spiritual heritage of England.[2] The

[1] Geoffrey Grigson, *Poems of John Clare's Madness*, p. 23.
[2] Aubrey L. Williams, in *Pope's Dunciad*, brings out with great clarity the moral and social implications of this splendid poem.

great Romantics all displayed an uneasy awareness that they
were misfits or outcasts, and as the century wore on poets
tended either to indulge in self-pity because they were cold-
shouldered by coarse-grained philistines, or to pride themselves on their defiant isolation. A poet of Baudelaire's stature
could endow such a myth with epic grandeur: lesser poets
announced their separation from society and proclaimed their
self-damnation with the jaunty, theatrical assurance of Kip-
ling's gentlemen-rankers. By the end of the nineteenth century the self-consciousness and self-justification of poets had
become an unhealthy obsession: it was more important to be
a poet than to write poems—a curious aberration which has
left its mark upon a swarm of contemporary Narcissi.

In the twentieth century most poets have become infected
with an ever-deepening consciousness of their isolation in a
society which they find utterly hostile and completely
meaningless. Yeats touches upon this theme in a passage of
fine dignity and restraint, tinged with a shade of bitterness:

> Better go down upon your marrow-bones
> And scrub a kitchen pavement, or break stones
> Like an old pauper, in all kinds of weather;
> For to articulate sweet sounds together
> Is to work harder than all these, and yet
> Be thought an idler by the noisy set
> Of bankers, schoolmasters, and clergymen
> The martyrs call the world.[1]

It is in Ezra Pound that we see the most tragic example of the
split between the contemporary poet and the society in which
he lives. Pound has always been one of those who, in Edwin
Muir's phrase, desire to connect everything with everything,
reiterating the inter-dependence of all aspects of life:

I can tell the bank-rate and component of tolerance for usury in
any epoch by the quality of *line* in painting . . .[2]

I loathe and always have loathed Indian art. Loathed it long before
I got my usury axis. Obnubilated, short curves, muddle, jungle etc.
Waaal, we find the hin-goddam-doo is a bloody and voracious usurer.[3]

---

[1] 'Adam's Curse.'
[2] *The Letters of Ezra Pound, 1907–1941*, ed. D. D. Paige, p. 397.
[3] Ibid., p. 427.

Unhappily this overmastering impulse to connect, to make sense of an incoherent world, degenerated into the obsessive belief that all the ills of the world had their root in usury, that all could be cured by currency reform and that only the machinations of Jews and wire-pulling democratic politicians were blocking such reform. Pound expressed his contempt for the democratic state as long ago as 1920:

> All things are a flowing,
> Sage Heracleitus says;
> But a tawdry cheapness
> Shall outlast our days . . .
>
> Faun's flesh is not for us,
> Nor the saint's vision.
> We have the Press for wafer;
> Franchise for circumcision.
>
> All men, in law, are equals.
> Free of Pisistratus,
> We choose a knave or an eunuch
> To rule over us.[1]

This contempt, which grew more and more frantic in the 1920s and 1930s, led him to venerate Mussolini, blinded him to the cruelties and the absurdities of Fascism, and finally consigned him to a prisoner-of-war's cage and to incarceration by his fellow countrymen.

The record of this increasingly lonely pilgrimage, which was finally to sunder Pound from the daily life of the world, is to be found in his *Cantos* which are, admittedly, among the most obscure poems of the century, fine passages of intense lyricism, and calm enunciation of moral and philosophical truths, alternating with reproductions of Chinese ideograms, quotations in several languages, extracts from Bank statements, summaries of economic history and doctrines, drab passages of contrived vulgarity, and cascades of wild, indecent abuse. Yet, in some ways, Pound recalls the writer who, of all the great poets in our language, is generally regarded as the supreme master of lucidity—

[1] 'E.P. Ode Pour l'Election de son Sepulchre.'

Alexander Pope. For Pope is at one with Pound in believing that the preservation of language from decay is a moral task, because a corrupt literature points to a fundamental inner disorder:

In his vision of the Augustan world as a world swamped by hack writings, muddy verse and party pamphlets, it appeared to the poet of the *Dunciad* that the whole great Western tradition of eloquence, symbol of inner sanity and wisdom, was endangered (in a manner to which we have now grown too much used) by incompetent and commercial-minded manipulators of the 'word'. And, like others before him, Pope regarded such a situation as symptomatic, thought that a chaotic and malformed rhetoric or poetic reflected an anarchic and malformed character or mind.[1]

In a similar vein Pound declares that:

the individual cannot think and communicate his thought, the governor and legislator cannot act effectively or frame his laws, without words, and the solidity and validity of these words is in the care of the damned and despised *litterati*. When their work goes rotten—by that I do not mean when they express indecorous thoughts—but when their very medium, the very essence of their work, the application of word to thing goes rotten, i.e. becomes slushy and inexact, or excessive and bloated, the whole machinery of social and of individual thought and order goes to pot.[2]

Pope resembles Pound in asserting that the unregulated activities of bankers and merchants are primarily instrumental in perverting the true order of society; and, again as in Pound, his scatological ferocity springs from an overpowering nausea in the face of the pollution of life by dunces and by usurers in a world where men scrabble for gold in sewers

And the fresh vomit runs for ever green.

What saved Pope from Pound's fate and preserved his poetry from obscurity? He was sustained in some measure by his religious faith, whereas Pound, after rejecting the distorting ugliness of plutocracy, has had to grope towards the tentative articulation of a private vision based partly upon

[1] Aubrey L. Williams, *Pope's Dunciad*. p. 156.
[2] *Literary Essays of Ezra Pound*, ed. T. S. Eliot, p. 21.

hatred of contemporary vulgarity, and partly upon the precepts of Confucius. In the 'Envoi' to *Hugh Selwyn Mauberley* he had contemplated the dusts of two lovers:

> Siftings on siftings in oblivion,
> Till change hath broken down
> All things save Beauty alone. . . .

and although his vision of beauty has grown deeper and more refined it has become no easier to communicate to the world at large, remaining a barrier between Pound and his reader rather than a union between them. More important still, Pope was fortunate in living in a society which, for all its grossness and shallowness, still honoured its poets and regarded them as the interpreters of the age. It is the sense of being isolated, unwanted, and irrelevant which, above all, distinguishes Pound from Pope, and which has brought him to the seclusion in which he now labours, composing his *Cantos* for a world which has largely ceased to listen to his voice—and not his voice only but that of all poets, living and dead.

Although no other poet of the century has reacted so violently as Pound against the civilization that bred him, a great many poets have felt that society as at present organized is a dreary chaos in which they are redundant. Eliot's Mr. Prufrock contemplates his isolation from the world with a wry self-mockery that slides imperceptibly into self-conceit; the narrator in 'Portrait of a Lady' squeezes ironical amusement from the popular newspapers:

> You will see me any morning in the park
> Reading the comics and the sporting page.
> Particularly I remark
> An English countess goes upon the stage.
> A Greek was murdered at a Polish dance,
> Another bank defaulter has confessed.
> I keep my countenance,
> I remain self-possessed . . .

Fifteen years later W. H. Auden, experiencing a similar isolation, begins to be infected by a feverish unease which he barely conceals beneath a spry self-assurance:

In my spine there was a base;
And I knew the general's face:
But they've severed all the wires,
And I can't tell what the general desires.
Here am I, here are you:
But what does it mean? What are we going to do?[1]

In a poem written a year or two later, Auden glances satirically at poets who indulge in private fantasies and in timid substitutes for genuine emotion, while cruelty and injustice triumph everywhere:

Unhappy poet, you whose only
Real emotion is feeling lonely
    When suns are setting;
Who fled in horror from all these
To islands in your private seas
Where thoughts like castaways find ease
    In endless petting.[2]

He returns to this theme in *Letter to Lord Byron* where he describes how, after the Industrial Revolution, poets freed themselves from the patronage of wealthy connoisseurs and rejoiced in their newly-gained independence. Unhappily, the 'Poets' Party' which began with such a swing has declined into a lugubrious affair:

To-day, alas, that happy crowded floor
    Looks very different: many are in tears:
Some have retired to bed and locked the door;
    And some swing madly from the chandeliers;
    Some have passed out entirely in the rears;
Some have been sick in corners; the sobering few
Are trying hard to think of something new.

The war of 1939–45 gave some men a spurious feeling of unity, encouraged professional patriots to puff any verse that might be reckoned a thrilling call to arms, and even inspired politicians to quote poetry as a sign of their emotional fervour: it left society even more incoherent than before and did

[1] *Poems*, IX. Not included in *Collected Shorter Poems, 1930–1944.*
[2] From 'A Communist to Others', printed in *New Country*. A revised version of this poem, without its old title and with these lines omitted, appeared in *Look, Stranger!* It is not included in *Collected Shorter Poems.*

nothing to assuage the poets' discontent at their isolation and insignificance in the modern world. G. S. Fraser spoke for a number of his fellow-poets when he attempted to explain why obscurity overwhelmed and choked so many poems written in the 1940s:

> We depend more and more on our own uncorroborated imaginings. Withdrawn from the public world (the army is only formally a world, it has a jargon but not an idiom), we are thrown back on the erratic judgments and uncertain impulses of a few intimate friends. . . . The obscurity of our poetry, its air of something desperately snatched from dream or woven round a chime of words, are the results of disintegration, not in ourselves, but in society . . . [1]

An unsympathetic critic might retort that this whining note is not to be detected in the works of the great Romantic poets who lived in a world disintegrated by war and revolution; and that the nearest parallel to the worst writing of the 1940s is to be found in Poe, Darley, and Beddoes, neurotic minor poets who, incidentally, flourished during a period of comparative tranquillity. We should not assume too readily that the plea of an unstable environment condones all poetic juvenile delinquency; nor should we be astonished if we discover that a self-assured and prosperous society gives birth to poetry of a subtle and obscure complexity. The relation between disintegration in society and obscurity in poetry cannot be reduced to a simple formula.

The establishment of the Welfare State has done nothing to reconcile the poets to the role for which they are cast in the modern world. Although twenty years separate Louis MacNeice's 'Turf-Stacks' from Roy Fuller's 'Poem to Pay for a Pen', a similar mood of sardonic disgust and self-mockery pervades them both:

> For we are obsolete who like the lesser things
> Who play in corners with looking-glasses and beads;
> It is better we should go quickly, go into Asia
> Or any other tunnel where the world recedes,
> Or turn blind wantons like the gulls who scream
> And rip the edge off any ideal or dream.

*　　*　　*

[1] *The White Horseman*, ed. J. F. Hendry and H. Treece, p. 30.

> I do not know which is the most obscene:
> Poets, profoundly sceptic, scared, unread;
> The leaders monolithic in their mania;
> Or the unteachable mass, as good as dead.

In *The White Goddess* Robert Graves contrasts a society wherein poets are honoured Bards, recognized as masters of a noble and difficult art, with one in which those who scorn to be either lackeys (political hacks) or gleemen (debased public entertainers) are driven into the wilderness. Once they have taken refuge there they may choose to live the life of a hermit or they may band together, forming a gang, a clique, or a *chapelle*.

The publication in 1932 of Michael Roberts's anthology, *New Signatures*, announced the formation of such a group, although it would be an error to suppose that Auden, Spender, Day Lewis, MacNeice, and their contemporaries were ever a highly-organized cabal. The literary politics of the 1930s need not detain us: our concern is to discover the characteristics which these poets had in common and the nature of the obscurity which vitiated some of their poetry.

One of the most noticeable traits which they shared was, as we might have guessed, a detestation of contemporary society with its mass unemployment and the futility of its alternating slumps and booms. W. H. Auden adopted the metre and imitated the dramatic Tennysonian declamation of 'Locksley Hall Sixty Years After' in order to deliver a youthful jeremiad upon the condition of England during the Depression:

> Get there if you can and see the land you once were proud
>   to own
> Though the roads have almost vanished and the expresses
>   never run:
>
> Smokeless chimneys, damaged bridges, rotting wharves
>   and choked canals,
> Tramlines buckled, smashed trucks lying on their side
>   across the rails;
>
> Power-stations locked, deserted, since they drew the
>   boiler fires;

Pylons falling or subsiding, trailing dead high-tension
    wires . . .[1]

The clearest expression of this general discontent is to be
found in Michael Roberts's preface to his second anthology,
which appeared soon after *New Signatures*. He emphasizes
the isolation of poets in a society governed by 'the proprietors
of Guinness, the Gaumont Palaces, Harrods, and the *Daily
Mail*', laments that 'the intellectual is turned to a petti-
fogging squabbler in Bloomsbury drawing-rooms or a recluse
"in country houses at the end of drives"', envisages the birth
of a new society and urges his fellow-writers 'to prepare the
way for an English Lenin'.[2]

Although there is in this manifesto an element of rhetorical
clap-trap (which Roberts speedily discarded), there is no
reason why poets holding such opinions should produce
obscure verse. The early poem by Auden which I have quoted
is over-simplified to the point of crudity, and Roberts himself
looks forward to a renascence of poetry that shall once more
appeal to a wide public: 'If these poets succeed in their
attempt to preserve their integrity without becoming obscure,
to speak simply without shoddiness or ambiguity, English
poetry may again become a popular, elegant, and contemporary art.'[3]

Among the poets represented in *New Signatures* is the
author of *Seven Types of Ambiguity*. Roberts ingeniously
argues that the obscurity of Empson's poetry 'is due solely
to a necessary compression . . . there is no scope for vagueness of expression, and its difficulty arises from this merit'.
In his eagerness to convince himself and his potential readers
that the audience for poetry is about to grow wider, Roberts
optimistically asserts that Empson's poems 'do something
to remove the difficulties which have stood between the poet
and the writing of popular poetry'.[4]

These hopes were frustrated because the poets of the
'thirties, to their credit, were resolved not to become pur-
veyors of shallow propaganda or to churn out facile answers

[1] *Poems*, XXII. Omitted from his *Collected Shorter Poems*, 1930–1944.
[2] *New Country*, ed. Michael Roberts, pp. 11–12.
[3] *New Signatures*, pp. 19–20.   [4] *New Signatures*, p. 12.

to the social problems which they were confronting in their poetry. Their dislike of the contemporary world, coupled with their inability to throw overboard the traditions of their cultural and educational background, reinforced their sense of belonging to a small group, isolated in an alien world, and linked by common sympathies. Many critics have remarked that the imagery and the atmosphere in Auden's early poems are tinged with memories drawn from the communal life of a school; Michael Roberts, Rex Warner, Isherwood, and Day Lewis were, like Auden, schoolmasters at some period of their careers; and it is therefore not surprising that so much of their early work is redolent of the school changing-rooms and dormitories, with their group loyalties and conspiratorial intensity, nor that we can discern so often the accents of the masters' common-room, where suppressed resentments, acrid personal feuds and oblique academic jokes sizzle and fume.

The consciousness of belonging to a tiny group, leagued together against the philistine ruling classes, yet incapable of communicating with the working classes, accounts for much that is trivial and strained in the work of these writers. One manifestation of their unease is the technique of larding verse with gossipy references to personal friends and enemies: the gayest and most irresponsible example of this device occurs in 'Auden and MacNeice, Their Last Will and Testament',[1] a slangy, rhyming burlesque, whose cryptic witticisms and allusive cultural chit-chat render it the Bloomsbury equivalent of 'Broadway Through a Keyhole'.

More serious, more ambitious, yet scarcely less parochial, was the verse that proclaimed their membership of a gang bent upon ridiculing and uprooting the stuffiness and stupidity of conventional *bourgeois* values. Auden celebrated the heroes of this underground movement in rollicking couplets that are curiously effective with their mixture of bathos and comic extravagance:

> Lawrence, Blake and Homer Lane, once healers in our
>   English land;
> These are dead as iron for ever; these can never hold
>   our hand.

[1] W. H. Auden and L. MacNeice, *Letters from Iceland*, pp. 236–58.

Lawrence was brought down by smut-hounds, Blake
    went dotty as he sang,
Homer Lane was killed in action by the Twickenham
    Baptist gang.[1]

Lacking belief in orthodox religion and deprived of the strength that adherence to a living tradition can offer, he was driven to invent the cult of 'ancestors' discernible in *The Orators* and to inhabit a day-dream world where dead writers were posthumously elected to membership of a secret society founded by his imaginary self. Isherwood's description of Mortmere, a fantastic world peopled by the creatures of his and Auden's brain, makes this clear:

And it wasn't merely a gang of medieval bogies what [sic] was on our side; we claimed the support of the ghosts of our favourite writers, particularly of Wilfred Owen, Katherine Mansfield and Emily Brontë . . . (Wilfred, Kathy and Emmy as we called them).[2]

In the light of this explanation some lines of Auden's which may at first appear insufferably patronizing are revealed as a young poet's endeavour to find consolation and reassurance in the words of the dead because, as Yeats had discovered, the living seem more shadowy than they:

'The poetry is in the pity', Wilfred said,
And Kathy in her journal, 'To be rooted in life,
    That's what I want.'[3]

This type of fantasy was less offensive than the references to Rex and Wystan which irritated many of those outside the circle of initiates. Men will respect the utterances of a prophet who bears the tokens of divine inspiration even if they cannot understand the precise significance of his vision: they will not tolerate the pretentious obscurity of young men who preen themselves upon their mental and moral superiority and, like the heaven-born Brahmins, disdain the intellectual untouchables:

Look west, Wystan, lone flyer, birdman, my bully boy!
Plague of locusts, creeping barrage, has left earth bare;

---

[1] *Poems*, XXII.   [2] *Lions and Shadows*, p. 72.
[3] 'The Malverns.'

Suckling and centenarian are up in air,
No wing-room for Wystan, no joke for kestrel joy.

Then I'll hit the trail for that promising land,
May catch up with Wystan and Rex my friend.[1]

*   *   *

But there waited for me in the summer morning
Auden, fiercely. I read, shuddered and knew . . .[2]

Even when these poets are exhorting their readers to embrace the proletarian cause, the voice which advocates universal brotherhood speaks in the accents of a *coterie*. At times one is reminded of a sporting parson jollying the lads into muscular Christianity:

. . . If anyone will come along to-night
To the local with me, honestly he'll know I'm right . . .

You watch, you cheer. But how much better in
The team itself. Half-time's late to begin.[3]

Occasionally the incitement to violent revolution resembles the speech of a harassed secretary whipping up enthusiasm for the club outing:

lovers of cricket, underpaid journalists,
lovers of Nature, hikers, touring cyclists,
now you must be men and women, and there is a chance.
Now you can join us, now all together sing All Power
not to-morrow but now in this hour, All Power
to lovers of life, to workers, to the hammer, the sickle,
the blood.
Come then companions. This is the spring of blood,
heart's hey-day, movement of masses, beginning of good.[4]

The best poetry of Auden, Day Lewis, Madge, and Warner is unflawed by this jejune freemasonry; and since it is fashionable to sneer at the poets of the 'thirties for their naïve

[1] C. Day Lewis, *The Magnetic Mountain*.
[2] Charles Madge, 'Letter to the Intelligentsia'.
[3] Charles Madge, 'Letter to the Intelligentsia'. The poem ends: 'Comrades, yours fraternally . . .'
[4] Rex Warner, 'Hymn'.

political enthusiasm it is worth stressing the fact that their sense of social responsibility was genuine and praiseworthy. Virginia Woolf, in her essay 'The Leaning Tower', pointed out how precariously they were balanced on their tightrope,[1] how insecure were the foundations on which they sought to build: for although by temperament and upbringing they shared Yeats's admiration for Villiers de l'Isle Adam's hero Count Axel, who declared, 'As for living, our servants will do that for us', they harboured grave doubts about their moral right to keep servants. Theirs was an honourable failure, for their very concern with social justice and desire to make poetry a popular art betrayed them into writing verse which hostile observers could stigmatize as intolerably cliqueish and obscure.

Wandering unhappily in No Man's Land, they were sniped at by sharpshooters of opposing camps. Empson's lampoon 'Just a Smack at Auden' caricatures, with malicious delight, the references to Marx, the parade of gang solidarity and the hearty prophecies of doom which were part of Auden's stock-in-trade at this time:

> What was said by Marx, boys, what did he perpend?
> No good being sparks, boys, waiting for the end.
> Treason of the clerks, boys, curtains that descend,
> Lights becoming darks, boys, waiting for the end.

In 'Autumn on Nan-Yueh' Empson returns to the charge:

> Besides, I do not really like
> The verses about 'Up the Boys',
> The revolutionary romp,
> The hearty uproar that deploys
> A sit-down literary strike . . .

Thoroughgoing Marxists, such as Christopher Caudwell, were equally scathing about public school revolutionaries who dabbled in communism and whose deepest affections were grounded in the social order that the revolution was pledged to destroy. Looking back on Auden's early poems, we are often moved to admire the fine poetic tension which

[1] For a brilliant analysis of the 'funambulism' of much contemporary literature, see G. Melchiori, *The Tightrope Walkers.*

vibrates in them and the emotional honesty which forbids him to resolve the tension by recourse to an empty slogan. Such ambivalence, such awareness of divided loyalties, such tenderness towards a dying culture merely irritated those who had committed themselves unreservedly to the revolutionary cause. Julian Bell argued that the morbid *bourgeois* determination of Auden and his friends to preserve their intellectual and emotional integrity in a decadent society had inevitably condemned them to write a private, fantastic kind of verse that meant no more to the masses than the sophisticated, erudite verse of T. S. Eliot:

> But how do you expect your proletarian audience in the theatre to understand the curious private jokes, the dream-transitions and incongruities, the personal intimate symbolism of *Noah*, the *Dog Beneath the Skin*, the *Dance of Death*? . . .
> And are you satisfied with all your mysticism of ancestors, of totems? And who is Mr. Auden's private war directed against? And what of your twisted, compressed, 'metaphysical' turns of wit and metaphor? . . .
> Indeed, it is a matter of common knowledge that private language, introspective subtlety of emotion and fantastic imagination and wit are as often refuges and façades for asylums as proofs of a native and personal force.[1]

I have suggested that some poets of the 'thirties, vainly desiring to escape from the isolation in which they found themselves, endeavoured to discover what values they held in common and to communicate with a large and unsophisticated audience. There were, however, other poets who, accepting their isolation as inevitable, turned their back upon the world that had rejected them and explored the solitary places of their own minds.

The most extreme form of this retreat from rational communication is visible in surrealist poetry for, as André Breton defined it in his *Surrealist Manifesto*, 'surrealism rests on the belief in the superior reality of certain hitherto neglected forms of association, in the omnipotence of the dream, in the disinterested play of thought'. The best examples of

[1] 'The Proletariat and Poetry: An Open Letter to C. Day Lewis.' Julian Bell, *Essays, Poems and Letters*, pp. 326–7.

English surrealist poetry are by David Gascoyne, who abandoned the style before he was twenty-one:

> The face of the precipice is black with lovers;
> The sun above them is a bag of nails; the spring's
> First rivers hide among their hair.
> Goliath plunges his hand into the poisoned well
> And bows his head and feels my feet walk
>   through his brain.
> The children chasing butterflies turn round and
>   see him there . . .[1]

> Supposing the breasts
> like shells on the oceanless shore
> at the end of the world
> like furious thrusts of a single knife
> like bread to be broken by hands
> supposing the breasts still untouched by desires
> still unsuckled by thirsts
> and motionless still
> breasts violently still and enisled in the
> night and afraid of both love and death.[2]

In the nineteenth century painters explored poetry for themes, whereas at the present time poets turn for inspiration to the visual arts. It is arguable that the rise of surrealist verse is a consequence or a sign of this revolution in artistic taste, and that such verse represents a pathetic effort of sterile writers to ape the painters of phantasmagorical visions:

> On the pale yellow sands
> There's a pair of clasped hands,
> And an eyeball entangled in string,
> And a bicycle seat,
> And a plate of raw meat
> And a thing that is *almost* a Thing.

It is possible that the objects mockingly catalogued by Lord Berners might, on a canvas, form a harmonious unity of shapes and colours, since the eye can delight in patterns which have no apparent meaning. Words, however, are saturated

---

[1] 'In Defence of Humanism.' To M. Salvador Dali.
[2] 'The Supposed Being.'

with rational meaning and even those readers who are most sensitive to their shape and sound obstinately demand that a poet's words should not throw overboard all logical and emotional coherence. Why, then, have so many gifted writers of Europe and America, in the past forty years, lavished their talents upon composing verse that alienates their readers and seems to deny the very nature of their art?

Changes in aesthetic theory are seldom dictated by aesthetic taste alone. Artists are frequently sensitive to the subterranean forces coiling and uncoiling beneath the surface of religion and politics, and surrealism in the arts was the first, frenzied twitching of the water-diviner's rod. Cyril Connolly's account of *Un Chien Andalou*, a ferocious surrealist film of the 1920s, brings out most vividly the nature of the compelling horror which it conveyed:

> This contemptuous private world of jealousy and lust, of passion and aridity, in which its beautiful occupants pattered about like stoats in search of blood, produced an indescribable effect, a tremendous feeling of excitement and liberation . . . the spectators had been treated to their first glimpse of the fires of despair and frenzy which were smouldering beneath the complacent post-war world.[1]

The surrealist poet, confronted by the aimless insanity of organized society, purposefully adopts the mask of insanity, like Pirandello's Henry IV, partly as a gesture of mockery, partly as an attempt to preserve his emotional integrity by evading all social responsibility. As Christopher Caudwell argued, in *Illusion and Reality*, only a poet who felt himself to be utterly and despairingly isolated in a society drained of all significance would deliberately reject the means of communing with his fellow-men. We must agree also with his contention that the surrealist poet attains only the narrowest and most illusory of freedoms, for the subconscious mind, with its limited range of recurring images, and its obsession with melodramatic patterns of experience, soon becomes a boring companion and an intolerably ruthless taskmaster.

William Empson, after attacking verses about 'Up the Boys', has a contemptuous flick at the surrealist poetasters:

[1] *The Unquiet Grave*, p. 88.

The other curly-headed toy's
The superrealistic comp.
By a good student who enjoys
A nightmare handy as a bike.
You find a cluster of them cloys.
But all conventions have their pomp
And all styles can come down to noise.[1]

Surrealism and gang-poetry are two sides of the same false penny, coined by poets with a grudge against a society which has no use for them. Good light verse often reveals truths which it does not aim at discovering, and one of Auden's ironical commentaries on surrealism casually illuminates a dark patch of mental turmoil:

Why association
Should see fit to set a
Bull-dog by a trombone
 On a grassy plain
Littered with old letters
Leaves me simply guessing,
I suppose it's La Con-
 dition Humaine.[2]

The human condition has been miserable for many centuries, but it is not wholly fanciful to believe that in the nineteenth century a note of deeper and more resonant anguish begins to echo through European poetry, and that one sign of this plangent desolation is what Lawrence Durrell has called 'the Semantic Disturbance', as a result of which we glimpse in Rimbaud, Laforgue, Nietzsche, and Lewis Carroll (strange bedfellows though they may be) a common dislocation of language.[3]

That dislocation mirrors a universe whose foundations have been split asunder, despite the scurrying of rationalists to paper over the chasms; and since we are all condemned to live alone in such a world the surrealists may claim that they are displaying more courage and honesty than their fellows in

[1] 'Autumn on Nan-Yueh.'
[2] Poem I in part TWO of *Another Time.* Entitled 'Heavy Date' in *Collected Shorter Poems,* where this stanza is omitted.
[3] See Lawrence Durrell, *Key to Modern Poetry.*

delineating the meaningless horror of an existence where the irrational and the absurd howl in triumph like hyenas. They might add that even those poets who disavow surrealism attain a rare force and intensity when they employ surrealist devices to convey the desolation of our lives and of our age:

> A woman drew her long black hair out tight
> And fiddled whisper music on those strings
> And bats with baby faces in the violet light
> Whistled, and beat their wings
> And crawled head downward down a blackened wall
> And upside down in air were towers
> Tolling reminiscent bells, that kept the hours
> And voices singing out of empty cisterns and
>   exhausted wells.[1]

T. S. Eliot

> O plunge your hands in water,
>   Plunge them in up to the wrist;
> Stare, stare in the basin
>   And wonder what you've missed.
>
> The glacier knocks in the cupboard,
>   The desert sighs in the bed,
> And the crack in the tea-cup opens
>   A lane to the land of the dead.[2]

W. H. Auden

What one may call either intellectual evasiveness or the wisdom of empiricism has traditionally guided our poets no less than our politicians. It is this quality of mind and temper which has restrained our contemporaries from embracing the more fanatical tenets of surrealism and counselled them to view its pretensions with a sceptical eye. The sense of isolation which has driven the surrealists to a ferocious despair has penetrated deep into the nature of the poets most sensitive to the anguish of our times, but their melancholy and their loneliness have assumed a gentler and more introspective character. Forced back upon themselves, divided from their audience by an impenetrable curtain of diffidence and ignorance, they are tempted to withdraw into the recesses of their

[1] *The Waste Land*, lines 377–84.   [2] 'As I Walked out one Evening.'

own being and to commune with themselves or with the phantoms that they have conjured out of the darkness.

One sign of their retreat from the stress of trying to interpret the nightmarish life of our epoch is their reliance upon childhood memories for their images. The celebration of childhood is a favourite theme with such visionary poets as Traherne and Wordsworth who recall this period of their lives in an effort to experience once again the glory and the vividness which they have lost. But whereas the poets of the past have tried to awaken in their readers the memory of a common heritage, poets in this century have cherished what was unique in their childhood. Traherne leads us back to an Eden we all once shared; so many of our contemporaries hide in a shadowed corner of the garden where secret rites are performed in solitude and the marks on the wall compose a picture whose significance reveals itself to one person alone.

Some poets who do not choose to celebrate the unique, lonely rituals of their childhood retire into a world of their own invention, peopled with mysterious figures. They may be symbols of extraordinary vividness and potency to their creator, but they are likely to remain baffling and faintly irritating to the world at large. In Frederic Prokosch's poem, 'The Masks', we are introduced to a succession of enigmatic men and women who, like the images on the cinema screen, loom up for a moment and are gone:

> Or wild grammarians travelling on the railway
> Swift to the yellow cities by the Caspian
> Blush, tremble; or the sisters who alone
> Shed tears and on the entry of the Countess
> Like owls rise and are gone.

It may be that the sisters and the Countess are characters from a novel or a play, or they may be figures from a dream, just as the apparition depicted by Stephen Spender may be derived from romantic literature or from a nightmare which demands a Freudian exegesis:

> If it were not too late!
> If I could mould my thought
> To the curved form of that woman

With gleaming eyes, raven hair,
Lips drawn too tight like a scar,
Eye sockets shadowed with migraine's
Memory of earlier loves and wars
And her smile learned with being so human.

W. H. Auden's 'Birthday Poem', addressed to Christopher Isherwood, recalls the fantastic world which they had invented some years before, in conspiratorial excitement and unease:

Our hopes were set still on the spies' career,
Prizing the glasses and the old felt hat
And all the secrets we discovered were
Extraordinary and false; for this one coughed
And it was gasworks coke, and that one laughed
And it was snow in bedrooms; many wore wigs,
The coastguard signalled messages of love,
The enemy were sighted from the Norman tower.

It is not surprising that in such a world as this enigmatic characters should make a momentary appearance, charged with a significance that Auden's readers can but dimly apprehend. In an early poem he invoked the impersonal force that is indifferent to our griefs and longings,

Though, calmer than us all, you move our lives;
Send back the writer howling to his art,
And the mad driver pulling on his gloves
Start in a snowstorm on his deadly journey.[1]

These images are also conjoined in 'Journey to Iceland':

Tears fall in all the rivers. Again the driver
Pulls on his gloves and in a blinding snowstorm starts
Upon his deadly journey, and again the writer
Runs howling to his art.

Given such a context, we are not completely baffled by the symbolical meaning of the mad driver, but there are figures in some modern poems who remain incomprehensible:

[1] 'The fruit in which your parents hid you, boy.' Printed in *New Verse*, No. 4, July 1933. Not reprinted.

The charming groans of ladies come to me
From the nursery sills of an invented climate;

My outlawed mother patient at the loom,
Behind her, oaks, their nude machinery,

The dark ones shining on their snowy tuffets.
I take this image on a screaming nib.[1]

One of Lawrence Durrell's books of verse is called *A Private Country*, and dotted throughout all his volumes there are passages which fulfil the threat implicit in this title. The poem, 'Cities, Plains and Peoples', contains marginal references to Kurseong, India, the Nepalese ayah, Kasim, Paris, H.V.M., Anaïs, Nancy, and Teresa. Another poem, 'Mythology', wittily conjures up the characters who stalk through the universe of his private imagination:

> All my favourite characters have been
> Out of all pattern and proportion . . .
>
> Tibble, Gondril, Purvis, the Duke of Puke,
> Shatterblossom and Dude Bowdler
> Who swelled up in Jaffa and became a tree:
> Hollis who had wives killed under him like horses. . .

T. S. Eliot employs a similar device for very different purposes in 'Gerontion', where he describes how

> In the juvescence of the year
> Came Christ the tiger
>
> In depraved May, dogwood and chestnut, flowering
>   judas,
> To be eaten, to be divided, to be drunk
> Among whispers; by Mr. Silvero
> With caressing hands, at Limoges
> Who walked all night in the next room;
> By Hakagawa, bowing among the Titians;
> By Madame de Tournquist, in the dark room
> Shifting the candles; Fraulein von Kulp
> Who turned in the hall, one hand on the door . . .

[1] 'The Sonnet of Hamlet.'

The naming of these sinister figures, which so effectively conjures up an atmosphere of curiously disturbing evil, resembles Durrell's mischievous catalogue in that it is the arcane celebration of a private liturgy. Perhaps the nearest parallel to it is the concatenation of grotesque names which Pascal maliciously forges in order to convince his readers that the Jesuits are both spiritually gross and ludicrous.

Sometimes when we read a contemporary poem it is as though we were standing on tip-toe outside the walled garden of a house where a ball is being held. Too far off to hear the music, we can occasionally glimpse a couple drifting by who are clearly moving in obedience to a dance rhythm, although to us their motions must appear strained and meaningless. The most baffling and tantalizing passages of modern verse are those whose intellectual precision and emotional force we can immediately sense even if we cannot perceive the significance of their imagery or the pattern of their argument. Two stanzas from Kenneth's Allott's poem, 'Offering', may serve to illustrate how a poem can be at once excitingly vivid and impenetrably dark:

> I offer you my forests and street cries
> with hands of double patience under the clock
> the antiseptic arguments and lies
> uttered before the flood, the submerged rock;
> the sack of meal pierced by the handsome fencer
> the flowers dying for 'a great adventure' . . .
>
> I offer you clouds of nuisance, fleurs de lys
> the opening lips of summer where pigeons rest
> the exploding office of the vast nebula
> the heraldic device under the left breast
> the taut string and the scribbler's Roman tread
> impinging on the slow shores of the dead . . .

C. Day Lewis is probably correct in maintaining that the proliferation of wild, incoherent imagery is yet another symptom of a collapsing social order in which poets feel isolated and despairing:

So, at the present time, we get the poets using a very great profusion of imagery, but with a minimum of support from the general imagination. That is perhaps the chief cause of the obscurity, the erratic touch, and the centrifugal strain we find in so much modern verse.[1]

In 1910 Valéry observed how confused and tentative modern literature must necessarily be until writers could begin to find a pattern in the flux of events:

> An important part of modern literature is given to communicating—not the final state of impressions, the state of something seized, unravelled, organized, cleared up—but the initial state, that of having still to understand (the encounter still to be met), the problematical state, confused, sentimental, sensorial.[2]

After nearly fifty years our poets have advanced scarcely a pace nearer the final state: it is easy to blame them, but juster to recall the weight and complexity of their task:

> In an unstable or disintegrating society the communal myth has collapsed and been replaced with a multitude of unrelated superstitions. The artists, the myth-makers, are then deprived of the established structure of symbol and are obliged to rediscover and revive ancient symbols and even to create symbols and myths of their own.[3]

George Herbert could use the traditional symbols of Christianity, secure in the knowledge that his readers would grasp their emotional and intellectual significance. Eliot ironically reveals his despair at trying to communicate his vision of life to a world in which the ringing of the sacring bell recalls only the muffin-man on his rounds:

> That is all we could see. But how many eagles! and how
>   many trumpets!
> (And Easter Day, we didn't get to the country,
> So we took young Cyril to church. And they rang a bell
> And he said right out loud, *crumpets*).[4]

Since there is no commonly-accepted body of symbols on which poets can draw, they will, as Whalley suggests, tend

---

[1] *The Poetic Image*, p. 108.
[2] *Note-Book* (1910). Quoted by George Whalley, *Poetic Process*, p. 184, n. 1.
[3] George Whalley, *Poetic Process*, pp. 183–4.
[4] 'Triumphal March.'

either to invent their own, or to use ancient symbols as decorative illustrations of their private myths. The first course subjects them to a strain which splits their verse into fragments; the second confuses their readers by introducing reminiscences of traditional religious beliefs into a highly individual pattern of thought. We have examined the way in which poets employ private images of their own invention, and must now consider the obscurities which are found when images consecrated by long usage are given an unexpected twist. Two stanzas from Louis MacNeice's poem, 'Hidden Ice', are particularly appropriate, since the poet himself has elucidated their meaning for us:[1]

> But some though buoyed by habit, though convoyed
> By habitual faces and hands that help the food
> Or help one with one's coat, have lost their bearings
> Struck hidden ice or currents no one noted.

> One was found like Judas kissing flowers
> And one who sat between the clock and the sun
> Lies like a Saint Sebastian full of arrows
> Feathered from his own hobby, his pet hours.

MacNeice tells us that his poem is in praise of those who live by routine. Some, however, may be unexpectedly destroyed by an obsession with politics, intellectual theories or emotional complexities. The image of a man kissing flowers is meant to depict a person who has neglected his routine duties for an alien preoccupation which may prove as fatal to him as kissing Christ proved to Judas. The clock and the sun are the symbols of time and routine, human and cosmic; the ticking of the clock has its equivalent in the dust-motes illuminated by the sun. MacNeice explains that, in certain moods, he finds both motes and ticking clocks hypnotic and sinister, Moreover, he has a mental image of a particular man, wrapped in suicidal thoughts, seated in a room; behind him, a clock on the mantelpiece is ticking, while through the window in front the sunlight comes pouring. The fatal arrows are feathered from the birds that the victim has

[1] *Modern Poetry*, pp. 175–7.

reared, for a man who is a cog in a machine must use a depre-
cating under-statement, even when he is on the edge of
destruction, and refer ironically to his obsession as a hobby.

The best Metaphysical poetry of the seventeenth century
delights us with a fusion of wit, fancy, sensibility, and passion,
but however dissimilar in meaning the images might be
which the Metaphysical poets allowed to clash and reverber-
ate in a single poem, they took care that the purport of the
images should be familiar to their readers. MacNeice's
failure to observe this precaution engenders a certain obscurity which muffles the impact of this poem and prevents our
accepting it unreservedly. The image of 'Judas kissing
flowers' implies a religious meaning which is not, in fact,
found in the poem, just as the reference to Saint Sebastian
evokes a set of associations and expectations which are incongruous in this context. When the reader discovers that he
has been left stranded in the marsh after pursuing these
religious will o' the wisps he may well feel cheated.

Even if he refuses to be distracted by these irrelevant
associations, the reader may still find these stanzas baffling.
He must indeed possess a remarkable agility on the trapeze if
he is to swing on the tenuous connexions that link the phrase
'feathered from his own hobby' to the expanded meaning
given by the poet in his prose explanation. For should we be
lucky enough to guess that the victim's hobby is bird-rearing,
we may still wonder who has affixed the feathers to the
arrows, and who has fired the arrows. And it is not unduly
captious to question the appropriateness of employing Saint
Sebastian as the symbol of a man with suicidal thoughts.

Finally, it is asking too much of a reader that he should
intuitively divine the emotions which animate the poet. He
cannot be expected to know that MacNeice considers clock-
tickings and dust motes to be hypnotic and sinister, even if
these phenomena were mentioned by name. Nor can he
possibly share MacNeice's private vision of the man contemplating suicide.

Whether a poet is justified in withdrawing to the inner
fastness of his mind, even if he thereby cuts himself off from
a potential audience, is a matter for debate. Some good poets

believe that they owe allegiance only to their Muse, and that in our present form of society any attempt at communicating with a mass audience would involve a betrayal of that allegiance. Perfect fidelity to one's own experience of truth is, on this view, the whole duty of a poet: that few of his fellowmen will pay heed to him is a matter of indifference. Robert Graves states this belief unequivocally in the Foreword to his *Poems 1938–45*:

> I write poems for poets, and satires or grotesques for wits. . . . To write poems for other than poets is wasteful. The moral of the Scilly Islanders who earned a precarious living by taking in one another's washing is that they never upset their carefully balanced island economy by trying to horn into the laundry trade of the mainland; and that nowhere in the Western Hemisphere was washing so well done.

Laura Riding, in her beautiful apology for private poetry, tells the Muse of Poetry that others can explore familiar country: hers is a rarer privilege and a harder task:

> Mistrust me not, then, if I have begun
> Unwontedly and if I seem to shun
> Unstrange and much-told ground:
> For in peculiar earth alone can I
> Construe the word and let the meaning lie
> That rarely may be found.[1]

Other poets have been tormented by a vague feeling of guilt, a belief that to remain immured in one's tower or to explore one's private country is a form of selfishness and weakness. It is this sense of moral obligation that lends a moving dignity to Auden's admission that an indulgence in private fantasy is no more admirable than an uncritical acceptance of conventional standards:

> Pardon the studied taste that could refuse
> The golf-house quick one and the rector's tea;
> Pardon the nerves the thrushes could not soothe,
> Yet answered promptly the no-subtler lure
> To private joking in a panelled room,

[1] 'As Well as any Other.'

The solitary vitality of tramps and madmen;
Believed the whisper in the double bed.
Pardon for these and every flabby fancy.[1]

Ever since the early seventeenth century, English poets
while growing more and more skilled in the power to
analyse their intellectual processes have steadily narrowed the
confines of their imaginative range. In Shakespeare we discover not merely the image of the whole Elizabethan and
Jacobean ages but the universe in miniature; in Pope the
world depicted for us, though still coherent and unified, is
limited and impoverished; Wordsworth's preface to *The
Excursion* is an admission that the poet, having abandoned
the attempt to interpret both the human and the divine
comedy, must now walk apart,

> On Man, on Nature, and on Human Life,
> Musing in Solitude.

Wordsworth's 'Human Life' is a poor, dim abstraction, compared with the passionate lives of Shakespeare's characters:
indeed Wordsworth gives up the pretence that he is concerned with the juice and joy of human existence by announcing the true subject of his poem as

> The Mind of Man—
> My haunt, and the main region of my song.

Four hundred years ago English poets, excited by the
prospects which the Renaissance seemed to offer, believed
that, having liberated themselves from the chafing restraints
of the schoolmen, they or their descendants might seize all
knowledge as their province. It is ironical to reflect that the
most gifted poets of our time have deliberately withdrawn
into an arcane world of private experience, which they proceed to explore less to illuminate the meaning of human life
for their fellow-men than to obey an overwhelmingly strong
compulsion that sends them burrowing into the darkness of

---

[1] 'Birthday Poem.' This poem, originally entitled 'To a Writer on his
Birthday', and addressed to Christopher Isherwood, is an interesting commentary on Isherwood's *Lions and Shadows*, which describes how he and Auden
constructed the elaborate fantasy-world of Mortmere.

their inner life. Cyril Connolly adopts a slightly different metaphor in his account of the artist's loneliness:

The artist of to-day in relation to his public is like the spelaeologist of the Peak or of the Causses of Southern France; he walks at first with his companions, till one day he falls through a hole in the brambles, and from that moment he is following the dark rapids of an underground river which may sometimes flow so near to the surface that the laughing picnic parties are heard, only to re-immerse itself in the solitude of the limestone and carry him along, not without evidence of previous exploration, until it gushes out through the hidden cave which he knows must exist, and sets him back in the sun.[1]

We cannot tell whether poets of the future will emerge from the cave and once again pass beyond the borders of their private country into the public world that we all share. If our society, as seems likely, has irrevocably become too complex and too hostile for poets to face and to subdue, we are condemned to inhabit an increasingly terrifying and lonely world without the fortifying reassurance of great poetry and, lacking Dante's redeeming faith, must wander through limbo without even the presence of his appointed guide.

[1] *Horizon*, vol. vii, No. 41 (May 1943), p. 296. Reprinted in a slightly modified version in *The Condemned Playground*, p. 287.

8

Themes and Images

A tumultuous stream of evocative, spell-bearing vocables, launched at your head—or poured into your Unconscious—is, finally, a dope only. It may be an auriferous mud, but it must remain mud—not a clear but a murky picture. As a literary medium it is barbaric.

WYNDHAM LEWIS, *Men Without Art*, p. 127

De la musique avant toute chose.

PAUL VERLAINE, 'L'Art Poétique'

Mere poets and mere musicians are as sottish as mere drunkards are, who live in a continual mist, without seeing or judging anything clearly.

JOHN DRYDEN, *Notes and Observations on the Empress
of Morocco*

I HAVE tried to indicate some of the ways in which recent social changes have fostered certain kinds of poetic obscurity, and have suggested that many poets, despairing of finding any coherent pattern in the chaos of modern life, have withdrawn into a baffled and baffling solitariness. Yet this is only half the story: art, though never entirely divorced from society, moves in response to its own rhythm, obeys its own logic and pays heed to the still, small voice within, impervious to the thunder of the world. It is impossible to understand the decline of polyphonic music, the brief glory of the Masque and the rise of heroic opera without some reference to the political and economic development of western Europe in the seventeenth century, but it was primarily a revolution in technique that so completely transformed the contours of music, just as another great technical development in the early seventeenth century—the separation of the lyric from its musical accompaniment—was more decisive for the future of English poetry than the Civil War. Nor can we hope to account for the obscurity of much contemporary poetry if we neglect to examine the most profound and pervasive revolution in poetic technique of the past hundred and fifty years.

The bulk of English poetry written between the middle of the sixteenth century and the late nineteenth century, despite a wide diversity of themes and styles, employed a basic technique that remained unaltered for over three hundred years. Poets working in this tradition constructed their poems upon a framework of logical statement and coherent narration; they laboured to make this framework memorable and beautiful by employing vivid images and by ordering the pattern of words into a melodious sequence. Modern poets (I use the words without intending praise or blame) have tended to eliminate this element of rational argument, replacing it by what one may call the logic of imagery and the manipulation of cadence. This technical revolution is of such importance that it is worth our while to trace in some detail the stages by which it was effected.

Hints of the device which I have singled out as being typically modern are found scattered here and there in poetry of the sixteenth and seventeenth centuries, notably in that fragment with the magical spell repeated three times:

> The bailey beareth the bell away;
> The lily, the rose, the rose I lay. . . .

in one or two songs from George Peele's plays, and in a singularly haunting song, 'The Seeds of Love', written in the late seventeenth century, possibly by Mrs. Fleetwood Habergham:

> In June there's a red rose-bud, and that's the
>   flower for me!
> But often have I plucked at the red rose-bud till
>   I gained the willow-tree;
> The willow-tree will twist, and the willow-tree
>   will twine—,
> O! I wish I was in the dear youth's arms that once
>   had the heart of mine . . .
>
> I'll make me a posy of hyssop,—no other I can
>   touch,—

> That all the world may plainly see I love one
>   flower too much;
> My garden is run wild! where shall I plant anew—
> For my bed, that once was covered with thyme is
>   overrun with rue?

A remarkable example of this leaping the fences of logical progression is to be found in *Othello*, where Othello addresses in turn the bewildered Lodovico and the weeping Desdemona:

> Concerning this, sir,—O well-painted passion!
> I am commanded home—Get you away;
> I'll send for you anon—Sir, I obey the mandate,
> And will return to Venice—Hence, avaunt!
> Cassio shall have my place. And, sir, to-night,
> I do entreat that we may sup together:
> You are welcome, sir, to Cyprus—Goats and monkeys!

The sudden cry of agonized disgust—'Goats and monkeys'— explodes soon after Othello has spoken the words 'Cassio shall have my place', which recall to him Iago's salacious description of the way in which Cassio has usurped his bed and enjoyed the pleasures that Desdemona has delighted to give him:

> It is impossible you should see this,
> Were they as prime as goats, as hot as monkeys,
> As salt as wolves in pride, and fools as gross
> As ignorance made drunk.

In T. S. Eliot's *The Cocktail Party*, a similar cry is torn from Edward, driven to a despairing fury by his unloved wife:

> And then you came back, you
> The angel of destruction—just as I felt sure.
> In a moment, at your touch, there is nothing but ruin.
> O God, what have I done? The python. The octopus.

On the stage these incoherent, broken cries can be given an added force and significance by the voice and gestures of a skilled actor, whereas non-dramatic poetry must rely solely upon the words printed on the page or, at the best, upon being read aloud in a room. Even in the theatre such anticipations of modern developments are rare, nor was it until the early nineteenth century that critics began to foreshadow a theory which might justify these departures from normal practice.

Schiller, Goethe, and Coleridge explored the possibility that the origin of a poem might be in something other than a thought or an idea; Shelley hinted at the close relationship between sounds and thoughts; Schopenhauer remarked that all art aspires to the condition of music; Coleridge insisted that what he called the sense of musical delight was the distinguishing mark of a poet.

Poe's intuitive divination of the paths that poetry was to follow has been noted by J. Isaacs,[1] who quotes from a review of Moore's poems in which Poe speaks of the mystic expression of a sentiment as having 'the vast force of an accompaniment in music'. Poe's use of this phrase and his notion of 'a suggestive indefiniteness' prove, according to Isaacs, that 'Poe has hit on the essential nature of modern poetry—the suggestive overtones or undertones of implication which lie parallel with the surface meaning.'

Strangely enough this concept of suggestiveness is to be found also in Whitman, who uses the very word in referring to *Leaves of Grass:*

> The word I myself put primarily for the description of them as they stand at last is the word Suggestiveness. I round and finish little if anything; and could not, consistently with my scheme. The reader will always have his or her part to do, just as much as I have mine.[2]

We must return later to the demands which this technique makes upon the reader; our present concern is with the stages by which these isolated and unsystematic observations hardened into a theory. In France, Baudelaire and Rimbaud explored the full range of language and of experience with a reckless passion that no English poet of the Victorian age dared to match, and the elaborate theory of Symbolism was formulated. English theory and practice were a pale reflection

---

[1] J. Isaacs, *The Background of Modern Poetry*, pp. 19–20.

[2] *A Backward Glance o'er Travel'd Roads* (Inc. Ed., p. 531). I owe this quotation to a review of Roger Asselineau's *L'Evolution de Walt Whitman* in *The Times Literary Supplement*, 27 January 1956, p. 54.

of the revolutionary pronouncements across the Channel, yet it is instructive to watch our own poets groping their way towards a new concept of poetry.

Sydney Dobell, who died in 1874, anticipated certain doctrines that were to become fashionable many years later when he remarked that his poetry was 'written on the principles of music, i.e. as a series of combinations that shall produce certain *states* in the hearer, and not a succession of words which he is separately to "intellectualate" by the dictionary'.[1]

His practice fails to fulfil the promise of his precepts, apart from one small masterpiece, 'The Orphan's Song':

> And again when nothing stirred,
> And not a word I said,
> Then my little bird
> Lifted up its head,
>
> And the little beak
> Loosed its stubborn pride,
> And it opened, it opened,
> With a yearning strong and wide.
>
> It lay in my breast,
> It uttered no cry,
> 'Twas famished, 'twas famished,
> And I couldn't tell why.
>
> I couldn't tell why,
> But I saw that it would die,
> For all that I kept dancing round and round,
> And singing about it so cheerly,
> With 'Hey my little bird, and ho my little bird,
> And ho but I love thee dearly!'

G. Brimley, G. H. Lewes, and F. H. Myers were three Victorian critics who intuitively sensed the way the current of poetic thought was flowing. Myers, in particular, displays a remarkable subtlety and penetration in a passage from his 'Essay on Vergil' (1879) where, having defined poetry as 'a system of rhythmical and melodious effects', he proceeds to indicate the nature and the complexity of the system:

[1] Quoted by Rosamond E. Harding, *An Anatomy of Inspiration*, p. 62.

And indeed in poetry of the first order, almost every word (to use a mathematical metaphor) is raised to a higher power. It continues to be an articulate sound and a logical step in the argument; but it becomes also a musical sound and a centre of emotional force. It becomes a musical sound;—that is to say, its consonants and vowels are arranged to bear a relation to the consonants and vowels near it,—a relation of which accent, quantity, rhyme, assonance and alliteration are specialized forms, but which may be of a character more subtle than any of these. And it becomes a centre of emotional force; that is to say, the complex associations which it evokes modify the associations evoked by other words in the same passage in a way quite distinct from grammatical or logical connection.

Swinburne at his best manipulates such a system with consummate virtuosity, as in 'The King's Daughter', where the cumulative effect of his imagery and his cadences lulls the reader into accepting without question the intellectual cloudiness and the narrative inconsequence of the poem:

> We were ten maidens in a field green,
>   Fallen fruit in the mill-water;
> Fairer maidens never have been,
>   Golden sleeves for the king's daughter.
>
> By there comes the king's young son,
>   A little wind in the mill-water;
> 'Out of ten maidens ye'll grant me one',
>   A crown of red for the king's daughter.
>
> 'Out of ten mays ye'll give me the best',
>   A little rain in the mill-water;
> A bed of yellow straw for all the rest,
>   A bed of gold for the king's daughter.

Isaacs has reminded us that we cannot hope to understand the nature of contemporary poetry unless we recognize in it 'the secret and invisible welding of the most contradictory elements, combined with that confusion of the senses, or rather fusion of the senses, which is the hallmark of modern suggestive writing'.[1]

It should have become apparent that by the end of the nineteenth century the elements of this suggestive writing

---

[1] J. Isaacs, *The Background of Modern Poetry*, p. 26.

had already been assembled by English poets, even if their full range had not yet been brought into play. In the present century our poets have developed a remarkable technical virtuosity which reveals itself most clearly in the dazzling vividness of their imagery and the sophisticated orchestration of their musical themes. Dame Edith Sitwell's *Façade*, which she has described as the poetical equivalent of Lizst's Transcendental Exercises, pushes the exploitation of word-music to outrageous lengths:

> Queen Victoria sitting shocked upon the rocking-horse
> Of a wave said to the Laureate, 'This minx of course
> Is as sharp as any lynx and blacker-deeper than the
>   drinks and quite as
> Hot as any hottentot, without remorse!
>
>   For the minx'
>   Said she,
>   'And the drinks,
>   You can see
> Are hot as any hottentot and not the goods for me!'

E. E. Cummings displays a comparable audacity and ingenuity:

> jake hates
>   all the girls (the
> shy ones, the bold
> ones; the meek
> proud sloppy sleek)
> all except the cold
>   ones
>
> paul scorns all
>   the girls (the
> bright ones, the dim
> ones; the slim
> plump tiny tall)
> all except the
>   dull ones
>
> gus loves all the
>   girls (the
> warped ones, the lamed

    ones; the mad
    moronic maimed)
    all except
            the dead ones.

    mike likes all the girls
       (the
    fat ones, the lean
    ones; the mean
    kind dirty clean)
    all
        except the green ones.

We shall find the equivalent of such *bravura* passages in the more overtly serious work of our time. Modern poets delight in employing, with a self-conscious technical brilliance, the full orchestral range of the language, just as they prize above all other qualities in imagery evocativeness, intensity, resonance, violence, and unexpectedness, even if, as in the following extract from Dylan Thomas, the profusion of heady images blurs the clarity and the coherence of the poetic argument:

    If I were tickled by the lovers' rub
    That wipes away not crow's-foot nor the lock
    Of sick old manhood on the fallen jaws,
    Time and the crabs and the sweethearting crib
    Would leave me cold as butter for the flies,
    The sea of scums could drown me as it broke
    Dead on the sweethearts' toes.

At its best, the reliance upon heavily-charged imagery, designed to stimulate our nerves and our perceptions, can produce extremely beautiful and vivid effects:

    And again morning announces amnesty over
    The serpent-kingdomed bed.
                      GEORGE BARKER

    Then in another city from the same
    Twice-used air and sheets, in the midst
    Of a parting: the same dark bedroom,
    Arctic chamber-pot and cruel iron bed,

I saw the street-lamp unpick Theodora
Like an old sweater, unwrinkle eyes and mouth,
Unbandaging her youth to let me see
The wounds I had not understood before.

LAWRENCE DURRELL

Nor need this imagery be sensuously rich: W. H. Auden has always been fond of employing abstractions that stab as sharply and unexpectedly as a stiletto:

Desire like a police-dog is unfastened.

*　　　*　　　*

The rigid promise fractured in the garden.

*　　　*　　　*

Scandal praying with her sharp knees up.

*　　　*　　　*

No chattering valves of laughter emphasised
Nor the swept gown ends of a gesture stirred
The sessile hush.

*　　　*　　　*

Pour out your presence, O delight, cascading
The falls of the knee and the weirs of the spine.

Far more significant and radical than the craving for vivid or even outrageously fanciful images and for verbal pyrotechnics are certain theories about the nature of poetry which have steadily been gaining ground since the early years of this century. Common to them all are a tendency to ignore or to depreciate the importance of a poem's overt, paraphrasable meaning and a corresponding eagerness to emphasize the supreme value of the meaning which unfolds itself as the images and the cadences gradually flower in the light of the understanding. Nor is this a mere fantastic speculation of critics: poets themselves have revealed that their poems' origin is to be sought in the play of evanescent images or in the counterpointing of rhythmical impulses. We need not inquire whether they have systematically and deliberately constructed their poems upon these critical principles, or whether they are content to accept these fashionable theories as a rough summary of a process which they know cannot be satisfactorily analysed. Our task is to indicate the main tenets of this new, elaborate doctrine and to examine some passages of verse animated by these modern principles.

We may take as a convenient starting-point for our discussion C. Day Lewis's account of a major difference between the Romantic and the Classical poet: 'With the Romantic poet the image-seeking faculty is unleashed and wanders at large, whereas with the Classical it is tethered to a thought, a meaning, a poetic purpose already clarified, and its radius of action is thus far limited.'[1] Judged by this definition almost all twentieth-century poetry is romantic, for it is precisely this enormous role allotted by contemporary poets to the evocative image and to other extra-logical elements that constitutes the modern element in poetry.

Sir Herbert Read has emphasized not only the evocative potency of the image but also its power to generate poetic meaning. In order to stress the fact that he is not simply echoing Aristotle's remarks on the prime importance of metaphor, Read distinguishes between the image and the metaphor and remarks that

the modern poet has passed beyond the metaphor to a new figure of speech. This has been called the *image*. Jacques Maritain . . . notes that the image thus conceived is the opposite of *metaphor*, which compares one known thing with another the better to express the former by comparing it with the latter. The image *discovers* one thing with the help of another, and by their resemblance makes the unknown known. But it is not a logical resemblance.[2]

Again, Read makes it clear that, in his view, a poet does not employ images in order to decorate a given argument: in a true poem the argument is visible only when the images have yielded the meaning folded within them: 'It is not merely a question of importing images into the stream of discourse to make it more vivid. Poetry is rather a crystallisation of the discourse into symbolic images.'[3]

Since this notion may still be unfamiliar to a great many readers it is worth recalling Nevill Coghill's bewilderment when his pupil, W. H. Auden, first read him some of his own poems:

[1] C. Day Lewis, *The Poetic Image*, p. 59.

[2] Herbert Read, 'Obscurity in Poetry', *Collected Essays in Literary Criticism*, pp. 90–99.

[3] Herbert Read, *The True Voice of Feeling*, p. 115.

I was brought up to demand a logical as well as a sensual meaning in poetry, so his recitation was completely incomprehensible to
me, though I was struck by some of the images that had a sudden
but seemingly irrelevant force. . . . Auden explained with clarity and
pity that to 'understand' a poem was not a logical process, but a
receiving, as a unity, a pattern of co-ordinated images that had
sprung from a free association of subconscious ideas private to himself. He again recommended the works of Mr. Eliot.[1]

This reference to Eliot may remind us that when Auden was
an undergraduate *The Waste Land*, published in 1922, was
regarded by conservative critics in the universities as a joke
in bad taste, or as the hideously cacophonous outpourings of
a diseased imagination. It is curious to notice that, while
correctly drawing his tutor's attention to the pattern of
images in Eliot's poetry, Auden omitted to stress the musical
pattern of *The Waste Land*, possibly because his passionate
love of music belongs to a later period of his life and because,
in the late 1920s, he was fascinated by the writings of Freud
and of Groddeck. In December 1923, Rilke passed a verdict
on his own *Duino Elegies* which one could apply without
modification to the early work of his great English contemporary:

The nature of these poems, their condensation and abbreviation,
the fact that they frequently name lyrical totals instead of enumera-
ting the various steps necessary to reach the result, seems to intend
them to be grasped generally by the intuition of a person with
similar tendencies, rather than by what is called the understanding.[2]

Sixteen years later, in a review of these *Elegies*, Auden suggests that another important lesson may be learned from a
study of Rilke. He begins by remarking that 'one of the constant problems of the poet is how to express abstract ideas in
concrete terms'. This insistence on the concrete, this fear that
the straightforward presentation of abstract ideas weakens
the intensity and the immediacy of a poem, is characteristic
of modern poetry and of modern critical theory. Having paid
the customary tribute to orthodox belief, Auden makes the

[1] Nevill Coghill, 'Sweeney Agonistes', in *T. S. Eliot: A Symposium*, compiled by Richard March and Tambimuttu, p. 82.
[2] Quoted by J. Isaacs, *An Assessment of Twentieth Century Literature*, p. 168.

observation that Rilke 'thinks of the human in terms of the non-human . . . one of [his] most characteristic devices is the expression of human life in terms of landscape. It is this kind of imagery which is beginning to appear in English poetry.'[1] Auden himself has employed imagery of this nature in a singularly beautiful poem, 'In Praise of Limestone', which ends:

> But if
> Sins can be forgiven, if bodies rise from the dead,
> These modifications of matter into
> Innocent athletes and gesticulating fountains
> Made solely for pleasure, make a further point:
> The blessed will not care what angle they are regarded from,
> Having nothing to hide. Dear, I know nothing of
> Either, but when I try to imagine a faultless love
> Or the life to come, what I hear is the murmur
> Of underground streams, what I see is a limestone landscape.

A statement by Dylan Thomas reveals the extent to which a poet may rely upon the dynamic power of images to sustain the impetus of a poem:

I make one image—though 'make' is not the word; I let, perhaps, an image be 'made' emotionally in me and then apply to it what intellectual and critical forces I possess; let it breed another, let that image contradict the first; make of the third image, bred out of the other two together, a fourth contradictory image, and let them all, within my imposed formal limits, conflict. Each image holds within it the seed of its own destruction, and my dialectical method, as I understand it, is a constant building up and breaking down of the images that come out of the central seed, which is itself destructive and constructive at the same time. . . . Out of the inevitable conflict of images—inevitable, because of the creative, recreative, destructive and contradictory nature of the motivating centre, the womb of war—I try to make that momentary peace which is a poem.[2]

It is clear from this declaration that Thomas, in throwing overboard the element of rational, discursive argument, was not relinquishing that sovereign control of his medium which

---

[1] In *The New Republic*, 6 September 1939. Quoted by Richard Hoggart, *Auden*, p. 27.

[2] Quoted by Henry Treece, *Dylan Thomas*, p. 47, n. 1.

distinguishes the artist from the undisciplined day-dreamer. Indeed, Thomas imposed upon himself far more strict formal limits than would commend themselves to conservative poets who still persist in thinking that his poems are as shapeless and aimless as a splurge of molten lava. Poets who develop their argument in a ratiocinative sequence set themselves a far easier task than poets who employ the rigorous, intricate, and unrelenting logic of images, if only because the former method of composition allows for a slackening of poetic tension from time to time, whereas the slightest relaxation by the poet who has chosen to leap from one image to another will prove fatal.

Many contemporary poets who have explored and exploited the latent resources of imagery more intensively and systematically than ever before have recognized that images can be resonant. They have deliberately chosen a word derived from one set of sense perceptions to evoke the effect produced by another set, in order to emphasize that interfusion of the senses which we have already singled out as a distinguishing mark of modern poetry. Moreover, the use of such a word draws attention to the original nature of poetry as defined by Sir Herbert Read—'the emotional sound-complex uttered in primitive self-expression'.[1] When Louis MacNeice tells us, in his essay 'Experience with Images', that he sometimes uses 'a set of basic images which crossfade into each other' we may recall that the word *crossfade* describes a technical device employed both in film-making and in radio production. Even more explicit is MacNeice's reference to a 'quasi-musical interlinking of images, with variations on contrasted themes.'[2] Hart Crane has described his attempt to endow poetry with the piercing, emotional, instantaneous quality of music, and to dispense with the clogging heaviness of prosaic explanation:

When I speak of 'adagios of islands' the reference is to the motion of the boat through islands clustered thickly, the rhythm of the motion etc. And it seems a much more exact and creative statement than any more 'logical' employment of words such as

[1] H. Read, *Collected Essays in Literary Criticism*, p. 347.
[2] L. MacNeice, 'Experience with Images', in *Orpheus*, II (1949), p. 131.

'coasting slowly through the islands', besides ushering in a whole world of music.

The two great English poets of this century, Yeats and Eliot, share the characteristically modern preoccupation with potent, reverberating imagery and with the musical resources of language. Yeats, despite his profound study of symbolist technique, never abandoned the structure of rational, intelligible argument in favour of a total reliance upon image and cadence. The reasons why he favoured a moderate conservatism in this matter can only be surmised. By temperament and by conviction a traditionalist who detested any slackness or shoddiness—

> Scorn the sort now growing up
> All out of shape from toe to top

he was aware that from Homer onwards great poets had found it necessary to preserve narrative and logical coherence in their poetry, and that the result of jettisoning so constant a principle might well be a faded, elegant, tinkling debility or a feverish procession of heterogeneous imagery. He was far too shrewd also not to be aware that the practice of Symbolism, for all its subtlety and richness, must weaken those elements which help to keep poetry rooted in the daily life and experience of mankind. In a letter to John Quinn, 16 September 1905, Yeats touches upon this theme: 'I believe more strongly every day that the element of strength in poetic language is common idiom, just as the element of strength in poetic construction is common passion.'[1] This conviction deepened after 1912, when a study of Donne taught him that poetry could be strong enough to bear the weight of even the most elaborate and difficult intellectual discourse and yet still retain its unbroken passionate and musical flow.

When Yeats desires to convey his horror at the cruelty and the chaos of the period after 1918 he is careful to preserve the normal structure of prose statement and to restrain his images from taking charge of the poem:

> Now days are dragon-ridden, the nightmare
> Rides upon sleep: a drunken soldiery

[1] *The Letters of W. B. Yeats*, ed. Allan Wade, p. 462.

Can leave the mother, murdered at her door,
To crawl in her own blood, and go scot-free:
The night can sweat with terror as before
We pieced our thoughts into philosophy,
And planned to bring the world under a rule,
Who are but weasels fighting in a hole.[1]

T. S. Eliot, surveying the desolation of Europe in those same
post-war years, employs a sequence of phantasmagorical
images and a long, sustained, rhythm of lamenting despair
to carry the burden of his threnody:

> Falling towers
> Jerusalem Athens Alexandria
> Vienna London
> Unreal
> A woman drew her long black hair out tight
> And fiddled whisper music on those strings
> And bats with baby faces in the violet light
> Whistled, and beat their wings
> And crawled head downward down a blackened wall
> And upside down in air were towers
> Tolling reminiscent bells, that kept the hours
> And voices singing out of empty cisterns
> and exhausted wells.[2]

The rapid shift from image to image, the absence of any
apparent logical sequence of ideas and the irregularity of the
versification disconcerted many readers of *The Waste Land*
when it first appeared in 1922. We have learned, in the past
thirty years, to accept the abrupt transitions and to recognize Eliot's extraordinary mastery of phrasing and cadence,
a mastery which has rightly been compared with that displayed by Milton in *Lycidas*.[3] Eliot himself, in a justly famous
passage, has laid his finger upon a fundamental virtue of
poetic style, which he calls the 'auditory imagination' and
which he defines as

[1] 'Nineteen Hundred and Nineteen.'
[2] *The Waste Land*, lines 373–84. In Chapter VII I quoted part of this passage
to indicate Eliot's employment of surrealistic devices.
[3] F. O. Matthiessen, *The Achievement of T. S. Eliot*, p. 47.

the feeling for syllable and rhythm, penetrating far below the conscious levels of thought and feeling, invigorating every word; sinking to the most primitive and forgotten, returning to the origin and bringing something back, seeking the beginning and the end. It works through meanings, certainly, or not without meanings in the ordinary sense, and fuses the old and obliterated and the trite, the current, and the new and surprising, the most ancient and the most civilised mentality.[1]

Of the many passages in Eliot's own verse which are distinguished by this quality I have chosen the opening lines of section III of *The Waste Land*, because they display also those sudden changes of tone and that rapid succession of images which we have remarked as being characteristic of modern poetry:

> The river's tent is broken: the last fingers of leaf
> Clutch and sink into the wet bank. The wind
> Crosses the brown land, unheard. The nymphs
>   are departed.
> Sweet Thames, run softly, till I end my song.
> The river bears no empty bottles, sandwich papers,
> Silk handkerchiefs, cardboard boxes, cigarette ends
> Or other testimony of summer nights. The nymphs
>   are departed.
> And their friends, the loitering heirs of city directors;
> Departed, have left no addresses.
> By the waters of Leman I sat down and wept . . .
> Sweet Thames, run softly till I end my song,
> Sweet Thames, run softly, for I speak not loud or long.
> But at my back in a cold blast I hear
> The rattle of the bones, and chuckle spread from
>   ear to ear.
> A rat crept softly through the vegetation
> Dragging its slimy belly on the bank.

Eliot's successors have been quick to follow his example, some relying upon the criss-crossing of broken images, others preferring to exploit the resonance of language in order to evoke the desired mood in their readers. A comparatively simple example of the way in which a poet flicks from one image to another occurs in Lawrence Durrell's 'Journal in Paris':

[1] *The Use of Poetry*, pp. 118–19.

> But today Sunday. The pit.
> The axe and the knot. Cannot write.
> The monster in its booth.
> At a quarter to one the mask repeating
> 'Truth is what is
> Truth is what is Truth'.

We are clearly not meant to dwell on any one of these feverish images, whose purpose is to convey the insecurity and anxiety of the diarist. This rapid switching from one jagged image to the next is in marked contrast to the technique employed by Dylan Thomas in his poem 'A Refusal to Mourn the Death, by Fire, of a Child in London', where the poet lingers upon each image as if to sound its depth and summons from the cunningly placed words that compose his verse a plangently funereal music:

> Never until the mankind making
> Bird beast and flower
> Fathering and all humbling darkness
> Tells with silence the last light breaking
> And the still hour
> Is come of the sea tumbling in harness
>
> And I must enter again the round
> Zion of the water bead
> And the synagogue of the ear of corn
> Shall I let pray the shadow of a sound
> Or sow my salt seed
> In the least valley of sackcloth to mourn
>
> The majesty and burning of the child's death.

Different again from the methods favoured by Durrell and by Thomas is Hart Crane's elaborately calculated manipulation of interlocking images, each of which secretes a wealth of meaning, in his poem 'At Melville's Tomb', which begins:

> Often beneath the wave, wide from this ledge
> The dice of drowned men's bones he saw bequeath
> An embassy. Their numbers as he watched,
> Beat on the dusty shore and were obscured.[1]

[1] For a discussion of this poem see J. Isaacs, *The Background of Modern Poetry*, pp. 80–83.

We have seen that, even as an undergraduate, Auden was fascinated by the latent potency of images and by the concept of poetry as a pattern of co-ordinated images. His early verse is notable for the violent, disturbing use of images, particularly grotesque images, which erupt into his poems like figures from a nightmare or a German film of the nineteen-twenties:

> The bolt is sliding in its groove,
> Outside the window is the black remov-
> ers' van.
> And now with sudden swift emergence
> Come the woman in dark glasses and the
> hump-backed surgeons
> And the scissor man.[1]

One feels that Auden's fondness for this type of imagery in the first period of his career sprang partly from a temperamental liking for melodrama, partly from a desire to convey the nature of our times by mingling the ridiculous with the menacing, and partly from a conviction that a series of unexpectedly sharp assaults upon the nervous system of his readers was more poetically effective than the leisurely unfolding of a philosophical argument. Instead of a statement about the impending collapse of our civilization or a discourse on the part played by science in the modern world we are given an image that has the vivid absurdity of a nightmare:

> For the wicked card is dealt, and
> The sinister tall-hatted botanist stoops at the spring
> With his insignificant phial and looses
> The plague on the ignorant town.[2]

As his art has matured, Auden's power of finding imagery and cadence that will bear the burden of what he wishes to express has grown correspondingly more assured. One of the finest examples of this power is a long passage in *The Age of Anxiety* where Rossetta, on her return from 'the big house which marks the end of their journey's fourth stage', recounts

[1] Chorus from *The Dog Beneath the Skin*. Printed as 'The Witnesses' in *Collected Shorter Poems*, 1930–1944.
[2] 'Epilogue', *Look, Stranger!*

what she has discovered there. The apparently disconnected images are, in fact, so cunningly ordered, and the verse moves to so poignant a rhythm, that we are overwhelmed by a feeling of utter sadness, of a desolation that has infected an entire spiritual landscape and all the creatures who dwell in it. The passage is too lengthy to quote, but a few stanzas may reveal something of the poet's art:

> Heavy the orchards; there's Alison pinching
> Her baby brother, Bobby and Dick
> Frying a frog with their father's reading-glass,
> Conrad and Kay in the carpentry shed
>   Where they've no business to be.
>
> Cold are the clays of Kibroth-Hattaavah,
> Babel's urbanities buried in sand,
> Red the geraniums in the rectory garden
> Where the present incumbent reads Plato in French
>   And has lost his belief in hell.
>
> From the gravel-pits in Groaning Hollow
> To the monkey-puzzle on Murderer's Hill,
> From the Wellington Arms to the white steam
>   laundry
> The significant note is nature's cry
>   Of long-divided love.
>
> I have watched through a window a World
>   that is fallen,
> The mating and malice of men and beasts,
> The corporate greed of quiet vegetation,
> And the homesick little obstinate sobs
>   Of things thrown into being.
>
> I would gladly forget; let us go quickly.[1]

If, as I have argued, the abolition of narrative statement and of logical argument, in favour of deeply suggestive musical cadence and of highly-charged imagery, is the most important characteristic of modern poetry we have still to inquire why poets have adopted this technique and whether in doing so they have led poetry down the wrong turning.

[1] *The Age of Anxiety*, pp. 75–76.

Some poets have discovered that they can best convey the speed and the incoherence of modern life by making their poetry ever more abrupt, disjointed, and bewildering, by switching rapidly from one image to another, by varying the tone and disrupting the smooth progression of their verse. The growing interest in psychoanalysis has concentrated their attention upon the subconscious and upon the image, which is the natural language of the *libido,* a revolution in thought thus coinciding with a transformation in our modes of daily life.

Moreover, the influence of other arts upon poetry has encouraged this new emphasis upon images and upon musical subtlety. Although the Imagists who flourished from 1910 until 1918 denied that they were a school of painters there is no doubt that, like almost every modern poet, they borrowed heavily from the theories of the French Impressionists. Nor have modern poets disdained to learn from the cinema and the radio, both of which have sharpened the wits and quickened the sense-perceptions of their audiences. We find in much contemporary verse an attempt to reproduce the characteristic technical devices of these new art-forms, notably the rapid cutting from image to image, the fading in and fading out of sounds, the juxtaposition of violently contrasting moods and themes, the effort to convey subtleties of meaning with the minimum of explanatory comment.

We may observe also that poetry, like other major branches of literature—philosophy, history, political theory, economics, and fiction—has become more and more highly specialized. It has ceased to be a means of conveying useful information about bee-keeping or husbandry, or a memorable way of telling a story, or a convenient repository of moral precepts and proverbs. Having stripped poetry of its last tattered remnants of didacticism and narration, many poets hope that its pure, essential nature will shine through the medium of a highly concentrated language cleansed from the accretions of prosaic muddiness.

Finally, it is worth considering Lawrence Durrell's speculation that the new techniques of verse reflect a profound change in our apprehension of time and of the psyche:

I am suggesting that the literature of our age is distinguished by two sorts of compression which reflect both the changes in the idea of time—which makes poets present their material not as argument but as direct and instantaneous statement impressionistically—and also the change in our attitude to the psyche. Thus you find not only the idea of a poem compressed but the sound-values as well, with the rhyme coming in the middle of the line instead of being set like a milestone at the end of every five stresses.[1]

Whether the systematic employment of post-symbolist technique has weakened or strengthened poetry is likely to remain a matter of dispute. The danger of relying exclusively upon vivid images was foreseen by Coleridge when he remarked that, however beautiful they may be, 'they become proofs of original genius only as far as they are modified by a predominant passion; or by associated thoughts or images awakened by that passion'. Again, Coleridge refers to 'the delusive notion that what is not imageable is not conceivable' and advises the poet to 'emancipate his mind from the despotism of the eye', a warning reiterated even more vehemently by Yeats in a letter to Frank Fay, dated 4 November 1905: 'I think the whole of our literature as well as our drama has grown effeminate through the over development of the picture-making faculty.'[2]

More recently, Donald Davie,[3] taking as his text Coleridge's observation about the despotism of the eye, has subjected to a most penetrating scrutiny the claim that poets can achieve a richer and subtler kind of verse if they replace conceptual thought and ordered syntax by music, imagery, and a tenuous syntax, in short, by what an apologist of symbolism has called 'psychological landscape':

. . . in psychological landscape the juxtaposition of various things and experiences becomes a precise means of orchestrating that which could never be rendered by systematic discourse. Landscape is the means of presenting, without the copula of logical enunciation, experiences which are united in existence but not in conceptual thought. Syntax becomes music, as in Tennyson's 'Mariana'.[4]

[1] *Key to Modern Poetry*, pp. 64–65.
[2] *The Letters of W. B. Yeats*, ed. Allan Wade, p. 466.
[3] Donald Davie, *Articulate Energy*.
[4] H. M. McLuhan, 'Tennyson and Picturesque Poetry', *Essays in Criticism*, I, 3 (1951), pp. 270–1, quoted by Davie, p. 150.

As Davie points out, this fondness for psychological landscape is linked with our contemporary insistence upon the merits of concentration in poetry, a quality not to be confused with the virtues of strength, compactness, and closeness of expression which were so much admired by good Augustan critics:

> 'Concentration' can come by many ways into poetry, down the avenues of dream, through the keyhole of innuendo, sidling through the false walls of irony, or shooting through a trapdoor from the cellarage of the unconscious. But none of these have much to do with 'closeness of expression' . . .

Nor, indeed, have they much to do with 'strength', which Davie defines as

> close and compact syntax, neither more nor less. And it is too a virtue of authentic syntax, not of the pseudo-syntax that is music. For a verse is strong only if it has 'strong sense'. . . . Verse may be 'strong' or it may 'aspire to the condition of music'; it cannot do both.[1]

Davie is right in claiming that verse which aspires to the condition of music will disregard the clogging redundancies of conventional grammar: he might have added that poets who rely heavily upon the evocative power of imagery will also become impatient of orthodox syntax. Alan Ross has criticized Lawrence Durrell's collection of poems, *The Tree of Idleness*, on precisely these grounds for, he says, the volume's 'recurrent defects' are mostly due to

> a syntactical over-compression which results, through the substitution of images for verbs, in the meaning being too often baffling. Mr. Durrell's mind moves rapidly from image to image, and in several poems the omission of a stage in the process of thought leaves a succession of bright ideas perched like birds on the branches of a tree that has grown too heavy for its trunk.[2]

The heirs of symbolism have fashioned a body of verse which, for musical subtlety, vividness of imagery, intensity, and technical virtuosity has seldom been equalled, yet the hold of poetry upon the interest and the affection of the

---

[1] Donald Davie, *Articulate Energy*, pp. 59–60.
[2] *The London Magazine*, vol. ii, No. 12 (December 1955), p. 83.

intelligent common reader has undeniably slackened in the past fifty years. It may be a mere coincidence that as the potency of symbolist theory and practice has grown the general appeal of verse has dwindled, but there are one or two reasons for supposing that poetry composed on the symbolist pattern will strike most readers as intolerably obscure and affected.

Man, though doubtless a passionate rather than a reasoning animal, has yet learned to construct a language that enables him to communicate with his fellows upon a rational plane. We have grown so accustomed to a logical framework of speech that any system of poetry seeking to kick away this support is likely to arouse feelings of bewilderment and resentment. Myers, while insisting that words in poetry should become musical sounds and centres of emotional force, took it for granted that they should contribute to the articulation of the argument: music and imagery, in his view, were an enrichment of logical discourse rather than a substitute for it.

Moreover, a poet who seeks to exploit the suggestiveness of words must, as Whitman recognized, call upon his readers to display great patience, and delicacy of perception. A poet expounding a coherent intellectual proposition or developing an argument can reasonably expect his readers to follow wherever he may lead them. It is asking a great deal that they should attune themselves to the evanescent moods that ripple across the surface of his being, respond as he responds to a sequence of images and move harmoniously with him to the cadence of his verse. The long passage which I quoted from *The Age of Anxiety* seems to me triumphantly successful, yet there may well be intelligent and sympathetic readers in whom its images and cadences awaken nothing but a puzzled boredom. The poet who shuns narrative and logical order, in an effort to establish by oblique suggestion a more subtle emotional order, may create only a series of disconnected intuitions, a few haunting, broken musical phrases, a handful of fragmentary images.

The hardest thing for a poet to achieve is what Coleridge called 'the passion and passionate flow of poetry', which is always being threatened by some new danger, some alluring distraction that tempts the poet from his proper task and entices him to pursue the veering dictates of fashion. 'Our faulty elder poets', says Coleridge, sacrificed this passionate flow 'to the subtleties of intellect and to the starts of wit', whereas the moderns sacrifice it to 'the glare and glitter of a perpetual, yet broken and heterogeneous imagery, or rather to an amphibious something made up, half of image, and half of abstract meaning.' Twentieth-century poets commonly fall into the second of these traps, although some have contrived to stumble into both.

The abandonment of logical discourse, far from enriching poetry, may in fact be a misguided though heroic attempt to attain a purity of utterance which can ultimately lead only to impoverishment and exhaustion. We may indeed discern in this rigorous pursuit of a poetic essence uncontaminated by any baser elements a type of extreme puritanism, although the greatest of Puritan writers was too humane and wise a poet to stultify his art by seeking an impossibly austere intensity. Milton, as C. S. Lewis has reminded us,

throws ideas together because of those emotional relationships which they have in the very recesses of our consciousness. But unlike the moderns he always provides a façade of logical connections as well. The virtue of this is that it lulls our logical faculty to sleep and enables us to accept what we are given without question.[1]

T. S. Eliot makes a similar observation:

The chief use of the 'meaning' of a poem, in the ordinary sense, may be . . . to satisfy one habit of the reader, to keep his mind diverted and quiet, while the poem does its work upon him: much as the imaginary burglar is always provided with a bit of nice meat for the house-dog.[2]

The danger of such a theory is that it may foster an undesirable kind of self-consciousness and of sophistication by tempting a poet to think of his meaning not only as something distinct from his poem but as a sort of low-quality bait for a stupid audience. When meaning has been reduced to playing

[1] C. S. Lewis, *A Preface to Paradise Lost*, p. 41.
[2] T. S. Eliot, *The Use of Poetry*, p. 151.

so minor and equivocal a role in poetry it is small wonder that
many poets should eliminate it as superfluous and false,
devoting their energy to perfecting their ingenious tessellation of images and elaborating their suggestive cadences.
There is no good reason why they should not do so unless
overt, communicable meaning still performs a genuine function in poetry and is not a decorative sham like the robes of
our judges and the flummery of the Lord Mayor's Show.

One characteristic of symbolist poetry is that it excludes
much which has for centuries proved the staple fare of great
verse—intelligible argument, narrative order, firm grammatical structure, didactic teaching, comment upon widely
shared problems, the illumination of humdrum, workaday
experience. Some poets have come to believe that a passage of
verse which one can readily paraphrase must be slackly constructed, since a poem should be so highly concentrated that
its enigmatic intensity ought to defy our attempts to render
its purport in prose. The formal perfection and self-sufficiency
of poems composed on this principle may give an exquisite
satisfaction: whether it is the finest or the most enduring kind
of satisfaction remains a matter of dispute. Donald Davie has
put the matter forcibly and concisely when he says of Wordsworth's poems:

> Their syntax is not 'pure' syntax because it refers to, it mimes,
> something outside itself, and outside the world of its poem, some-
> thing that smells of the human, of generation and hence of corrup-
> tion. It is my case against the symbolist theorists that, in trying to
> remove the human smell from poetry, they are doing harm. For
> poetry to be great, it must reek of the human, as Wordsworth's
> poetry does.[1]

Wyndham Lewis used a similar metaphor in his satirical
description of 'pure' poetry:

> In any medium except that of verse
> Forthwith I could enlighten you. Too terse,
> And as it were compact, this form of art—
> Which handles the finished product only—the hard
> Master-material of selected sound.

[1] D. Davie, *Articulate Energy*, p. 165.

The intellect has its workshops underground;
We cannot go back, out of this dance of words,
To become the teacher. Here we behave as birds—
The brain-that-sweats *offends*, it breaks our spell,
You do see that? we really must not *smell*.[1]

Perhaps the most eloquent and convincing testimony comes
from Nikos Kazantzaki who, as a Greek, has been nourished
upon a tradition that includes not only the primal vigour of
the Homeric epics but also the most refined and esoteric
subtleties of Alexandria and of Byzantium. The hero of his
novel is reflecting on the poetry of Mallarmé:

In religions which have lost their creative spark, the gods eventu-
ally become no more than poetic motifs or ornaments for decorating
human solitude or walls. Something similar had happened to this
poetry. The ardent aspirations of the heart, laden with earth and
seed, had become a flawless intellectual game, a clever, aerial and
intricate architecture. . . . All these things which had formerly so
fascinated me appeared this morning to be no more than cerebral
acrobatics and refined charlatanism. That is how it always is at the
decline of a civilisation. That is how man's anguish ends—in masterly conjuring tricks: pure poetry, pure music, pure thought. . . .
The last man has emptied himself; no more seed, no more excre-
ment, no more blood. Everything having turned into words, every
set of words into musical jugglery, the last man goes even further:
he sits in his utter solitude and decomposes the music into mute
mathematical equations.[2]

If this judgement appears too harsh we should remember that
Mallarmé, who warned Valéry against pushing courage to
the brink of suicide, passed an even more severe verdict upon
himself when he said: 'Mon art est une impasse.'

Yet whatever view we may take about the modern emphasis upon imagery and musical themes, there is no excuse
for a niggling, argumentative disparaging of poetry that at
first glance seems illogical and difficult. T. S. Eliot, in re-
minding us that genuine poetry can communicate before it is
understood, is only repeating an observation by Coleridge:
'When no criticism is pretended to, and the Mind in its

[1] Wyndham Lewis, *One-Way Song*, XXIV.
[2] Nikos Kazantzaki, *Zorba the Greek*, p. 142.

simplicity gives itself up to a Poem as to a work of nature, Poetry gives most pleasure when only generally and not perfectly understood.'[1] The first half of this sentence gives a salutary warning that poetry is not simply a vague magic devoid of intellectual content, yet Coleridge is right in implying that criticism must follow, not precede, this surrender of the questioning intellect to a poem's total harmony. Poetry, as Robert Frost has said, begins in delight and ends in wisdom: nothing can kill that initial delight so effectively as the unrelenting coldness of mind which surveys a poem as suspiciously as a prosecuting counsel treats a hostile witness. F. O. Matthiessen has described how he came to love the poetry that he was later to criticize so perceptively:

> I am also thankful that my first introduction to Eliot's poetry came through my friends, the poets Phelps Putnam and Maxwell Evans Foster, who made me listen to it read aloud, thus enabling me to feel from the outset its lyric sound and movement, instead of letting me begin by losing the poetry in a tortuous effort to find a logical pattern in its unfamiliar structure.[2]

Only when we have learned to relax our speculative curiosity, to suspend the operation of our meddling intellect, can we respond to the intimations that a poem may bring:

> It is a great pity that we cannot inhale poems like scents—for crude as their medium is, their message, their content, is something which owes little to reason. That is why one should, if possible, allow poems to impact themselves upon one without too much dissection of detail. Let them be totals to experience first of all . . .[3]

This is particularly true of the mode of poetry which we have been considering in this chapter. Much of its obscurity will vanish if we recognize sympathetically the principles upon which it is composed; and to the impatient and stiff-necked who persist in judging it by rigid and inappropriate categories of logic and of prosaic good sense we can only

---

[1] Only the second part of this sentence is quoted in *Anima Poetae*. See *Inquiring Spirit*, edited by Kathleen Coburn, p. 156 and p. 424, note; also H. House, *Coleridge*, pp. 29–30.

[2] F. O. Matthiessen, *The Achievement of T. S. Eliot* (2nd ed.), p. xi.

[3] Lawrence Durrell, *Key to Modern Poetry*, p. 84.

murmur the lines that Wordsworth addressed to those who, in his day, murdered to dissect:

> Enough of science and of art;
> Close up these barren leaves;
> Come forth, and bring with you a heart
> That watches and receives.

9

The Nature of Poetry

Church-bels beyond the starres heard, the souls bloud,
The land of spices; something understood.
                                                        GEORGE HERBERT

Peacefull, and young, Herculean silence bore
His craggie Club; which up aloft hee hild;
With which, and his forefingers charme, hee stild
All soundes in ayre; and left so free mine eares
That I might heare the musique of the Spheares,
And all the Angels, singing, out of Heaven.
                                                        GEORGE CHAPMAN

As the waifs cast up by the sea change with the changing season,
so the tides of the soul throw up their changing drift on the sand,
but the sea beyond is one for ever.
                                                        D. G. ROSSETTI

And though thy soul sail leagues and leagues beyond,—
Still, leagues beyond those leagues, there is more sea.
                                                        D. G. ROSSETTI

I HAVE suggested in previous chapters that poetry is commonly found to be obscure when, for one or more of several reasons, there is a breakdown in the flow of communication between a poet and his readers. We must now consider the possibility that, judged by normal standards of prose clarity, there will always remain an element of obscurity in poetry; that poetry, in obeying the very laws of its nature, must preserve the right to be obscure.

If it were possible to express in prose every shade of meaning, every emotional inflection and every tone of sensibility, there would be little point in writing poetry except to titillate the ear with the jog-trot of metre and the vain repetition of jangling sounds. Poets, however, believe that they can attain in verse a precision and a subtlety which are beyond their reach in prose; they will therefore refuse to limit themselves to the codified rules of syntax which govern prose, or to the habits of logical exposition which regulate a barrister as he argues a point of law or an army instructor as he demonstrates the mechanism of a tommy gun. Poetry is much more closely related to vivid, informal, conversational speech for, as Louis MacNeice has put it, the ordinary man makes a poetic pattern, however rudimentary,

when he himself is poeticising, i.e., talking; he will then use all sorts of hidden allusions, double meanings, irony, hyperboles and fancy variations from baby-talk to 'meaningless' swear-words; he will also play many tricks with rhythm.[1]

He can also, by making bodily movements, and facial gestures, even by refraining from speech, convey the fullest and most exact of meanings—it is not for nothing that we speak of an eloquent silence.

Poets, being unable to use any of these devices, and feeling the need for auxiliary support, occasionally summon to their aid unorthodox typography and dubious embellishments designed to stimulate the visual faculties of their readers or to point the sense and rhythm of their verse. These stratagems are not revolutionary aberrations of modernist poets: Elizabethan versifiers enjoyed writing acrostics; George Herbert laid out one of his poems in the shape of a bird's wing; and John Quarles's elegy on Charles I, King and Martyr, was printed in a book whose alternate pages were entirely black.[2]

Most good poets, recognizing that spectacular tricks of this kind can have only a limited and transient appeal, have known that the proper exercise of their art lies in the mastery of language, in their ability to express the subtlest concepts, the most evanescent moods, the minutest fluctuations of feeling by controlling the pace, the colour, the timbre, and the rhythms of their chosen words. Poets care passionately for words because they depend upon them so utterly; whereas most of us can rub along somehow with a slack use of a limited vocabulary channelled into codified formulae and

[1] Louis MacNeice, 'Poetry, the Public and the Critic', *New Statesman.* 8 October 1949, pp. 380–1.
[2] I owe this detail about Quarles to D. Davison, *Andrew Marvell*, p. 33.

eked out with a series of conventional gestures. They may, like Keats and Wilfred Owen, be fascinated by the sensuous, evocative quality of words; or, like W. H. Auden who in youth believed that there was an inherent magic in the word *pyrites* and who, in later years, noted down scores of abstruse words for use in his poems, they may reverence words because they are the source of power to a poet, as they were to Adam when he named the creatures. Another type of poet, exhibiting the temper of the collector, will linger over rare and curious words, often displaying a particular fondness for out-of-the-way dialect words which he savours for their picturesque antiquity. Other poets, more intelligently and more fruitfully, will emulate Barnes and Hopkins, studying words scientifically, engaging in comparative philology, seeking to re-animate their own tongue by importing new phrases, compound adjectives, metres, rhyming schemes, and stanzaic patterns from other literatures. Above all they will exploit the possibilities of language as a plastic medium, not hesitating to wrench and twist language out of its customary shape in order that they may mould it to the exact pattern which alone can satisfy their intellectual and emotional demands.

We have grown accustomed to the idea that a man's subconscious mind may be a chaos of warring impulses, that ambivalent emotions may contend within him for mastery and that he may scarcely be aware of the intense strain to which his divided nature is being subjected. In moments of extreme joy or sorrow, at times of severe emotional stress, on those occasions when we dart out a lightning repartee or crack a fantastic joke, our words seem to weld together fragments of disparate, contradictory experience and an instantaneous flash of revelation courses through our being. Good poets habitually enjoy such moments of exhilarating certainty and unifying power, as Coleridge makes clear when he describes the imagination performing its work of synthesis, and fusing 'the sense of novelty and freshness with old and familiar objects; a more than usual state of emotion with more than usual order; judgement ever awake and steady self-possession with enthusiasm and feeling, profound or vehement'.

When a poet's mind is working under this kind of intense

pressure we may well find the resulting poetry obscure because, to use a mathematical expression, he is raising language to a new power. He will shift from one metaphor to another, or develop more than one metaphor simultaneously; he may swerve from a thought to a metaphor and back again to a variation of the original thought; his quick, darting perceptions enable him to divine tenuous connexions that link apparently irreconcilable emotions and ideas; overt and submerged puns will suddenly reveal to him hitherto unsuspected networks of curious relationships. In such moments he rises and falls through different levels of consciousness, leaping enormous gaps between discontinuous orders of experience, like a desperate climber who, having clawed his way to safety, looks back in wonder, unable to believe that he has made so perilous and athletic a progress.

Some readers may object that I am merely describing the convolutions of those modern poets whom they detest, judging them to be painfully self-conscious, obsessed with Freudian jargon, intellectually brilliant but emotionally sterile. I shall therefore illustrate my belief that poets of high stature employ language in this way by quoting passages from Shakespeare and from other poets of equally venerable respectability.

Shakespeare is the supreme master in English of that rigorous and daring compression which seems to me so characteristic of poetic language. If it were not so, editors of his plays would not be able to earn their keep by expanding and diluting his meaning until it is acceptable to the literally-minded who can't take their poetry straight.

I begin with a relatively simple example from *Troilus and Cressida*, IV, iv, 38–47.

> We two, that with so many thousand sighes
> Did buy each other, must poorely sell our selves
> With the rude brevitie and discharge of one.
> Injurious time now, with a robbers haste,
> Crams his rich theeverie up, he knowes not how:
> As many farwels as be stars in heaven,
> With distinct breath, and consign'd kisses to them,
> He fumbles up into a loose adiew;

> And scants us with a single famisht kisse,
> Distasted with the salt of broken teares.

This is of moderate difficulty only, because although the language is closely packed the content of the argument is straightforward, and the metaphors are neither mixed nor conjoined with abstractions to make a baffling amalgam.

Nor is it much more obscure when Shakespeare abruptly switches metaphors, even if incorrigible visualizers may be disconcerted by trying to follow the transmutations of avarice in these lines from *Macbeth*, IV, iii, 84–87:

> This Avarice
> Stickes deeper, growes with more pernicious roote
> Than Summer-seeming lust: and it hath bin
> The Sword of our slaine kings.

The screw is turned perceptibly tighter when violently incongruous metaphors follow each other in rapid succession, as if Shakespeare deliberately yokes them together in order that they may rend each other apart:

> The hearts
> That spaniel'd me at heeles, to whom I gave
> Their wishes, do dis-Candie, melt their sweets
> On blossoming Caesar.[1]

Yet, by some inexplicable stroke of genius, Shakespeare compels us to accept the seemingly absurd trope which portrays hearts first as trotting like dogs and then as melting like toffee. He has so concentrated his scorn for the false friends of Antony into a couple of metaphors that we are borne onward by a wave of contempt for the fawning timeservers and carried triumphantly over the shoals and quicksands of logical usage.

Although in the compressed ferocity of his loathing Antony pours out a flood of scalding words, his emotional state is relatively uncomplicated. Shakespeare reaches an even fiercer degree of intensity when Angelo, in *Measure for Measure*, scrutinizes the horrifying maze of sin where he is wandering. Forced by the goad of lust to probe his heart, Angelo at last admits the depth of his degradation; after speculating whether

---

[1] *Antony and Cleopatra*, IV, xii, 21–24.

the tempter or the tempted is more guilty, he acknowledges that his evil nature is corrupted by the very radiance of Isabella's purity:

> . . . nor doth she tempt: but it is I,
> That, lying by the Violet in the Sunne,
> Doe as the Carrion do's, not as the flowre,
> Corrupt with vertuous season.[1]

These lines mime to perfection the self-disgust of an intelligent man, subtle enough to peer into the recesses of his being, and sensitive enough to recoil in horror at what he finds there.

There are passages in Shakespeare which violate conventional processes of thought and normal ordering of speech so outrageously that editors have covered up the scandal by judicious emendation. A speech of the Duke to Friar Thomas has caused more than one commentator to wag a reproving finger at so irregular a use of language:

> We have strict Statutes, and most biting Laws,
> (The needfull bits and curbes to headstrong weedes),
> Which for this foureteene yeares we have let slip,
> Even like an ore-growne Lyon in a Cave.[2]

The eighteenth-century editor Theobald (whom Pope called 'pidling Tibalds') altered *weedes* to *steeds* and *slip* to *sleep*, for which he was commended in the Arden edition of the play published in 1905: 'To apply bits and curbs to garden weeds is an intolerable confusion of metaphors to our ears. But the whole speech is a jumble of them.' William Empson has analysed these lines so ingeniously and suggestively[3] that further discussion of them here would be a waste of time. What is worth noting is the admission by the Arden editor that the whole speech, whose authenticity is unquestioned, is as much a jumble as the particular mixed metaphor which he finds so offensive. We are then confronted with an inescapable dilemma: Shakespeare is either, in this and in similar passages, revealing himself as a careless, incompetent, muddle-headed

---

[1] *Measure for Measure*, II, ii, 165–8.
[2] Ibid., I, iii, 19–21.
[3] *Seven Types of Ambiguity*, pp. 106–8.

botcher; or deliberately using words in a riddling, ambiguous style for highly subtle purposes.

If we adopt the first alternative we must then explain why
a similar intolerable confusion occurs in lines which most
people regard as one of the consummate achievements of
Shakespeare's art, when Cleopatra, knowing that all is lost,
begins to recognize the nature of mortality:

> My desolation does begin to make
> A better life. 'Tis paltry to be Caesar;
> Not being Fortune, hee's but Fortune's knave,
> A minister of her will: and it is great
> To do that thing that ends all other deeds,
> Which shackles accedents and bolts up change:
> Which sleepes, and never pallates more the dung,
> The beggers Nurse, and Caesars.[1]

Many editors, made uneasy by the word *dung*, have preferred
to read *dug*, which placidly carries us on to the image of the
nurse in the next line. Other commentators recognize that
Shakespeare is probably displaying here his characteristic
delight in sketching one metaphor, leaving us to complete the
train of thought which he has initiated and, before we have
had time to do so, whirling us away to contemplate an entirely
dissimilar metaphor. We are expected to follow him unquestioningly as he darts from one order of experience to
another; to hold in our mind's eye a sequence of rapidly
dissolving images; to retain in the memory the criss-cross of
reverberating echoes. Those who adopt the reading *dung* give
slightly differing explanations of the passage's meaning. The
New Cambridge edition of the play (1950), commenting on
the last four lines, remarks that 'by a natural transition, the
deed becomes the doer' and gives, as a paraphrase of the final
two lines, 'nevermore eats the fruit of this dungy earth,
nurse of beggar and Caesar alike'. The New Arden edition
(1954), shrewdly fearing that if you call the transformation
of a deed into a doer 'a natural transition' you are encourag-
ing modern poets to imitate an unbridled poetic licence
tolerable only in the Bard, tells us that *which sleeps* is a bold

[1] *Antony and Cleopatra*, V, ii, 1–8.

equivalent for 'which is a sleep emancipated from need of the base food . . .'.

An impartial observer can only conclude that Shakespeare knew perfectly well what he was doing when he violated the decorum of conventional language. It is significant that this kind of riddling intensity occurs most frequently in his later plays, when his technical mastery proclaims itself in almost every line; and even more significant that such passages are no mere decorative adornment of the text, but a means whereby character and situation develop in all their complexity. The brilliant set-pieces of the early plays, Biron's celebration of love in *Love's Labour's Lost*, or Mercutio's Queen Mab speech in *Romeo and Juliet*, bring the action of the play to a standstill while the poetry coruscates and sings, just as in *Rigoletto* the famous quartet is a sensuous delight rather than an integral part of the dramatic action. In the supreme moments of the great tragedies the bravura passages are woven into the texture of the play as closely as the unending flow of melody in Verdi's *Otello* is wedded to the musical structure of the complete opera. And the tremendous power which lies coiled within Shakespeare's tragic poetry has a still more vital function to perform. Blake says that energy is eternal delight. It is because Shakespeare's verse crackles and pulsates with compressed energy that we can find joy in what would otherwise be the intolerable spectacle of extreme suffering delineated in the tragedies, where the poetry consumes the dead tinder of broken sorrow in a blaze of splendour:

> Grief is the word that separate letters make,
> By reading them with care, you rightly say,
> A scholar's accurate heart must bend and break,
> Because they read unclouded their vile day,
> Ophelia, Lear and Timon all go mad.
> Yes, but their dying makes the audience glad
> Who see their separate letters burn away
> First in a sentence, then a paragraph
> And lastly the whole bonfire of the play.[1]

The concentration of language, the huddling of turbulent images into a confined space and the simultaneous presentation

[1] Thomas Blackburn, 'The Unabiding'.

of contradictory experiences are to be found in certain other early seventeenth-century poets. It is forty years since T. S. Eliot, in his essay 'Tradition and the Individual Talent',[1] drew attention to a passage from *The Revenger's Tragedy* in which Tourneur amalgamates into a magnificent unity a bewildering variety of strongly contrasted emotions:

> And now methinks I could e'en chide myself
> For doting on her beauty, though her death
> Shall be revenged after no common action.
> Does the silkworm expend her yellow labours
> For thee? For thee does she undo herself?
> Are lordships sold to maintain ladyships
> For the poor benefit of a bewildering minute?
> Why does yon fellow falsify highways,
> And put his life between the judge's lips,
> To refine such a thing—keeps horse and men
> To beat their valours for her?

Although it would be easy to find in Chapman, Webster, Middleton, and Massinger a similar combination of intellectual rigour and palpable sensuous vitality, I have preferred to draw my last example from Ben Jonson, who is not commonly reckoned an obscure poet; yet the following lines from *The Alchemist* are so tightly knit that it is hard to prise apart the constituent elements of their meaning. Face is jeering at Subtle for his failure to make enough money to keep himself in clothes: so much is clear, but in the final two lines Face hurls one jibe after another at Subtle without bothering to make any logical or grammatical connexion between them:

> When all your alchemy, and your algebra,
> Your minerals, vegetables and animals,
> Your conjuring, cozening and your dozen of trades,
> Could not relieve your corps with so much linen
> Would make you tinder but to see a fire.

The most casual study of the Metaphysical poets would of course yield numerous passages even more closely and intricately knotted than my examples from Shakespeare and his contemporaries. I have refrained from quoting these poets

---

[1] *Selected Essays*, p. 20.

because I wanted to show that the 'Metaphysical' style, far from being an affectation cultivated by a handful of clever versifiers deficient in true poetic feeling, is a mode of apprehension perfectly adapted to express a wide range of bewilderingly varied emotions. Whenever a civilization reaches a high degree of complexity; whenever poets become aware of the tensions within such a society and within themselves; above all when they are conscious that a more brutal and vigorous civilization is threatening to destroy the finer and more beautifully poised values of their own world—then poetry is likely to be 'Metaphysical' and to find in the conceit the only instrument sharp enough for the operations which it must perform:

For the conceit exists not just to shock or startle, though that is one of its valuable attributes. It is an integral element of the metaphysical style since it is the most compelling means of making the desired union of emotion and thought by bringing together widely divergent material in a single image. Instead of being ornamental, it is wholly functional: only by its use does the poet feel that he can express the precise curve of his meaning. If the reader objects that the meaning would be much better conveyed in plain speech without resort to such tortuous comparisons, let him bear in mind Hulme's remark that 'Plain speech is essentially inaccurate. It is only by new metaphors . . . that it can be made precise.'[1]

I have suggested that metaphysical poetry flourishes when society is in a state of fierce emotional and intellectual tension, and when self-conscious, complex, subtle poets try to embody that tension in their verse. There must come a time when the strain grows too acute and incoherence follows: or when, all their uncertainties resolved, men begin to acquire a simplicity and an assurance less rich but more comforting than the painful excitement which animated their predecessors. Once a society has moved into this phase, the older metaphysical poetry will seem odd and contorted to a generation untormented by the stress of inner conflict.

Yet even if there is no ferocious impulse driving a man to seek that compression and intensity of language which I have shown to be so characteristic of the great Jacobean writers,

[1] F. O. Matthiessen, *The Achievement of T. S. Eliot* (2nd ed.), p. 29.

good poets are never content to use words slackly or conventionally. Painters, sculptors, composers, and poets are always trying to explore the potentialities of their medium, to see what they can do with colours, or notes or lumps of clay; to learn the limits to which they can push new combinations and shapes and tones; to liberate unsuspected powers that may lie imprisoned within the material of their art. Poetry, as T. E. Hulme proclaimed, is the advance-guard of language, forever alert and foraging, travelling light and risking disaster in order to spy out the territory which the heavily-armoured troops may seize and fortify.

There are times when the natural tendency of artists to experiment for the sheer hell of it will have ludicrous results. Few figures are more comic than the dupe who is always panting after the latest fashion, terrified that he may be missing a new revelation, and ignorant of the truly revolutionary work that men are doing far away from the splutter and froth of self-advertising innovators. Even serious artists may go astray in their attempts to extend the frontiers of their art, and although poets must continually try to renew and to reinvigorate the language, probing always for fresh sources of poetic energy, some of their experiments are bound to be unsuccessful. Samuel Butler poked fun at a writer whose use of words ran athwart the natural genius of the English tongue:

It is no mean Art to improve a Language, and find out Words, that are not only removed from common use, but rich in Consonants, the Nerves and Sinews of Speech, to raise a soft and feeble Language like ours to the Pitch of *High Dutch* as he did, that writ

Arts rattling Foreskins shrilling Bagpipes quell.[1]

It is worth remembering that Butler mocked at all genuine passion, whether it was the burning Puritan zeal for holiness or the concentrated desire for scientific knowledge which inspired the founders of the Royal Society, whom Butler delighted to ridicule as charlatans peering through cob-webbed telescopes. The restless anxiety to experiment with the English language goads some poets to write High Dutch

[1] *Genuine Remains: A Small Poet* (1759 ed.). Quoted by Daniel George, *Alphabetical Order*, p. 151.

or double Dutch, but from that same imperative need have flowered the richest triumphs of Shakespeare, Donne, Milton, Keats, Tennyson, and Hopkins; and when our writers no longer answer to the tug of that impulse English poetry will swallow an overdose of caution and good taste and quickly die.

I have tried to explain why poetry, though nearer to informal conversation than to the dehydrated prose of newspapers, business letters, and official documents, is more exact, highly organized, and impassioned than the common run of speech. Paul Valéry's observation on this theme may help us to carry our inquiry a stage further:

. . . the *given* language acquired in childhood, being of a statistical and communal origin, is generally not well fitted to express shades of thought far from practical: such a language scarcely lends itself to ends more profound or more precise than those which determine the actions of everyday life. Therefore technical languages come into being—and among them literary language.[1]

The concept of poetry as a technical language, fruitful as it may be, at once raises an awkward question. If poetry is a technical language, how does it differ from other technical languages and, in particular, from scientific prose, which is specifically designed to express the most precise shades of thought? We may agree that poetry is far more elaborately and beautifully articulated than the sloppy vagueness of workaday conversation: must we also admit that in exactitude and intellectual clarity it is greatly inferior to the rigorous logic of mathematical and scientific demonstration; that the obscurity which some apologists have found enshrined in the very nature of poetry is a proof that poetry is a messy and inefficient mode of expression fit only for the scrap-heap along with the tangle of other rusty junk?

The story of the running fight between poetry and science for the past three hundred and fifty years is too long and bewildering for us to cram into a few pages. It is enough to remember that poets have never sought the type of clarity and of certainty which scientists try to achieve by close analysis

[1] From an article in the *Nouvelle Revue Française*, May 1932. Quoted by Herbert Read, 'Obscurity in Poetry', *Collected Essays in Literary Criticism*, p. 97.

and unambiguous definition. Warton, in his commentary on Milton's shorter poems (1785), seems to have apprehended this truth, crude and unsatisfactory as his terminology may seem. After quoting two lines from *Paradise Lost*, Book IV:

> His stature reached the sky, and on his crest
> Sate HORROR plum'd

and criticizing Dr. Newton for his pedantic, literal interpretation of the image, he adds:

> . . . we have no precise or determinate conception of what Milton means. And we detract from the sublimity of the passage in endeavouring to explain it, and to give a distinct signification. Here is a nameless terrible grace, resulting from a mixture of ideas and a confusion of imagery.[1]

Sir Joshua Reynolds grants a similar licence to poets in the seventh of his *Discourses*: 'We will allow a poet to express his meaning, when his meaning is not well known to himself, with a certain degree of obscurity, as it is one source of the sublime.' Blake's marginal note on this pronouncement is terse and unequivocal: 'Obscurity is Neither the Source of the Sublime nor of any Thing Else.' Recalling that elsewhere Blake defends the right of the poet to be obscure, we may surmise that he is here displaying a cantankerous fondness for quarrelling. This is unfair to Blake. He loved the bold, wiry line of energy, despised vagueness and, above all, loathed Reynolds for his patronizing tone, and for his avuncular tolerance which implied that all sensible men expect poets to be a bit muddle-headed.

George Chapman's defence of obscurity is finer and more radical than the easy commonplaces of Sir Joshua:

> . . . that Poesie should be as perviall as Oratorie, and plainness her speciall ornament, were the plaine way to barbarisme. . . . Obscuritie in affectation of words and indigested concets, is pedenticall and childish; but where it shroudeth it selfe in the hart of his subject, uttered with fitnes of figure, and expressive Epethites; with that darkness will I still labour to be shadowed.[2]

[1] Quoted by Herbert Read, 'Obscurity in Poetry', *Collected Essays in Literary Criticism*, p. 94.
[2] Epistle Dedicatory of *Ovid's Banquet of Sence*.

Nearly three hundred years later Hopkins once again defines the place of obscurity in poetry:

Obscurity I do and will try to avoid so far as is consistent with excellencies higher than clearness at first reading.[1]

One of two kinds of clearness one should have—either the meaning to be felt without effort as fast as one reads or else, if dark at first reading, when once made out *to explode*.[2]

Ever since Coleridge began to speculate about the poetic imagination, and more particularly in the past fifty years, poets have discovered increasingly elaborate reasons for believing that poetry must be shrouded in darkness. Most intelligent readers, if they are not themselves poets, assume that a poem is a translation into rhyme and metre of ideas, feelings, and sensory perceptions; and would accept Dryden's account of the creative process as a reasonable description of how a poet begins to shape a poem: '. . . thoughts, such as they are, come crowding in so fast upon me, that my only difficulty is to choose or to reject; to run them into verse, or to give them the other harmony of prose'.[3] Most contemporary poets, on the other hand, would agree that Dryden's remarks are not merely imprecise but positively misleading in their implication that a poem is simply a statement which could have been made in plain prose if the poet had not arbitrarily chosen to stud it with images and set it to a pretty tune. According to the modern critical theory to which almost all poets of the present age subscribe, a poem comes into being by necessity rather than by choice, in answer to a demand which no other form of expression can satisfy. The tacit assumption held by readers is that a poem, though more melodious than a straightforward utterance in prose, bears a close resemblance to it. This cuts clean across the axiomatic belief of poets that a poem is a unique mode of speech, not subject to the same conventions which govern the workaday world of prose.

Unhappily, few poets seem aware of their readers' naïve perplexities, and few readers make the effort to understand or

[1] *Letters to Robert Bridges*, ed. C. C. Abbott, p. 54.   [2] Ibid., p. 90.
[3] *Preface to the Fables* (1700).

to sympathize with the passionate convictions which poets hold about the nature of their art. It may help to remove this mutual incomprehension and hostility if we try to discover what these convictions are and why they give rise to obscure poetry. We can wish for no better evidence than the testimony of good contemporary poets, especially if they are of different generations, share no common background and display violently dissimilar temperaments.

Robert Graves has argued that poetry was originally a sacred mystery practised by initiates who had undergone a long and arduous training:

> The Irish ollave's chief interest was the refinement of complex poetic truth to exact statement. He knew the history and mythic value of every word he used and can have cared nothing for the ordinary man's appreciation of his work.[1]

Since, in our arrogant rationalism, we have trampled upon the holiness of life-giving myth, we have necessarily simplified and degraded the ancient concept of poetry:

> . . . in England, as in most other mercantile countries, the current popular view is that 'music' and old-fashioned diction are the only characteristics of poetry which distinguish it from prose: that every poem has, or should have, a precise single-strand prose equivalent. . . . And from the inability to think poetically—to resolve speech into its original images and rhythms and re-combine these on several simultaneous levels of thought into a multiple sense— derives the failure to think clearly in prose.[2]

It is difficult to imagine a poet more unlike Robert Graves than Ezra Pound, yet he also has emphasized the multiple complexity of poetry. His essay, 'The Serious Artist', a little masterpiece of thrillingly exact observation, contains a number of brilliant aphorisms: 'Poetry is a centaur. The thinking, word-arranging, clarifying faculty must move and leap with the energizing, sentient, musical faculties.'[3] He says of certain lines of poetry:

[1] *The White Goddess*, p. 19.
[2] Ibid., p. 203.
[3] 'The Serious Artist', *Literary Essays of Ezra Pound*, ed. T. S. Eliot, p. 52.

These things have in them that passionate simplicity which is beyond the precisions of the intellect. . . . In the verse something has come upon the intelligence. In the prose the intelligence has found a subject for its observations. The poetic fact pre-exists.[1]

Poetry obeys the laws of its nature, as Coleridge perceived, and Pound stresses the harmonious discipline of poetry when he speaks of 'this orderliness in the greatest poetic passages, this quiet statement that partakes of the nature of prose and is yet floated and tossed in the emotional surges'.[2]

Yet the order of poetry is less clearly definable, more subtle and fugitive, than the logic of prose, and nearer to the condition of music. Lawrence Durrell suggests that

a good poem is a congeries of symbols which transfers an enigmatic knowledge to the reader. At its lowest power you can find the faculty in the nickname or the nursery rhyme: at its highest it reflects a metaphysical reality about ourselves and the world.[3]

I quoted earlier in this chapter Hulme's contention that a poet finds plain language inaccurate and seeks new metaphors in his desire to attain precision. If we accept what Graves, Pound, and Durrell assert about the nature of poetry we shall recognize that Hulme was indulging in no rhetorical flourish but stating a fact known to every poet. Herbert Read carries the attack still further into the enemy's country:

We see, therefore, that essentially obscurity lies not in the poet, but in ourselves. We are clear and logical at the cost of being superficial or inexact. The poet, more exactingly, seeks absolute precision of language and thought, and the exigencies of this precision demand that he should exceed the limits of customary expression, and therefore *invent*—invent sometimes words, more frequently new uses of words, most frequently phrases and figures of speech which reanimate words, and among these, above all, *metaphor*.[4]

Critics from Aristotle onwards have recognized that a command of metaphor is an unmistakable mark of a poet. If we regard metaphor as simply a fanciful word-picture we shall be

---

[1] 'The Serious Artist', *Literary Essays of Ezra Pound*, ed. T. S. Eliot, p. 54.
[2] Ibid., pp. 53–54.   [3] *Key to Modern Poetry*, p. 90.
[4] 'Obscurity in Poetry', *Collected Essays in Literary Criticism*, p. 98.

at a loss to explain why good judges esteem so highly this mastery. The most original and penetrating analysis of metaphor known to me occurs in George Whalley's *Poetic Process*, a major work of criticism which has had less than its proper share of praise. He draws a distinction between what he calls 'the pointing metaphor' and metaphor at its richest:

The pointing metaphor makes for intense clarity, but a clarity somehow visual, static and sterile. The full process of metaphor— the 'ringing' metaphor as I shall call it—makes for resonance, a pervasive *tone* which spreads outward in rings of sound and light to bring into sympathetic vibration other or all features of the poem.[1]

According to Whalley the tyranny of the eye has so enslaved us that we use far too often the term *image* in our criticism of poetry, when a sound-word would more accurately represent the elemental principle of articulation in Poetic. With true Coleridgean inventiveness and optimism Whalley coins the word *sone* and hopes that it may achieve a wide circulation. Even if it does not displace more orthodox terminology the existence of such a word may help us to understand the nature and the purpose of metaphor:

The end of metaphor is not acute *visual* clarity, nor even is it intense sensory clarity: it is a process in which words and images are made incandescent and resonant. . . . It is through the ear that the most profound and characteristic features of Poetic are grasped. Once the ear is engaged the other senses are roused to a tenebrous activity which precludes both the static character of what is merely *seen* and the unmuscularity of what is merely *thought*.[2]

Yet it would be misleading to construe metaphor in terms derived from any one of the five senses:

Although the terms of Poetic must have sensory character, metaphor disorients the individual senses so that they excite and fertilize each other. In this way Poetic establishes a novel interpenetration of thought and feeling, and—through the inter animation of sound, rhythm, meaning, and sensory qualities—evokes complex meanings and paradoxical implications. In Poetic, sight can be converted into sound and texture and even scent; single words can assume

[1] *Poetic Process*, p. 148.   [2] Ibid., pp. 155-6.

physical shape, contour, fibre; groups of words may take on meanings not implied by their grammatical relations; savour, aroma, cachet may be conveyed in texture and rhythm. All this occurs in the transmuting crucible of feeling; the mouth of that crucible is the ear.[1]

Those who object that Whalley is according the ear too much reverence may profitably study a celebrated passage from Coleridge:

Imagery (even taken from nature, much more when transplanted from books . . .) affecting incidents, just thoughts, interesting personal or domestic feelings, and with these the art of their combination or intertexture in the form of a poem, may all by incessant effort be acquired as a trade by a man of talents and much reading. . . . But the sense of musical delight, with the power of producing it, is a gift of imagination; and this, together with the power of reducing multitude into unity of effect, and modifying a series of thoughts by some one predominant thought or feeling, may be cultivated and improved, but can never be learned. It is in these that 'poeta nascitur non fit'.[2]

The contemporary obsession with imagery has distracted poets and readers from paying heed to that inner harmony and melodic flow which are the life of poetry:

. . . it is the music which most gives to poetical sense its curious capacity to captivate our beings by suggesting more than the sense seems to declare and by prolonging the reverberations of that sense in memory. Even such poetry as possesses no particular felicity of image has yet power to stir us if the music is excellent. Conversely the power of even the most felicitous image is sadly diminished where there exists little melody to carry the image in its flow and little orchestration to enhance that image's power by exploitation of the analogies in sound of those syllables from the heart of which the image disengages.[3]

My purpose in quoting these extracts from Whalley, Coleridge, and Nichols is not to exalt the claims of poetic music and to depress the status of the poetic image, but to

---

[1] *Poetic Process*, p. 155. The chapters on 'Metaphor' and on 'Science and Poetic' merit careful study.

[2] *Literary Remains*.

[3] Robert Nichols, *Such Was My Singing*, pp. 11–12.

correct the distorted theorizing which gazes rapturously at the image and turns a deaf ear to the music. For poetry is a unity of all the senses, pointing beyond the senses; alternatively, one can say that there are three kinds of poetry united in an indissoluble trinity:

MELOPOEIA, wherein the words are charged, over and above their plain meaning, with some musical property, which directs the bearing or trend of that meaning.

PHANOPOEIA, which is a casting of images upon the visual imagination.

LOGOPOEIA, 'the dance of the intellect among words'.[1]

At this stage, the common reader, bewildered and half-convinced by the weight of the testimony, may allow that when poets robe themselves in their singing garments they will inevitably be cloaked in obscurity. He may then legitimately ask whether such costuming has any deeper significance than the preparation for a fancy-dress ball, and whether poetry is more than a superior entertainment puffed up into a spurious cult by a clever minority possessing the gift of the gab. Poetry may indeed operate simultaneously on any number of levels; it may work through metaphor, either imagistic or resonant; it may even be a peculiarly complicated technical jargon spangled with tinselly phrases: but what is the point of it all? Let us grant that poetry is elaborate, intricately ordered, and satisfying to a highly refined sensibility: so was the ceremonial at Versailles in the age of Louis XIV. One day, as he left the Court, Saint-Simon paused to watch a dog gnawing a bone, and rejoiced to see genuine emotion. Moreover, the minute inquiry into shades of meaning, exquisite splitting of tenuous hairs and nice gradations of poetic texture, in which so many apologists for poetry delight, savour too strongly of the antics of that precisian whom Samuel Butler mocked three hundred years ago. Sir Hudibras had mastered

> A Babylonish dialect
> Which learned pedants much affect

[1] Ezra Pound, 'How to Read', *Literary Essays of Ezra Pound*, ed. T. S. Eliot, p. 25.

and vied with twentieth-century critics of poetry in self-conscious subtlety:

> He could raise scruples dark and nice,
> And after solve them in a trice:
> As if Divinity had catch'd
> The itch, of purpose to be scratch'd.

Are those who harp upon the profoundly enigmatic quality of poetry less ridiculous and obscurantist than Sir Hudibras?

One answer to these questions is to say that even if poetry is only a superior entertainment it is preferable to an inferior entertainment. Bentham asserted that it was neither better nor worse than pushpin: intelligent men have discovered that, at the very least, it surpasses pushpin in the duration and intensity of the pleasure it affords. Nor need we bog ourselves in the mud of hedonistic ethics. As Traherne remarks, 'it is of the nobility of man's soul that he is insatiable'; and the desire for perfection is ingrained very deep in our nature. A woman arranging flowers, a labourer scything, a rider urging his mount over a fence are all responding to the feeling for order, pattern, and rhythm which pulses within us. We look for a similar rightness and sense of achievement in language; and the child who revels in the crispness, vividness, and rhythmical vitality of a nursery rhyme is enjoying a genuine, though simple, poetic delight, akin to that which we experience in the greater range and complexity of mature poetry. In such poetry, at its finest, we can glimpse men exercising to the full their faculty of speech, and since any display of consummate skill demands our respect we may claim that poetry would justify its existence even if it did no more than embody men's richest perceptions, and reveal the most splendid potentialities of language:

> A terrible Child-bed thou hast had, my deare,
> No light, no fire, th' unfriendly elements
> Forgot thee utterly, nor have I time
> To give thee hallowd to thy grave, but straight
> Must cast thee scarcly coffind in the ooze,
> Where for a monument upon thy bones,
> And e'er remayning lampes, the belching Whale

And humming Water must orewelme thy corpes,
Lying with simple shels.

WILLIAM SHAKESPEARE

All other things, to their destruction draw,
    Only our love hath no decay;
This, no to-morrow hath, nor yesterday,
Running it never runs from us away,
But truly keepes his first, last, everlasting day.

JOHN DONNE

The lizard and the lazy lurking bat
Inhabit now perhaps the painted room . . .

JOHN CUNNINGHAM

Beyond the shadow of the ship,
I watched the water-snakes:
They moved in tracks of shining white,
And when they reared, the elfish light
Fell off in hoary flakes.

Within the shadow of the ship
I watched their rich attire:
Blue, glossy green, and velvet black,
They coiled and swam; and every track
Was a flash of golden fire.

COLERIDGE

There, the eyes are
Sunlight on a broken column
There, is a tree swinging
And voices are
In the wind's singing
More distant and more solemn
Than a fading star.

T. S. ELIOT

In alternating bells have you not heard
All hours clapped dense into a single stride?
Forgive me for an echo of these things,
And let us walk through time with equal pride.

HART CRANE

211

Yet poetry can do more than dazzle us with the beauty of its achievement. Poets have for long believed that it is a way of communicating truths which men might otherwise fail to perceive. Not that it is didactic for, as De Quincey remarked in his 'Essay on Pope', poetry 'can teach only as nature teaches, as forests teach, as the sea teaches, as infancy teaches,—viz. by deep impulse, by hieroglyphic suggestion'. Nor can the truth that it seeks to impart be seized except by the strategy of indirect approach, as Donne well knew:

> On a huge hill,
> Cragged, and steep, Truth stands, and hee that will
> Reach her, about must, and about must goe;
> And what the hills suddennes resists, winne so.

Poets do not urge that poetry is the advance-guard of language solely because they wish to justify their pleasure in experimenting with words and to display their technical virtuosity. They desire above all to break the crust of custom and to rouse man from dully acquiescing in stale modes of thought and feeling. This does not mean that a poet must be a reckless innovator bent on destroying hallowed associations and traditional certainties. De Quincey indeed singles it out as a mark of Wordsworth's genius that he 'awakens into illuminated consciousness ancient lineaments of truth long slumbering in the mind, although too faint to have extorted attention', and contrasts him with the author who 'perplexes men by truths drawn from fountains of absolute novelty— truths as yet unsunned, and from that cause obscure'.[1] We might even argue that we are living in an age when we should discourage the frantic scrabbling for novelty and the preoccupation with the unexpected and the far-fetched which end in exhaustion and sterility:

> Obscurely yet most surely called to praise,
> As sometimes summer calls us all, I said
> The hills are heavens full of branching ways
> Where star-nosed moles fly overhead the dead;
> I said the trees are mines in air, I said

[1] I owe these quotations to Donald Davie, *Purity of Diction in English Verse*, p. 193.

See how the sparrow burrows in the sky!
And then I wondered why this mad *instead*
Perverts our praise to uncreation, why
Such savour's in this wrenching things awry.
Does sense so stale that it must needs derange
The world to know it? To a praiseful eye
Should it not be enough of fresh and strange
That trees grow green, and moles can course in clay,
And sparrows sweep the ceiling of our day?[1]

Yet poets must face these occupational risks. De Quincey, knowing that Wordsworth's power to stir half-forgotten perceptions is only one side of the medal, directs us to study the obverse of his genius:

A volume might be filled with such glimpses of novelty as Wordsworth has first laid bare, even to the apprehension of the *senses*. For the understanding, when moving in the same track of human sensibilities, he has done only not so much.[2]

To extend the frontiers of human sensibility in this manner may, by some, be considered a prerogative of Romanticism: it is in fact the province of all poetry. The famous passages from *Tamburlaine*, with their reiteration that men's souls are

Still climbing after knowledge infinite,
And always moving as the restless Spheres,

and that, despite the utmost essay of men's aspiring minds,

Yet should there hover in their restless heads,
One thought, one grace, one wonder at the least,
Which into words no virtue can digest

are proof that Marlowe's exploring poetic intelligence had recognized the nature of its task. We still commonly think of Pope as the master of a formal but limited perfection: Dr. Johnson's splendid and just encomium acknowledges that Pope's genius is 'always investigating, always aspiring; in its widest searches still longing to go forward, in its highest flights still wishing to be higher, always imagining something greater than it knows'.

[1] Richard Wilbur, 'Praise in Summer'.
[2] *De Quincey's Literary Criticism*, ed. Helen Darbishire, p. 240.

Poetry which thus faithfully obeys the law of its nature is bound at times to be obscure; and to complain of this is like bemoaning the wetness of water or the hardness of stone. We should rather honour the poet who, sooner than falsify his vision, has the courage and perception to embrace obscurity:

Obscurities *not inherent* in the matter, obscurities due not to the thing but to the wording, are a botch . . .

Obscurities inherent in the thing occur when the author is piercing, or trying to pierce into uncharted regions; when he is trying to express things not yet current, not yet worn into phrase; when he is ahead of the emotional, or philosophic sense (as a painter might be ahead of the colour-sense) of his contemporaries.[1]

It is important not to confuse obscurity of this kind with the vagueness that accompanies incompetence. Some of the best modern poets, indeed, have been accused of obscurity because they have aimed at a precision too exacting and unsentimental for their contemporaries to understand or to endure. T. S. Eliot has called our attention to this neglected truth in a memorable though comparatively little-known observation. In the course of an unpublished lecture on 'English Letter Writers', delivered in New Haven, Connecticut, during the winter of 1933, he quoted from a letter of D. H. Lawrence's:

. . . the essence of poetry with us in this age of stark and unlovely actualities is a stark directness, without a shadow of a lie, or a shadow of deflection anywhere. Everything can go, but this stark, bare, rocky directness of statement, this alone makes poetry.

Then, in a revealing autobiographical fragment, he said:

This speaks to me of that at which I have long aimed, in writing poetry; to write poetry which should be essentially poetry, with nothing poetic about it, poetry standing naked in its bare bones, or poetry so transparent that we should not see the poetry, but that which we are meant to see through the poetry, poetry so transparent that in reading it we are intent on what the poem *aims at*, and not on the poetry, this seems to me the thing to try for. To get *beyond poetry*, as Beethoven, in his later works, strove to get *beyond music*. We never succeed, perhaps, but Lawrence's words

[1] Ezra Pound, 'Early Translators of Homer', *Literary Essays of Ezra Pound*, ed. T. S. Eliot, pp. 268–9.

mean this to me, that they express to me what I think that the forty or fifty original lines that I have written strive towards.[1]

There is no need for me to labour the relevance of that passage to our inquiry or to the theme of *Four Quartets*, and in particular to the closing lines of 'East Coker', which announce the task of poets as well as of saints:

> We must be still and still moving
> Into another intensity
> For a further union, a deeper communion
> Through the dark cold and the empty desolation,
> The wave cry, the wind cry, the vast waters
> Of the petrel and porpoise. In my end is my
>   beginning.

We are nearing the borders of a region where literary criticism begins to stumble. The fact that most great verse hints at the existence of a realm where supernatural values are supreme does not prove that such a realm is more than a figment of our imagination, an elaborate confession of our ignorance, a deluded attempt to remedy our inner uncertainty. Nor can we derive from a study of poetry the assurance that any one religion or system of dogmatic theology has a monopoly of truth. All we can say is that the language of poetry approximates closely to the language of religious faith and that men have long since recognized the links between them. John Dennis, in his *Grounds of Criticism in Poetry* (1704), declares that 'Poetry is the natural language of Religion', and laments that, 'by divesting itself of Religion', poetry 'from the greatest Production of the Mind of man is dwindled to an extravagant and a vain Amusement'. Plutarch had made a similar diagnosis in the twilight of classical civilization: 'God hath now taken away from his Oracles Poetry, and the variety of dialect, and circumlocution and obscurity.'

Some modern critics, steeped in Coleridgean terminology, have affirmed the primary creative power of poetry. George Whalley has made very large claims for poetry,[2] endowing it

---

[1] Quoted by F. O. Matthiessen, *The Achievement of T. S. Eliot* (2nd ed.), p. 90.

[2] *Poetic Process*, pp. 222–4.

with a unique status: 'Poetry is metaphysical; its primary function is directly to "body forth" reality and Being. No other mode of human expression can fulfil this function.'[1] Others, with more humility, have been content to reaffirm the ancient belief in the enigmatic, oracular nature of poetry: 'In the last analysis great poetry reflects an unknown in the interpretation and understanding of which all knowledge is refunded into ignorance.'[2]

The significance of this unknown remains a matter of conjecture. The Christian mystic will hold, with Vaughan, that it is of divine origin:

> There is in God (some say)
> A deep, but dazzling darkness.[3]

A Greek poet of our own day, who enriched English poetry with his native intensity, believed that his art drew strength from that darkness: 'It is the infinite depth of the unknown, called by religious people God, which gives depth to poetry.'[4] He suspected also that the pursuit of artistic creation, like the pursuit of love, 'may lead one to the space in which the meaning of our life is hidden—and who can say that this space may not be the land of death?'[5]

What matters, above all, is to have the courage to explore that land, and to accept those contradictions and ambiguities which frustrate the optimistic rationalist in his search for neat solutions. We must learn to follow the way of the prophets:

> The prophets wept, forgetting all their bliss:

> 'The days of hope have only led to this.
> The pattern of man's dream is mere convention;
> We thought the Lover bound to take a kiss,
> That God should look divine in His Ascension.

---

[1] *Poetic Process*, p. 224. For a warning against such a sweeping generalization, see John Holloway, *The Victorian Sage*, pp. 8–9.

[2] Lawrence Durrell, *Key to Modern Poetry*, p. 90.

[3] 'The Night.'

[4] Demetrios Capetanakis; 'A View of English Poetry', *Demetrios Capetanakis: A Greek Poet in England*, p. 131.

[5] 'Notes on Some Contemporary Writers', *Demetrios Capetanakis: A Greek Poet in England*, p. 138.

But God does not conform. The night grows deep
While common sense extols the joys of rest.
We had our human dignity to keep
And sent our souls on this unheard-of quest,

In which there are no dreams and no escape
In holidays from fate, no time to cure
The watchful wound: the precipices gape
And all the answers break or sound impure.

But those who see His face in all its terror
Will die for that, yet not before they give
A cryptic message to the world in error
With hints of what to hope and how to live.'[1]

Poetry can never give us more than hints. Wordsworth in later life was always eager to explain why Coleridge had failed as a poet, though some of us may find Coleridge's failure more illuminating and sympathetic than Wordsworth's success. Coleridge at least recognized, with more humbleness than Wordsworth could command, why all poets in a sense are failures and why all poems are bound in some degree to be obscure: to God's eye, says Coleridge,

what to our short sight appears strait is but a part of the great Cycle—just as the calm sea to us *appears* level, though it be indeed only a part of a *Globe*. Now what the Globe is in Geography, miniaturing in order to *manifest* the truth, such is a poem to that image of God, which we were created with . . .[2]

St. Augustine, in the plenitude of his faith, envisages a state in which we might apprehend God, 'not through any tongue of flesh, nor Angel's voice, nor sound of thunder, nor in the dark riddle of a similitude, but might indeed hear Him, whom in these things we love, Himself without these'.[3]

Since poetry flowers only upon the lips of living men it must always speak through tongues of flesh and in the dark riddle of a similitude; and although it struggles continually to pass beyond the limitations of its nature it can never hope to discard that element of obscurity which is the shadow thrown by an ampler and diviner radiance.

[1] Demetrios Capetanakis, 'Prophets'.
[2] *Unpublished Letters of S. T. Coleridge*, ed. E. L. Griggs, vol. ii, p. 128.
[3] *Confessions*, vol. ix, p. 10.

BIBLIOGRAPHY

The footnotes to the body of the text indicate the sources of my quotations and my specific debts to other writers. I owe a more general debt to the books which are included in this bibliography.

BATESON, F. W. *English Poetry: A Critical Introduction*. Longmans, 1950.

BETHELL, S. L. *The Literary Outlook*. Sheldon Press, 1943.

BLACKSTONE, B. *English Blake*. C.U.P., 1949.

BOWRA, C. M. *The Heritage of Symbolism*. Macmillan, 1943.

— *The Creative Experiment*. Macmillan, 1948.

BRONOWSKI, J. *William Blake: A Man Without a Mask*. Secker and Warburg, 1943.

CAPETANAKIS, D. *A Greek Poet in England*. John Lehmann, 1947.

CAUDWELL, C. *Illusion and Reality*. Macmillan, 1937.

DAVIE, D. *Articulate Energy*. Routledge and Kegan Paul, 1955.

DOBRÉE, B. *The Broken Cistern*. Cohen and West, 1954.

DURRELL, L. *Key to Modern Poetry*. Peter Nevill, 1952.

ELIOT, T. S. *Selected Essays*. Faber, 1932.

— *The Use of Poetry and the Use of Criticism*. Faber, 1933.

— *On Poetry and Poets*. Faber, 1957.

ELLMANN, R. *Yeats: The Man and the Masks*. Macmillan, 1949.

— *The Identity of Yeats*. Macmillan, 1954.

EMPSON, W. *Seven Types of Ambiguity*. Chatto and Windus, 1930.

GARDNER, H. *The Art of T. S. Eliot*. Cresset Press, 1949.

GRAVES, R. *The White Goddess*. Faber, 1948.

— *The Common Asphodel*. Hamish Hamilton, 1949.

— *The Crowning Privilege*. Cassell, 1955.

GRIERSON, H. J. C. *The Poems of John Donne*. O.U.P. 1912.

— *Metaphysical Lyrics and Poems of the Seventeenth Century: Donne to Butler*. O.U.P., 1921.

GRIGSON, G. *The Harp of Aeolus*. Routledge and Kegan Paul, 1947.

HENN, T. R. *The Lonely Tower: Studies in the Poetry of W. B. Yeats*. Methuen, 1950.

HOGGART, R. *Auden: An Introductory Essay*. Chatto and Windus, 1951.

HOPKINS, G. M. *Letters to Robert Bridges*. Ed. C. C. Abbott. O.U.P., 1935.

— *The Correspondence of Gerard Manley Hopkins and Richard Watson Dixon*. Ed. C. C. Abbott. O.U.P., 1935.

— *Further Letters of Gerard Manley Hopkins*. Ed. C. C. Abbott. O.U.P., 1938.

— *The Notebooks and Papers of Gerard Manley Hopkins*. Ed. H. House. O.U.P., 1937.

HOUGH, G. *The Last Romantics*. Duckworth, 1949.

HOUSE, H. *Coleridge*. Rupert Hart-Davis, 1953.

HUXLEY, A. *Texts and Pretexts*. Chatto and Windus, 1932.

ISAACS, J. *An Assessment of Twentieth Century Literature*. Secker and Warburg, 1951.

— *The Background of Modern Poetry*. Bell, 1951.

ISHERWOOD, C. *Lions and Shadows*. Hogarth Press, 1938.

JONES, J. *The Egotistical Sublime*. Chatto and Windus, 1954.

KERMODE, F. *Romantic Image*. Routledge and Kegan Paul, 1957.

LEAVIS, F. R. *Revaluation*. Chatto and Windus, 1936.

LEWIS, C. DAY. *The Poetic Image*. Cape, 1947.

LEWIS, C. S. *De Descriptione Temporum*. C.U.P., 1954.

MACNEICE, L. *Modern Poetry: A Personal Essay*. O.U.P., 1938.

MATTHIESSEN, F. O. *The Achievement of T. S. Eliot*. O.U.P., 1935.

MELCHIORI, G. *The Tightrope Walkers*. Routledge and Kegan Paul, 1956.

NICHOLS, R. *Such Was My Singing*. Collins, 1942.

NICOLSON, H. *Tennyson*. Constable, 1922.

POUND, E. *The Letters of Ezra Pound*. Ed. D. D. Paige. Faber, 1952.

— *Literary Essays of Ezra Pound*. Ed. T. S. Eliot. Faber, 1954.

READ, H. *Collected Essays in Literary Criticism*. Faber, 1938.

— *The True Voice of Feeling*. Faber, 1953.

RICHARDS, I. A. *Practical Criticism*. Routledge and Kegan Paul, 1929.

ROBERTS, M. *New Signatures*. Hogarth Press, 1932.

— *New Country*. Hogarth Press, 1933.

— *Critique of Poetry*. Cape, 1934.

— *The Faber Book of Modern Verse*. Faber, 1936.

SITWELL, E. *A Notebook on William Shakespeare*. Macmillan, 1948.

SPARROW, J. *Sense and Poetry*. Constable, 1934.

WHALLEY, G. *Poetic Process*. Routledge and Kegan Paul, 1954.

WILSON, F. A. C. *W. B. Yeats and Tradition*. Gollancz, 1958.

YEATS, W. B. *The Letters of W. B. Yeats*. Ed. Allan Wade. Rupert Hart-Davis, 1954.

INDEX

Addison, Joseph, 70
Allott, Kenneth, 156
Arnold, Matthew, 114
Atterbury, Bishop, 75
Auden, W. H., allusions, 51; attitude
to society, 127–8, 129, 132; early
poems, 38–39, 142–8; fascinated
by words, 193; images, 171, 180–1;
indifference to his readers, 104–5;
Isherwood on, 65, 104; Marxism,
63–64; modelled himself on Hardy
and Edward Thomas, 124; obscurity of references, 62–65; Oxford
Chair of Poetry, 74; private
images, 154, 160–1; punctuation,
15; quotes De Tocqueville, 119–20;
syntax, 21–22. *On:* Churchill,
127 n.3; Eliot, 173; images,
172–4; isolation of poets, 139–40;
Rilke, 172–4. *The Age of Anxiety,*
180–1, 185; *Another Time,* 151
n.2; 'As He Is', 39 n.3; 'As I
Walked Out One Evening', 152
n.2; 'Birthday Poem', 154, 161 n.1;
'A Bride in the Thirties', 126
n.1; *Collected Shorter Poems,* 21 n.1,
140 n.1, 180 n.1; 'A Communist
to Others', 140 n.2; *The Dog Beneath the Skin,* 63 n.2, 180 n.1;
'A Happy New Year', 127–8;
'Heavy Date', 151 n.2; 'In Praise
of Limestone', 174; 'Journey to
Iceland', 154; 'Letter to Lord
Byron', 63 n.1, 140; *Letters from
Iceland,* 104 n.1, 144 n.1; *Look,
Stranger!* 180 n.2; 'The Malverns',
145 n.3; *New Year Letter,* 66,
105 n.1; *The Orators,* 145; *Paid
on Both Sides,* 21, 62, 104–5;
Poems, 21, 47, 62 n.1–4, 64 n.1,
140 n.1, 143 n.1, 145 n.1; 'The
Questioner Who Sits So Sly', 39
n.2; 'Too Dear, Too Vague',
39 n.1; 'The Truest Poetry is the
Most Feigning', 68; 'Under Which
Lyre', 69 n.1; 'The Witnesses',
180 n.1

Augustine, St., 217. *Confessions,* 217
n.3

Bacchylides, 97
Bacon, Lord, *Advancement of Learn-
ing,* 4
Balzac, Honoré de, 71
Barker, George, 170
Barnes, William, 193
Bartlett, Phyllis, *Poems in Process,*
20 n.1
Bateson, F. W., *English Poetry,*
30 n.1, 86 n.1
Baudelaire, Charles, 121, 136, 166
Beddoes, T. L., 141
Bell, Julian, *Essays, Poems and Letters,*
148 n. 1
Benthem, Jeremy, 210
Bentley, Richard, 75–76
Betjeman, John, 1
Blackburn, Thomas, 198 n.1
Blackstone, Bernard, 55. *English
Blake,* 55 n.2, 100 n.1
Blake, William, admired obscure
passage in Wordsworth, 99–100;
cosmology, 25, 28–30; mythology,
52–55; Prophetic Books, 49, 53–55.
On: Bacon, 53; energy as eternal
delight, 198; Locke and Newton,
54–55; obscurity, 69–70, 203;
Bishop Watson, 53. 'Earth's
Answer', 30; 'Mock on, Mock on,
Voltaire, Rousseau', 53
Boswell, James, 69, 76
Bottrall, Ronald, 118–19
Breton, André, 132, 148
Breton, Nicholas, 71 n.1
Bridges, Robert, 12, 20, 37–38
Brimley, G., 167
Brittain, Robert, *Poems by Christopher
Smart,* 28 n.2, 76 n.1
Bronowski, J., *William Blake: A Man
Without a Mask,* 55 n.3
Brown, Ivor, 73. *I Commit to the
Flames,* 73
Browning, Elizabeth Barrett, 19–20,
107

PRINTED IN GREAT BRITAIN
BY WESTERN PRINTING SERVICES LTD. BRISTOL